Learn Programming With Unreal Script

Written By:
Kyle Langley

Contributing Editor:
Genevieve Green

ISBN-13: **978-1491262665**
ISBN-10: **1491262664**

Introduction

The Unreal Development Kit (UDK) is a versatile tool that offers many features which allows the process of making videos a slightly less daunting task. UDK offers a straight forward editor with many designer tools to create many genres of video games. While some game types are going to take more work than others, Epic is a fantastic company who is nothing but happy to show support for those who have a game that needs some help to launch.

This book is aimed at those who are looking at learning the beginning aspects of object-oriented programming, while also wanting to understand how to make video games with UDK. The early chapters are aimed at those who have no programming experience at all. The later chapters are the process of programming an example game.

The example game will be a fully function game that is aimed at what it takes to create something custom.

You will also need a basic understanding of what it is to install a program on Windows and be able to follow along with simple install instructions. This is a beginners book for programming and is not aimed at those who do not have a basic understanding of Windows and computers in general.

The teaching approach taken for this book is a step by step based format. Each notable block of code will be followed with an explanation of how it works, as well as any other aspect of beginner looking to learn how to program.

If you want to run the examples, you will need a computer that is running Windows.

Here is a list of the minimum requirement for computer specifications:

- Windows XP SP3 (32-bit only) with DirectX 9.0c
- 2GHz or better CPU
- 2+ GB RAM
- Graphics card with Shader Model 3.0 support, such as nVidia GeForce 7800

If you do not meet these requirements, you can still follow along with the book but running the editor and seeing what the code is doing within the game will be challenging (if not impossible). You will however be able to run the software used to program, as well as compile the code, to see if it is correct.

By the end of this book, you should have grasped the concepts of passing data through functions and from classes, in order to perform tasks for game characters, weapons, game states, and simple Artificial Intelligence. You should also understand the basic concepts behind how the different game classes are related to each other, as well as how each of these classes are designed to function.

I have tried to create an accurate representation of the thought process and the practice related to object-oriented programming and the process used to make video games, using Unreal Script. It is plausible that the descriptions and practices explained within this book will be unique and not necessarily the general programmers "correct" way. I am often describing what is my way of programming something. With this in mind, if you find anything that needs some improvement, such as a compiling error, grammatical error, syntax error, or anything else that comes across as confusing or inaccurate, please contact me. I will do my best to correct it and I will try to have it included in a future version of this book.

I can be contacted at:

Kyle@EmotionalRobots.com

Acknowledgments

I would like to thank all of the game design students who came to me with questions.

I would also like to thank everybody at Emotional Robots, Inc, for giving me a place to progress in such a challenging field.

Table of Contents

What is Unreal Script?
Chapter One

What is Unreal Script?

Unreal Script is an object-oriented programming (OOP) language that takes some of its principles from Java and C++, in syntax. Though the concepts of OOP are almost always transferable between other OOP Languages, some of the Unreal Script language is unique to the game engine. Including features such as timers and states. If you have experience with other OOP languages, you will be able to pickup and understand Unreal Script easier than starting from not knowing anything.

Getting setup:

There are many different Integrated Development Environment (IDE) options when it comes to programming with Unreal Script.

If any of these links do not work, a Google search will find them.

For these tutorials I will be using nFringe.

> http://pixelminegames.com/nfringe/

Here is many more that you can also use, to follow along:

> http://tinyurl.com/Unreal-X-Editor
> http://tinyurl.com/UnrealSED

http://tinyurl.com/UDKIDE
http://tinyurl.com/CodePlexIDE

The reason I like nFringe is out of personal preference. It was the first IDE option I chose to learn with and as a result, is the one I continue to use. There is a license fee if you do decide to use nFringe on projects that will release but for learning purposes it is free.

Installing nFringe:

Download and install the Microsoft Visual Studio 2008 Shell (Integraded Mode):

http://tinyurl.com/MVS2008Shell

If you do NOT have .NET framework 3.5 SP1, download and install it:

http://tinyurl.com/3-5SP1NET

Install nFringe (make sure all Visual Studio instances are closed).

http://tinyurl.com/PixelMine-nFringe

Installing UDK:

There are *many* different versions of UDK though using the most recent is probably the best. Here is a link to the current installer, as of July 2013:

http://tinyurl.com/UDK2012-02

(You can also access UDK through Steam. After opening Steam go to Library →Tools →scroll to the bottom. DOUBLE-CLICK "Unreal Development Kit". While this is an option, I do recommend going through the **www.UDK.com** website).

DOUBLE-CLICK the downloaded UDK installer and follow the steps to install. When it asks if you would like to install a "custom game" or "include UT example game" please choose to install the UT example game or you will get lost later on in these lessons. The reason you should install the UT example game is not for the code, it is for the example game at the end of the book, which needs this art.

You can skip when it asks to install "Perforce" as we will not be using it.

(Perforce is a tool used by teams to keep track of who is working on what as well as keeping version control of all work, in case anything goes wrong. This service is fantastic for those in need of it. We do not).

At the end of the installation it will ask to "open UDK" or "return to desktop". Go ahead and select "return to desktop" and hit finish.

At this point, UDK, Microsoft Visual Studio 2008 (Integraded Mode) and nFringe should all be installed.

Setting up our editor:

Open up the directory you installed UDK to (if you kept the default naming, it will resemble: UDK-2013-02). Open up the "Binaries" folder then "WIN64" folder. (You may also use the "WIN32" folder).

Scroll down near the bottom, find the "UDK.exe", RIGHT-CLICK it, and then "Copy". Go to anywhere you want to save a short-cut for the editor (I use the location where I installed UDK because I like to have more than one UDK install at a time and it is easier to keep track of) RIGHT-CLICK and then "Paste short-cut".

RIGHT-CLICK the short cut and go to "Properties". In the "Target" line, move the cursor end of the file path, press space, and then add: editor.

It should resemble: **Target: C:\UDK\UDK-2013-02\Binaries\UDKLift.exe editor**

Target: :\UDK\UDK-2013-02\Binaries\UDKLift.exe editor

If you want, double-click (or if it is already selected, press Enter) to open the editor. If you did open it, feel free to look around but make sure to close it before the next step(s).

Setting up our game project:

Navigate to your UDK install location. Open up "Development" folder and then "Src" folder. This is the folder that stores all of the available code for the UDK.

RIGHT-CLICK in the "Src" folder and "New". Then, select " Folder".

Name this folder: **UnrealScriptLesson**

The name of the folder can be anything but if you choose not to follow my naming chances are you will end up with some confusion down the line. I recommend that you follow the same naming as what I use, especially if you're new to this.

Open up your new "UnrealScriptLesson" folder and RIGHT-CLICK →new →folder. Name this folder: classes

The naming of this folder is important. If you do not name this folder "classes" the compiler will not be able to find your code.

Open up your Visual Studio 2008 Shell. You will see a screen such as:

You will also get a notification that you have not registered nFringe and will need to have a license before you are able to use it. In order to do this, go to the "Help" tab then to "Pixel Mine nFringe Licensing" option. Press the "Add" button and follow the steps.

It will ask for what type of usage that you plan on using this for and relevant information. If all you are doing is following this book, choose "I am using nFringe for a non-commercial project" then fill in your name, project name, and email.

You will then need to validate your email. Do this by following the steps in the email you receive.

If you are having an issue with this, refer to the Pixel Mine wiki, here:

http://tinyurl.com/PixelMineFAQ

You can also go to the root site, here:

http://pixelminegames.com/nfringe/

If you are still having issues at this point, I recommend downloading and installing either of these IDE's, as they are more contained and easier to install. Though a bit less stable because they are always being updated, they are fine alternatives to nFringe.

http://tinyurl.com/Unreal-X-Editor
http://tinyurl.com/UnrealSED

We are ready to setup our code project. To do this, press "File →new →project" in Visual Studio. This prompt should show:

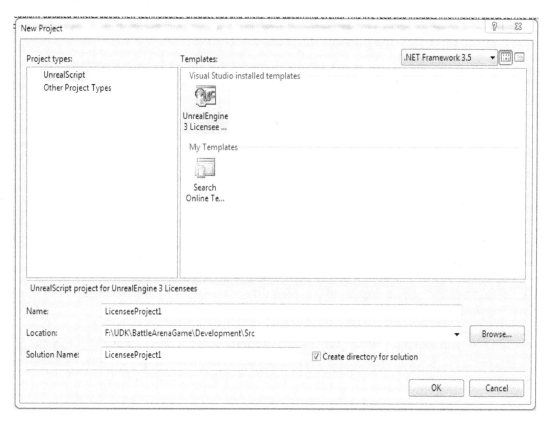

If it doesn't, make sure to select the "UnrealScript" option on the top left.

Instead of naming the solution "LicenseeProject" name it "UnrealScriptLesson". Change the location of the project by using the "Browse" button to the location of your UDK install then go to: Development →Src folder. Un-check "Create directory for solution" and then press "OK".

Go to "My Computer" and navigate to the location of the UDK folder →development →src folder. There is a folder named "UnrealScriptLesson" in this location.

Open the "UnrealScriptLesson" folder and RIGHT-CLICK →cut the files named:

UnrealScriptLesson.sln

UnrealScriptLesson.suo
UnrealScriptLesson.ucproj

Go back to the Src directory and paste these files there. You may get a warning that you cannot move these because Visual Studio is still open. Close Visual Studio and then press "retry".

This is how the three files should look in the **Src** folder.

        UnrealScriptLesson.suo
        UnrealScriptLesson.ucproj
        UnrealScriptLesson.ucproj.user

DOUBLE-CLICK the UnrealScriptLesson.ucproj file and Visual Studio will open again. This time your "Solution explorer" (on the right side of the Visual Studio Window) will have a category of folders that are the same as your Src folder. This is how we will be accessing and creating our code from now on.

We must setup UDK to "see" our game which allows the engine to compile the code we will be adding.

Go to "My Computer" and navigate to the UDK directory →UDKGame →Config → DefaultEngine.ini.

These .ini files can look quite intimidating at first. Try not to worry about them too much now. They serve a great purpose. Which you may appreciate one day. For now, find the line that says:

```
[UnrealEd.EditorEngine]
```

Under this you will see:

```
+EditPackages=UTGame
+EditPackages=UTGameContent
```

Follow the format of what is already here and add your own version under the list that is already there. Like:

```
+EditPackages=UnrealScriptLesson
```

"UnrealScriptLesson" is the name of your game project folder – the one that holds the "classes" folder.

The entire block will look like

```
[UnrealEd.EditorEngine]
+EditPackages=UTGame
+EditPackages=UTGameContent
+EditPackages=UnrealScriptLesson
```

Once your custom game is added, save this .ini file and close it.

To setup our debug settings, so we are able to test the game via Visual Studio, open Visual Studio and your code project. This can be done by double-clicking the UnrealScriptLesson.ucproj file in your Src folder or by going to "File →open project " and finding your UnrealScriptLesson.ucproj file through Visual Studio.

Once that is done, RIGHT-CLICK on your solution, in the top right of Visual Studio.

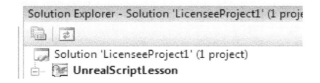

Then, go to "properties".

This window can look complicated but this is a very useful tool. You will be glad to understand it.

In the "General" tab, the UCC Path will be empty. Select the (...) button and navigate to your UDK install location. Go to the "Binaries" folder →Win32 →UDK.exe and select OK.

Skip the "Build Events" and "Build" tabs and open the "Debug" tab.

The two top drop downs should be:

Click the (...) button for the "Start Game Executable". Navigate to the "Binaries" folder of your UDK install →Win32 →UDK.exe and select OK.

Click the box for "Load map at startup" then type: TestMap

Click the box for "Start with specified game type" then type:

UnrealScriptLesson.USL_GameInfo

Click the box for "Disable Sound" if you do not wish to hear any game sounds.

Click the box for "Disable startup movies" if you do not wish to see the Unreal Engine movie every time you start the game.

Click the box for "Force windowed mode" and choose a resolution you like. The default is fine though I use 1600 x 900 because it's a bit easier to see things with a higher resolution.

If you have TWO monitors, click the box for "Open log window at position" and for "Left" enter: 1980. If you have ONE monitor, keep this setting as is.

If you want to keep a log output, click the box for "Log output to file" and then press the "... " button and select where you want it to go. I do not use this as often the log window itself is enough. This is handy for more complicated projects, though. Click the "Save all" button. On the top tool bar of Visual Studio. Then, close Visual Studio.

Setting up our TestMap:

Go to "My Computer" and navigate to your UDK short-cut location. Open the UDK editor. If you have not opened the editor yet, you will be met with a few windows. One is the Content Browser, another is a entry page for new people to get recourse information related to UDK, and the last is the editor itself. Close the "Whats new" and Content Browser windows. On the top left of the editor press the "Create a new level" button. Select the "Blank Map" option.

You will see a black world, with a blue grid, and a red box in the middle. If you do not see the red box, press "B" on your keyboard.

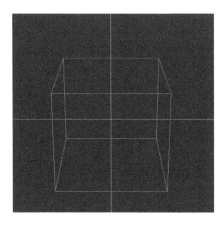

On the left side of the editor, RIGHT-CLICK the "Cube" button.

You will see a new "Brush Builder – Cube" window. In these options, input this:

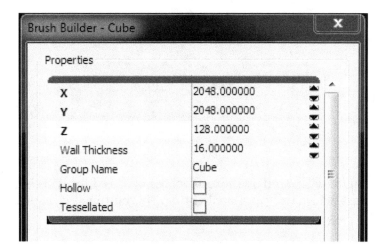

 Then click the CSG Add button, on the left side of the editor, under CSG, or press "CTRL + A".

Nothing should change because the default lighting is set to "Wireframe".

Press the Unlit button, or press "ALT + 3", to change to the "Unlit" setting.

You should now see a big unlit cube in the level. RIGHT-CLICK on the cube, Then LEFT-CLICK →Add Actor →Player Start.

Press the "View" dropdown on the top of the editor window. Go to "World Properties → Lightmass →Lightmass Settings →click on the black bar under "Environment Color" Slide both the top and bottom bar all the way to the right, then hit OK.

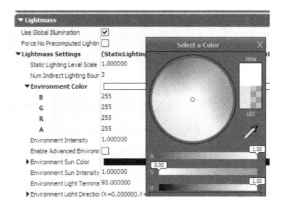

Press the "Build All" button on the top tool bar of the editor. This is going to open the Unreal Lightmass, which will calculate lighting. This button also rebuilds all CSG brushes and builds paths.

When that is done, press the "Save" button and save it in the "Maps" folder, within the "Content" folder, inside of your UDK install location, and name it: "TestMap".

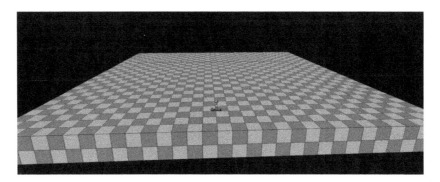

Once the map is saved close the editor. Open Visual Studio then open up your code project. You can do this in Visual Studio by pressing: File →Open Recent Project.

In the Solution Explorer, on the right side of Visual Studio, use the (+) to open up your code project folder. The only thing in there should be the "classes" folder. RIGHT-CLICK on the classes folder →Add →New Item.

Make sure the UnrealScript File is selected for the "Template", then name it:

USL_GameInfo

Press "Add".

nFringe will auto-create a base class for you to use. We will need to change this in order to work for us. The default format looks like:

```
class USL_GameInfo extends Object;

DefaultProperties
{
}
```

Change it to:

```
class USL_GameInfo extends GameInfo;

DefaultProperties
{
}
```

Create three more files to our classes folder. Name them:

> **USL_PlayerController**
> **USL_Pawn**
> **USL_HUD**

Then do the same thing we did with the GameInfo class. Change "Object" to the corresponding class type.

The three new classes should start like:

```
class USL_PlayerController extends PlayerController;
class USL_Pawn extends Pawn;
class USL_HUD extends HUD;
```

Keep the "DefaultProperties" in all of these, if you wish.

All of these are their OWN class file. If you put everything into one file it will not work. Make sure you follow the steps of creating a new Unreal Script file, name it what the name of the class should be, then press "OK". Exactly what we just did for the GameInfo class.

There is one more step to tie the Player Controller, Pawn, and HUD to the GameInfo.

Add the following inside of the DefaultProperties bracket, of the USL_GameInfo class.

```
DefaultProperties
{
    HUDType = class'UnrealScriptLesson.USL_HUD'
    PlayerControllerClass=class'UnrealScriptLesson.USL_PlayerController'
    DefaultPawnClass = class'UnrealScriptLesson.USL_Pawn'
    bDelayedStart = false
}
```

This tells the GameInfo class what classes it needs to be referencing when the game is running.

 Press the "Start Debugging" button, on the top tool bar of Visual Studio.

This should open up the UDK game with our TestMap, running our GameInfo, and related classes. The log window should also load. Don't worry if you see some yellow text in the log window, those are some warnings caused for various non-related reasons.

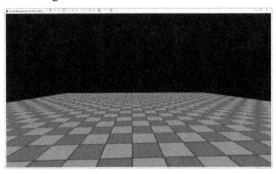

The HUD should be blank and you should be able to move around using your mouse and the W, A, S, D or UP, DOWN, LEFT, RIGHT keys. - Just as the picture above.

Your log window should read something similar to this, as well:

```
[0006.20] Log: LoadMap: TestMap?Name=Player?Team=255?game=UnrealScriptLesson.USL_GameInfo
[0006.24] Log: Game class is 'USL_GameInfo'
```

```
[Log: LoadMap: TestMap?Name=Player?Team=255?
game=UnrealScriptLesson.USL_GameInfo]
[Log: Game class is 'USL_GameInfo']
```

We have yet to do any "real" programming, though we did learn a lot about setting up our Unreal Script IDE and setting up UDK.

The next chapter will begin with the very basics of programming.

Additional Reading:

What is computer programming?
http://www.bfoit.org/itp/Programming.html
http://en.wikipedia.org/wiki/Computer_programming

If you want to know more about building levels:
http://udn.epicgames.com/Three/GettingStartedLevels.html
http://udn.epicgames.com/Three/CreatingLevels.html

If you want to know more about the editor and game engine:
http://udn.epicgames.com/Three/WebHome.html

If you want to know more about the toolbars and options within the editor:
http://udn.epicgames.com/Three/MainEditorToolbar.html
http://udn.epicgames.com/Three/ViewportToolbar.html

If you want to know more about CSG / BSP:
http://udn.epicgames.com/Three/UsingBspBrushes.html
http://en.wikipedia.org/wiki/Constructive_solid_geometry
http://en.wikipedia.org/wiki/Binary_space_partitioning

If you want to know more about Lightmass:
http://udn.epicgames.com/Three/Lightmass.html
http://udn.epicgames.com/Three/LightmassTools.html

If you want to be a part of a UDK / Unreal community:
http://forums.epicgames.com/forums/366-UDK
http://www.reddit.com/r/udk
http://www.3dbuzz.com/forum/forums/277-Unreal-Technology

Variable Types

Chapter Two

A variable is a way for the programmer to store a specific type of data. As an example, if you need a whole value between ZERO and TWO-HUNDRED and FIFTY-FIVE, you can use the **byte** variable. If you needed a variable that is still a whole number but needed to be a negative value or something much bigger than TWO-HUNDRED and FIFTY-FIVE, you could use a **int** variable. If you need to use a floating point variable (a positive or negative value that also has a decimal point), you can use a **float** variable. There are also variables for holding text, holding many types of the same variables together in a group or, you can even use a "class" as a variable. The premise is that in order for you to perform tasks within the program, you must use variables (also called data types) to both store and "send" data between functions and classes.

To begin, these are all "basic data type" variables. These will constitute much of what you see in this chapter.

- **Byte**: Single byte value ranging from **ZERO** to **TWO-HUNDRED** and **FIFTY-FIVE**.
- **Int**: A 32-bit integer value. Stores **WHOLE** numbers.
- **Bool**: A boolean value which is either **FALSE** or **TRUE.** This can also be represented by a **ZERO** or **ONE,** with **ZERO** being **FALSE**.
- **Float**: A 32-bit floating point number. Stores positive or negative numbers with decimal points.
- **String**: A string of characters. Holds characters.
- **Constant**: A variable that cannot be changed.
- **Enumeration**: A variable list that can take on a name in place of a integer value.

- **Array:** Stores a list of the same type of variable.
- **Struct**: Allows the programmer to create a new variable type that contain sub-variable types. Can store different types of variables.
- **Name**: A variable unique to Unreal Script. Holds a simple **string** up to **SIXTY FOUR** characters.
- **Object and Actor references**: A variable that refers to another **Object** or **Actor** in the world.
- **Delagate**: Holds a reference to an Unreal Script function.

To start, open Visual Studio and your code project. Then, open up the USL_HUD.uc file. Add this string variable, so the class looks liked:

```
class USL_HUD extends HUD;

// This will be our "Testing" text.
var private string text;
```

The green text that starts with the TWO slashes (//). This is referred to as a "comment", which is a way for the programmer(s) to keep a note within the program. It is a common practice to comment your code as it is difficult to remember every single detail. This is especially true if the program is big or there is more than one programmer working on it. Comments are ignored by the compiler (the program that allows the computers hardware to "read" the code) and is purely for the human element of programming. It allows you to come back or pass along your code and know what portions of that code is doing.

In this instance, this comment will remind us that "text" will be used for testing.

If you are following along, you do NOT have to write all of the comments out. These are here to help you understand what the code is doing and are not crucial for getting the code to compile.

We have a "var" name "text", that is a type "string". The Unreal keyword for variables is "var" and our type of variable is "string". Strings are used to store normal text, just like what you're reading. There is also another **specifier** called **private**. Private is a term that programmers can use to tell the program that this variable is to be modified and accessed by this class. This practice will be explained more, when we get to functions. For now, remember that it means no other class but our USL_HUD.uc class can modify or access it.

At the moment, our string variable is not assigned. If you were to run the game now, nothing would happen.

Add this to the DefaultProperties:
```
DefaultProperties
```

```
{
    text = "Hello Unreal!"
}
```

To see text on the screen, a **function** needs to be added to the USL_HUD class.

A function is a named part of a program that is designed to perform a specific task. A function starts with the specifier "function", followed by the name of a function, then a open and closed parenthesis ( ), which may or may not hold variables. Each function has a "body" which is represented by an open and closing bracket { }, or "curly brace". If any one of these is missing (aside from the optional variables within the parenthesis), the function will be incomplete and will not compile. As you follow along, remember to have all of the correct formatting in place.

We will talk about functions more during the "functions" chapter. For now, make sure your USL_HUD class looks liked:

```
class USL_HUD extends HUD;

// This will be our "Testing" text.
var private string text;

// This is the HUD class "Main" draw loop - For now, used to
// draw HUD elements to the screen.
function DrawHUD ( )
{
    Canvas.SetPos( Canvas.SizeX * 0.45, Canvas.SizeY * 0.5 );
    Canvas.SetDrawColor( 255,255,255,255 );
    Canvas.DrawText( text );
}

DefaultProperties
{
    text = "Hello Unreal!"
}
```

▸ Press the "Start Debugging" button. The game should open and display, in small white text, "Hello Unreal!".

16

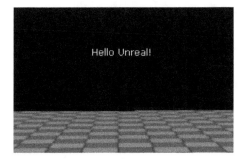

Our program is simple. We have a string variable that is assigned the text "Hello Unreal". This is displayed by DrawHUD( ) function.

The DrawHUD( ) function is that it is called "every frame". This means that if your game is running at SIXTY frames per second (FPS) the DrawHUD( ) function will be calculated SIXTY times per second. If your game is running at TWO FPS the DrawHUD() function will be called TWO times per second.

This is often a difficult thing to comprehend when starting to use these types of functions when programming specific aspects of the game HUD. For now, try to remember that what is called in this function will be calculated per frame.

Lets explore some other types of variables.

Add this under the "string text" variable:

```
// Ranges from 0 to 255
var byte red;
var byte green;
var byte blue;
var byte alpha;
```

Byte variables are used for values between ZERO and TWO-HUNDRED and FIFTY-FIVE. This means they are used in much more precise way, as this is a limited range. One good way of using byte values is for the making of colors.

Add this variable under our byte list:

```
// Color used for our "Testing" text.
var Color TestingColor;
```

You'll notice that Color specifier is a different color within the IDE. This is because the Color variable is a **struct**. A struct is a way for programmers to keep a list of variables inside of a "wrapper". This so called wrapper then can be accessed and used as a variable.

For now, keep in mind that it is a way to change the color of our text using RGB (Red, Green, Blue) colors.

In the DefaultProperties add this:

```
DefaultProperties
{
   // Default color values
   red = 128
   green = 52
   blue = 224
   alpha = 255
}
```

This will serve as our new text color values. I chose random numbers between ZERO and TWO-HUNDRED and FIFTY-FIVE. You can do so, as well.

Under our new color variable, add this function:

```
// A function called right after this class is created.
simulated function PostBeginPlay( )
{
   super.PostBeginPlay( );

   TestingColor.R = red;
   TestingColor.G = green;
   TestingColor.B = blue;
   TestingColor.A = alpha;
}
```

This PostBeginPlay( ) function is a way for programmers to perform actions directly after the class is created. In this instance, our class will be created as soon as the game begins. This means we can use this function to assign our TestingColor variable a value.

Super is another specifier to access the same function of the class this came from. For instance, the HUD class extends Actor (just as USL_HUD extends HUD) and because we sometimes would like a way to either access or re-write parts of functions from our "parent" (the class our class extends) classes, we have this keyword to do so.

Since PostBeginPlay( ) does some important things higher up the class tree (or hierarchy), we don't want to overwrite them by not including the previous classes code from the same function we are using (PostBeginPlay( )).

Another way to look at super is, instead of re-writing or copying a lot of code over and over, we can use the one simple keyword to tell the compiler to go ahead and run that code we need from the previous class. We will touch on the subject later as well. For now, try not to worry about it too much about it, just remember that when we use PostBeginPlay( ), we are doing so with the mind set that this function will be called for us, when we start the game.

Inside of PostBeginPlay( ), TestingColor had to be assigned in an interesting way. Because TestingColor is a struct variable type, we cannot tell it to be ONE value. We have to access the elements of the struct in order to assign each one with the value we want. In order to assign the TestingColor values we had to use the dot (.) operator, to access the Color struct elements. In this case, the Color struct takes four values (R,G,B,A) between ZERO and TWO-HUNDRED and FIFTY-FIVE. We then assigned our related byte variables to each of the TestingColor elements.

The color struct is made up of FOUR byte variables, though any other number value that fits the same rules as a byte will work. Such as an int assigned from ZERO and TWO-HUNDRED and FIFTY-FIVE.

Such as:

```
// EXAMPLE: Ranges from 0 to 255
var int red;
var int green;
var int blue;
var int alpha;
```

This brings up a good question, *why use bytes?* The reason is if you use byte values for our color, it is impossible to accidentally change that value in code to something outside of the scope a byte: ZERO to TWO-HUNDRED and FIFTY-FIVE.

Make sure all of our TestingColor values are of the variable type byte. If you changed any bytes to int, change them back.

In order for our text to change color, we have to change a variable assignment in the DrawHUD( ) function. Change this:

```
Canvas.SetDrawColor( 255,255,255,255 );
```

to this:

```
Canvas.DrawColor = TestingColor;
```

An alternative way to do this would be to change Canvas.SetDrawColor( ) to:

```
Canvas.SetDrawColor( red,green,blue,alpha );
```

Though this will end up ignoring our TestingColor variable.
Here is our entire class, at the moment. If you are having compiling issues, check your class verses this:

As stated in the previous chapter, you do NOT have to write out the comments if you do not want to. They are there to help you know what the code is doing but have no effect on the program.

```
class USL_HUD extends HUD;

// This will be our "Testing" text.
var private string text;

// Ranges from 0 to 255
var byte red;
var byte green;
var byte blue;
var byte alpha;

// Color used for our "Testing" text.
var Color TestingColor;

// A function called right after this HUD class is created.
simulated function PostBeginPlay( )
{
   super.PostBeginPlay( );

   TestingColor.R = red;
   TestingColor.G = green;
   TestingColor.B = blue;
   TestingColor.A = alpha;
}

// This is the HUD class "Main" draw loop. Used to draw HUD
//elements to the screen.
function DrawHUD( )
{
   // Set location to display text
   Canvas.SetPos( Canvas.SizeX * 0.45, Canvas.SizeY * 0.5 );

   // Set color to display text
   Canvas.DrawColor = TestingColor;

   // Draw text
   Canvas.DrawText( text );
}

DefaultProperties
```

```
{
    // Default color values
    red = 128
    green = 52
    blue = 224
    alpha = 255

    text = "Hello Unreal!"
}
```

If you press the "Start Debugging" button and used the same values as I did, you will see our text in a darker shade of purple and pink.

Our program is a bit more complex than the original version but it is essentially the same thing. We are using the DrawHUD( ) function to display our text at the center of the screen. We are using our assigned TestingColor variable (from the byte variables) to tell Canvas what color we want our text to show as and we are using the DrawText( ) function to display the text to the screen.

To reiterate, a variable is a way to **store data** that is associated by a name. This name tells the compiler what sort of data this variable is supposed to hold and each has its own set of rules. We also touched on the idea of structs, which is a group of variables that refer back to the struct name. The variables (or elements) inside of the struct allow the programmer to access and modify what information the struct holds.

Lets modify some aspects of our class so we can further modify the way our text is displayed on the screen.

Start by changing the way our color byte variables are setup.

Remove these class variables:

```
// Ranges from 0 to 255
```

```
var byte red;
var byte green;
var byte blue;
var byte alpha;
```

and add:

```
// An array to hold our color variables
var byte ColorArray[4];
```

Also, remove this in DefaultProperties:

```
// Default color values
red = 128
green = 52
blue = 224
alpha = 255
```

And add:

```
// Default color values
ColorArray[0] = 128
ColorArray[1] = 52
ColorArray[2] = 224
ColorArray[3] = 255
```

Change:

```
// A function called right after this HUD class is created.
simulated function PostBeginPlay( )
{
   super.PostBeginPlay( );

   TestingColor.R = red;
   TestingColor.G = green;
   TestingColor.B = blue;
   TestingColor.A = alpha;
}
```

to:

```
// A function called right after this HUD class is created.
simulated function PostBeginPlay( )
{
   super.PostBeginPlay( );

   TestingColor.R = ColorArray[0];
```

```
    TestingColor.G = ColorArray[1];
    TestingColor.B = ColorArray[2];
    TestingColor.A = ColorArray[3];
}
```

If you run the game now, nothing should have changed, even though there was a lot done within the program that has changed.

We are now using an **array** to store our byte variables. An array is a collection of data types (variables) of the same type. The one tradeoff in our current approach is that the naming of our variables is not as clear as it was previously. Though it is a way to clean up our variable declaration and makes it more difficult to confuse any of the byte variables since they are all a part of the same array group. I am using the same Red, Green, Blue, Alpha order for the array.

You will notice that we gave our array FOUR byte variables but when we assign them in the DefaultProperties the last number is [3]. This is because arrays start at ZERO. This can become a bit tricky to understand at first but it is important to remember that when you want to access portions of an array, the array starts at ZERO and ends ONE before the size of the array.

For instance, if you create a byte array with FIFTY elements.

```
var byte myArray[50];
```

The last accessible element in that array is going to be FORTY-NINE.

```
MyByte = myArray[49];
```

If you were to try:

```
MyByte = myArray[50];
```

The game is going to compile and may even assign a value to MyByte. However, this is not going to be something you want. You will also get a "ScriptWarning" in the log, such as:

```
[0021.57] ScriptWarning: Accessed array 'USL_HUD_0.myArray' out of bounds (50/50)
        USL_HUD TestMap.TheWorld:PersistentLevel.USL_HUD_0
        Function UnrealScriptLesson.USL_HUD:DrawHUD:0032
```

The same is true if you want to go **BELOW** zero.

```
[0012.96] ScriptWarning: Accessed array 'USL_HUD_0.myArray' out of bounds (-10/50)
        USL_HUD TestMap.TheWorld:PersistentLevel.USL_HUD_0
        Function UnrealScriptLesson.USL_HUD:DrawHUD:0035
```

23

To explore some other variables, lets display a "HealthValue", "GameTime", and a bool value (bool variables represent TRUE or FALSE) for if the player is moving or not.

To start, delete everything inside of the DrawHUD( ) function, leaving just this:

```
// This is the HUD class "Main" draw loop
function DrawHUD( )
{

}
```

Add these class variables:

```
// A 32 bit integer value : is a whole number, no decimal point
var int iHealthValue;

// A 32 bit floating point value : can have a decimal point
var float fTimer;

// A booleon value : either true or false
var bool bOnOff;
```

Add to the DefaultProperties:

```
// default health value
iHealthValue = 100
```

The HUD class now looks like this. If you are having compiling errors, check your code with the follow:

```
class USL_HUD extends HUD;

// This will be our "Testing" text.
var private string text;

// An array to hold our color variables
var byte ColorArray[4];

// Color used for our "Testing" text.
var Color TestingColor;

// A 32 bit integer value : is a whole number, no decimal point
var int iHealthValue;

// A 32 bit floating point value : can have a decimal point
var float fTimer;
```

```
// A bool value : either true or false
var bool bOnOff;

// A function called right after this HUD class is created.
simulated function PostBeginPlay( )
{
   super.PostBeginPlay( );

   TestingColor.R = ColorArray[0];
   TestingColor.G = ColorArray[1];
   TestingColor.B = ColorArray[2];
   TestingColor.A = ColorArray[3];
}

// This is the HUD class "Main" draw lOOP. Used to draw HUD //elements
to the screen.
function DrawHUD( )
{

}

DefaultProperties
{
   // default health value
   iHealthValue = 100

   // Default color values
   ColorArray[0] = 128
   ColorArray[1] = 52
   ColorArray[2] = 224
   ColorArray[3] = 255

   text = "Hello Unreal!"
}
```

Add the following to the DrawHUD( ) function:

```
// This is the HUD class "Main" draw loop Used to draw HUD
//elements to the screen.
function DrawHUD( )
{
   // Display Health Value
   Canvas.SetPos( Canvas.SizeX * 0.01, Canvas.SizeY * 0.01 );
   Canvas.DrawColor = TestingColor;
   Canvas.DrawText( "Health: " $ iHealthValue );

   // Display Timer
```

```
Canvas.SetPos( Canvas.SizeX * 0.01, Canvas.SizeY * 0.03 );
Canvas.DrawColor = TestingColor;
Canvas.DrawText( "Game Time: " $ fTimer );

// Display if player is moving or not
Canvas.SetPos( Canvas.SizeX * 0.01, Canvas.SizeY * 0.05 );
Canvas.DrawColor = TestingColor;
Canvas.DrawText( "Player Moving: " $ bOnOff );
}
```

If you debug the game now, you will see the default values for each of our variables. Such as:

```
Health: 100
Game Time: 0.0000
Player Moving: False
```

As you can see, the Health value is the same as what we set it in the DefaultProperties. The GameTime float defaults at 0.0000 and the default value for bool variables is FALSE.

Before we go any farther, I am going to change the text color back to White. In order to do this, change all of the elements in our ColorArray in DefaultProperties to "255". This will make the text easier to see.

Such as:

```
// Default color values
ColorArray[0] = 255
ColorArray[1] = 255
ColorArray[2] = 255
ColorArray[3] = 255
```

Let's introduce some logic to increase the fTimer variable, which will count up in seconds.

Add this to the top (above // Display Health Value) of the DrawHUD( ) function:

```
fTimer += RenderDelta;
```

We are using a "Compound assignment" operator to take the value of fTimer and add it to itself PLUS the value of RenderDelta. As a comparison, this is the same as typing:

```
fTimer = fTimer + RenderDelta;
```

If you play the game now, you will see the value after Game Time count up in seconds. This is one of the cool aspects of using "Per frame" rendering. Regardless of how fast or slow your game is running, the fTimer will show seconds count up in the games time.

Let's add some logic so the "Player Moving" bool will change, the players velocity is GREATER than ZERO.

Above "fTimer += RenderDelta;" add the following:

```
local Pawn P;
```

Under fTimer += RenderDelta;, in the DrawHUD( ) function, Add the following:

```
foreach WorldInfo.AllPawns( class'Pawn', P )
{
   if ( VSize( P.Velocity ) > 0 && P != none )
   {
      bOnOff = true;
   }
   else
   {
      bOnOff = false;
   }
}
```

The DrawHUD( ) function should look like:

```
// This is the HUD class "Main" draw lOOP. Used to draw
// HUD elements to the screen.
function DrawHUD( )
{
   // Used to reference the Pawn class, within our game world
   local Pawn P;

   // Used to keep track of time
   fTimer += RenderDelta;

   // Used to access ALL Pawn actors in the world.
   foreach WorldInfo.AllPawns( class'Pawn', P )
   {
      // If the magnitude ( speed ) of our Pawn is greater than ZERO
      //and our Pawn doesn't equal none
      if ( VSize( P.Velocity ) > 0 && P != none )
      {
         // Set bOnOff to true
         bOnOff = true;
      }
```

```
        // If the speed of the Pawn is 0 or the Pawn doesn't exist
        else
        {
                // Set bOnOff to false
                bOnOff = false;
        }
    }

    // Display Health Value
    Canvas.SetPos( Canvas.SizeX * 0.01, Canvas.SizeY * 0.01 );
    Canvas.DrawColor = TestingColor;
    Canvas.DrawText( "Health: " $ iHealthValue );

    // Display Timer
    Canvas.SetPos( Canvas.SizeX * 0.01, Canvas.SizeY * 0.03 );
    Canvas.DrawColor = TestingColor;
    Canvas.DrawText( "Game Time: " $ fTimer );

    // Display if player is moving or not
    Canvas.SetPos( Canvas.SizeX * 0.01, Canvas.SizeY * 0.05 );
    Canvas.DrawColor = TestingColor;
    Canvas.DrawText( "Player Moving: " $ bOnOff );
}
```

This is a big step from the last example of displaying text at the center of the screen.

This is the first time we have used a **local variable**. Local variables need to be at the top of the function. This is one of the rules that Unreal has that cannot be broken. If you try to put a local variable below any of the code in a function block, you will get a compiling error.

```
// Used to reference the Pawn class, within our game world
local Pawn P;
```

Within programming, there is a term called **scope**. Scope is a way for the programmer to manage when a variable declaration has an effect. Instead of creating a "global" or "class" variable, as we have done previously, this example shows that we can create a variable within a function, to use in that function.

For instance, if you wanted to use the Pawn variable in more than one function, you could create it as a class variable. As of now, it is a local variable because it is only being used within the DrawHUD() function.

Scope is one of the more challenging aspects of programming, as it can be difficult to understand how to manage "talking" with other classes or functions. The reason for this is because the program runs one line at a time and will manage blocks of code one at a time.

To further explain, look at the DrawHUD( ) function. This function is called every frame and during this frame, it calculates everything in the "block" (represented by the { } brackets). Then, it deletes everything from memory. For each frame, the function is called, calculated, and deleted. This is quite fascinating, as it is going through the code, line by line, and calculating each called function then coming back to the DrawHud( ) function.

For instance, the line:

```
Canvas.SetPos( Canvas.SizeX * 0.01, Canvas.SizeY * 0.01 );
```

While this is in the DrawHUD( ) function when it is calculated, the game will go to the **Canvas** class being created by our HUD, find the function SetPos( ), then use our "parameters" or "arguments" (another word for variables when they are "passed" into a function) which also search the Canvas class, attached to our HUD, for the variables of SizeX and SizeY, then return to SetPos, which will then return back to our DrawHUD( ) function.

As you can see, to calculate this one line, the program will have to jump around to a few places to calculate and access the variables data.

(Canvas is a class that helps to render elements to the screen, such as text).

Another example of using scope to "talk" with another class, is the block of code, in DrawHUD( ):

```
// Used to access ALL Pawn actors in the world.
foreach WorldInfo.AllPawns( class'Pawn', P )
{
   // If the magnitude ( speed ) of our Pawn is greater than ZERO and
   //our Pawn doesn't equal none
   if ( VSize( P.Velocity ) > 0 && P != none )
   {
      // Set bOnOff to true
      bOnOff = true;
   }
   // If the speed of the Pawn is 0 or the Pawn doesn't exist
   else
   {
      // Set bOnOff to false
      bOnOff = false;
   }
}
```

This **iterator** will search for all of the instances of the class "Pawn" and then we give it a local reference of the same class type (local Pawn P;), so we can now reference each Pawn within the game world with the variable "P", for each iteration or cycle of this iterator.

(A iterator is a way to search and get a reference to many different instances of the same class. If you had TEN Pawn classes in the world, this is a way to get access to each one of them without directly knowing each one).

One thing that must be clear here is that this iterator cycles through EVERY Pawn class in the game world. In our instance, we only have ONE Pawn so using it in this way is not a big deal. If we happened to have TWENTY Pawns in our game world it would calculate this block of code for each of them. This is important to remember because if you did have TWENTY Pawns in a game world, there is a good chance you don't want to reference all of them.

As an example, this iterator works by cycling through each relevant class (Pawn). If it finds ONE, it calculates the relevant code within the iterator block, with the reference variable declared in the foreach statement, then looks for another. If it finds another, it will do the same thing for it, with the same reference variable. If it doesn't find another, it will **break** from this block and continue through the rest of the function.

Chances are this is still a bit confusing. I will touch on it further when we talk about creating and using functions, as well as when I talk about "loops".

The purpose of the iterator is to know when our Pawn is moving. In order to do this with use another Unreal function called VSize( ). This function will take a vector (a struct of THREE float variables that represent X, Y, and Z space within the game world) and convert it into a float variable, represented as "magnitude", which is a speed.

The magnitude of velocity is speed.

We take our float magnitude (speed) value and make sure it is above ZERO, meaning the player is moving, and we check to make sure that our Pawn has been referenced in the iterator. If both are TRUE, the code continues into the block of the iterator.

```
// Set bOnOff to true
bOnOff = true;
```

If either the speed is equal to ZERO or the Pawn reference comes back as NONE (it doesn't find any Pawns in the world), then:

```
// Set bOnOff to false
bOnOff = false;
```

The DrawHUD( ) function calculates all of the data we have set to show our three variables.

```
// Display Health Value
Canvas.SetPos( Canvas.SizeX * 0.01, Canvas.SizeY * 0.01 );
Canvas.DrawColor = TestingColor;
Canvas.DrawText( "Health: " $ iHealthValue );

// Display Timer
Canvas.SetPos( Canvas.SizeX * 0.01, Canvas.SizeY * 0.03 );
Canvas.DrawColor = TestingColor;
Canvas.DrawText( "Game Time: " $ fTimer );

// Display if player is moving or not
Canvas.SetPos( Canvas.SizeX * 0.01, Canvas.SizeY * 0.05 );
Canvas.DrawColor = TestingColor;
Canvas.DrawText( "Player Moving: " $ bOnOff );
```

To explain again, each of these "groups" of code do pretty much the same thing. The first line calls the SetPos( ) function, which stores the location on the screen to display the text. Then we assign the Color we want to display the text as. We then use the DrawText( ) function to draw the variable. One thing you will notice is the RED text, within the quotation marks. This is a way to have "static" (non changing) text on the screen, before the variable that can change.

Challenges:

To further educate yourself, here is a few things you can try to do, in order to get a better understanding of variables.

1) Change the color that is displayed for each of the variables, so that the static quotation text is white but the variable being displayed is a different color.
2) Move the text from the top left corner of the screen, to the bottom right.

Next is possible answers for these three challenges, if you need them. They are written to follow the same sort of pattern we see in this chapter. There are more advanced ways to do this but these answers will be something you should be able to follow along with.

1: "Change the color of the variables "

This is inside the DrawHUD( ) function:

```
// Display Health Value
Canvas.SetPos( Canvas.SizeX * 0.01, Canvas.SizeY * 0.01 );
Canvas.DrawColor = TestingColor;
Canvas.DrawText( "Health: " );

Canvas.SetPos( Canvas.SizeX * 0.075, Canvas.SizeY * 0.01 );
Canvas.SetDrawColor( 255,0,255,255 );
```

```
Canvas.DrawText( iHealthValue );

// Display Timer
Canvas.SetPos( Canvas.SizeX * 0.01, Canvas.SizeY * 0.03 );
Canvas.DrawColor = TestingColor;
Canvas.DrawText( "Game Time: " );

Canvas.SetPos( Canvas.SizeX * 0.075, Canvas.SizeY * 0.03 );
Canvas.SetDrawColor( 255,0,255,255 );
Canvas.DrawText( fTimer );

// Display if player is moving or not
Canvas.SetPos( Canvas.SizeX * 0.01, Canvas.SizeY * 0.05 );
Canvas.DrawColor = TestingColor;
Canvas.DrawText( "Player Moving: " );

Canvas.SetPos( Canvas.SizeX * 0.075, Canvas.SizeY * 0.05 );
Canvas.SetDrawColor( 255,0,255,255 );
Canvas.DrawText( bOnOff );
```

2: "Move the text from the top left to the bottom right "

Add this to the DrawHUD( ) function:

```
  // Display Health Value
Canvas.SetPos( Canvas.SizeX * 0.9, Canvas.SizeY * 0.95 );
Canvas.DrawColor = TestingColor;
Canvas.DrawText( "Health: " );

Canvas.SetPos( Canvas.SizeX * 0.95, Canvas.SizeY * 0.95 );
Canvas.SetDrawColor( 255,0,255,255 );
Canvas.DrawText( iHealthValue );

// Display Timer
Canvas.SetPos( Canvas.SizeX * 0.9, Canvas.SizeY * 0.93 );
Canvas.DrawColor = TestingColor;
Canvas.DrawText( "Game Time: " );

Canvas.SetPos( Canvas.SizeX * 0.95, Canvas.SizeY * 0.93 );
Canvas.SetDrawColor( 255,0,255,255 );
Canvas.DrawText( fTimer );

// Display if player is moving or not
Canvas.SetPos( Canvas.SizeX * 0.9, Canvas.SizeY * 0.9 );
Canvas.DrawColor = TestingColor;
Canvas.DrawText( "Player Moving: " );

Canvas.SetPos( Canvas.SizeX * 0.95, Canvas.SizeY * 0.9 );
```

```
Canvas.SetDrawColor( 255,0,255,255 );
Canvas.DrawText( bOnOff );

// Display the magnitude ( speed ) of the Pawn
Canvas.SetPos( Canvas.SizeX * 0.9, Canvas.SizeY * 0.87 );
Canvas.DrawColor = TestingColor;
Canvas.DrawText( "Player Speed: " $ fPlayerSpeed );
```

Additional Reading:

More on formatting programs:
http://en.wikipedia.org/wiki/Programming_style

More on naming conventions for programming:
http://en.wikipedia.org/wiki/Naming_convention_(programming)

More about variables in UnrealScript:
http://udn.epicgames.com/Three/StringsInUnrealScript.html
http://udn.epicgames.com/Three/UnrealScriptVariables.html

More about using iterators in UnrealScript:
http://udn.epicgames.com/Three/UnrealScriptIterators.html

More about variables in computer programming:
https://en.wikipedia.org/wiki/Variable_(computer_science)
http://en.wikipedia.org/wiki/Data_type

More about Arrays:
http://en.wikipedia.org/wiki/Array
http://en.wikipedia.org/wiki/Array_data_structure

More about Canvas:
http://udn.epicgames.com/Three/CanvasTechnicalGuide.html

More about scope;
http://en.wikipedia.org/wiki/Scope_(computer_science)

More about RGB color:
http://en.wikipedia.org/wiki/RGB_color_model

Loops, Conditional, and Switch Statements

Chapter Three

Last chapter introduced the idea of variables; the way of storing data within specific types, by using a keyword (also called a specifier). In this chapter will start to develop a better understanding how to use these variables to make more impressive things happen in the game world.

The first thing that needs to be setup is an addition to our TestMap. Ipen up the UDK editor by using the short-cut you created in chapter one.

When you open the editor, you should see a "Content Browser" window. If you do not, click the Content Browser button.

Open your map by either selecting the "Open Map" button, or by going to File →Open, and choosing your TestMap.

In the Content Browser, you should see a few tabs on the top.

| Content Browser | Actor Classes | Levels | Scene | Layers | Documentation |

Select the "Actor Classes" tab and on the top, there is a search window. Search "Note".

You should now see:

Select the Note name and then in your level, RIGHT-CLICK on the ground and select: Add Note Here.

Since it may be partially in the ground, raise it above the ground a bit. You can do this with the translation widget. When the Note is selected. Use your LEFT-CLICK to select the Note. You can then hover over the Z Axis Widget line (the blue vertical line), HOLD down LEFT-CLICK, and drag the Note up off the ground.

Once the Note is off the ground and the Note selected, hold down ALT + LEFT-CLICK, while selecting the Y Axis widget (the green horizontal line) and drag to the RIGHT. This will duplicate your Note. Do this until you have FIVE Notes, spread out in a line, within the scene.

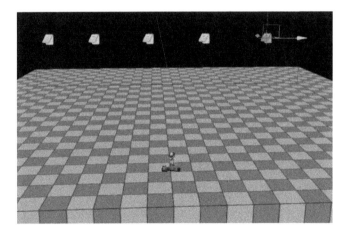

Save your scene by pressing the save button or by going file →save, and close down the editor. If you press CTRL + S you will NOT be saving your level, you will be adding a subtraction brush to your scene, which may "remove" your floor.

If you did press CTRL + S on accident, press ALT + 1 to enter "wireframe mode" and select the YELLOW brush, and press delete. Then press ALT + 3 to enter "unlit" mode and rebuild your level by pressing the "Build All Button".

Then save your map through the save button or by file →save and close the editor.
We are going to be using both the GameInfo and HUD class, for this example. Open the
USL_GameInfo.uc file, in Visual Studio.

You should see this:

```
class USL_GameInfo extends GameInfo;

DefaultProperties
{
    HUDType = class'UnrealScriptLesson.USL_HUD'
    PlayerControllerClass=class'UnrealScriptLesson.USL_PlayerController'
    DefaultPawnClass = class'UnrealScriptLesson.USL_Pawn'
    bDelayedStart = false
}
```

Add the following, after the class declaration and before DefaultProperties:

```
simulated function PostBeginPlay( )
{
    super.PostBeginPlay( );

    SetTimer( 3.5,, 'LoopTesting' );

}

function LoopTesting( )
{

}
```

After the class is created, we will use the SetTimer( ) function to set a delay before our
LoopTesting( ) function will be called. This will give us a little time to experience what is
going on.

As explained last chapter, PostBeginPlay( ) is a way for the programmer to call functions,
assign values, or do anything just after the class is created.

The function LoopTest( ) will be our way of testing different methods of using loops.

To get started, create three local variables in the LoopTesting( ) function:

```
function LoopTesting( )
{
    // Help to show us what our loops are doing by firing rockets
    local UTProj_Rocket proj;
```

```
   // Used to keep track of our loops
   local int i;

   // Used to reference the Pawn within our world
   local Pawn P;
}
```

The **for loop** works a lot like our foreach iterator in the previous chapter, though it has more precise ways to manage it. A for loop is also called a iterator, which is a method to repeat code. One of the unique aspects of the for loop, compared to the previous chapters iterator is the ability to manage how many times the loop will run. This is done by the initial statement.

Add this to our LoopTesting( ) function:

```
function LoopTesting( )
{
   // Help to show us what our loops are doing by firing rockets
   local UTProj_Rocket proj;

   // Used to keep track of our loops
   local int i;

   // Used to reference the Pawn within our world
   local Pawn P;

   // A for loop : cycles five times
   for( i = 0; i < 5; i++ )
   {

   }
}
```

In the for loop, we initially assign the variable "i" to ZERO. Then we finish that assignment with a semi-colon (;). After that, we want to check if i is less than FIVE, also followed by a semi-colon. At last, we say i++, which will take the value of "i" and add ONE to it, allowing the loop to continue. This is followed by checking the value of "i" again. Only when the condition within the for loop is FALSE will the for loop stop iterating.

Another way to write this, that may make more sense to what is going on, though not practical, because for loops were made because of this, is:

```
i = 0;

if ( i < 5 )
```

```
{
   i++;
   LoopTesting( );
}
```

This fundamentally will NOT work because of **scope**. This is because we will not be able to manage our local variable "i" in the same way as the for loop would be able to. The variable would be "destroyed" after each iteration of calling it (remember last chapter, each line of code is called, in order, by block. When the program reaches the end of the block, the memory of that block is deleted).

If you were to have "i" be a class variable this method would work, though I don't recommend going down that road. It can be a bad practice and for loops are much easier to handle.

You'll notice this function would call itself. There is an expression for calling this, it is called "recursion". This practice can be dangerous, as getting caught having a function loop itself forever can happen. If you are interested in learning more about this, look at the end of this chapter for additional reading. I won't be touching on recursion, as it is outside of the practices involved in beginning programming.

Another advantage of the for loop is that they are contained. This means that even though "i" starts at ZERO, the loop will manage adding to it, without any worry of it being reset or manipulated outside of that loop.

The i++ expression is new. This operator is called a **Arithmetic Increment Operator**. Essentially, the ++ means that it takes the value of what is before it, and adds ONE to it.

It is the same as:

```
i = i + 1;
```

Or:

```
i += 1; // Another shortcut to add a value on top of itself
```

We will touch on the (++) operator later, as there is many ways to use it.

Add this inside of our for loop:

```
// A for loop : cycles five times
for( i = 0; i < 5; i++ )
{
   DebugMessagePlayer( "Value Of i: " $ i );
```

```
}
```

If you run the game now using the "Start Debugging" button, after THREE point FIVE seconds you will see this appear on the bottom left side of the game window:

Where did ZERO go? If you press the Tilde key (`), above the Tab key, you will open the Console Window and there will be the list of ZERO to FOUR. The reason ZERO is not seen, is that the display for debug messages shows FOUR lines, which end up being the last FOUR.

Let's add some things so we can use this for loop in a more visual way. Make a class variable below the class declaration, as such:

```
// An array to store world Note actors
var array<Note> NoteArray;
```

This is a **Dynamic Array**, which is a way to store alike variables (data types) without worrying about how many you might have. In the last chapter we worked with an array but we managed it statically, by declaring that it had FOUR elements. In this Dynamic Array we will manage it differently during "run time". This means we will populate and manage the array when the game is running.

To do this, create a new function:

```
// A function at add all of the world Note actors to a Dynamic Array
function FindNoteActors( )
{
   // Used to reference each Note in the world.
   local Note N;

   // Iterates through all of the Notes and using our reference, will
   // add each to the Dynamic Array.
   foreach WorldInfo.AllActors( class'Note', N )
   {
      NoteArray.AddItem( N );
   }
}
```

We will also want to set this up so our Dynamic Array will be populated as soon as the game starts. Inside of the PostBeginPlay( ) function, after the super.PostBeginPlay( ), add:

```
// Add all the Notes to the Dynamic Array
FindNoteActors( );
```

Now that we are adding all of our Note Actors to the Dynamic Array, lets use them in our for loop.

Change the for loop, within the LoopTesting( ) function, to:

```
// Get a reference to our pawn
foreach WorldInfo.AllPawns( class'Pawn', P )
{
   // A for loop : cycles five times
   for( i = 0; i < NoteArray.Length; i++ )
   {
      // Spawn a projectile at the location and given the rotation of
      //the pawn
      proj = Spawn( class'UTProj_Rocket', P,,
            P.Location, P.Rotation );

      // Tell the projectile which way to go
      proj.Init( Normal( NoteArray[i].Location - P.Location ) );
   }
}
```

This might be a moment where you think, *you can use iterators within iterators?* The simple answer is yes; however, the practical answer is to try to avoid it (especially when it comes to large or complicated loops). These can be a hefty cost on performance if not managed well enough. Since the explained knowledge of Unreal Script at the moment is not too in depth, this should be a straightforward way to accomplish this and will work adequately. Keep in mind that later on, we will find better references for our Pawn class, so we will not have to run iterators to access it.

Our for loop statement has changed, instead of "i < 5;" we are now using "i < NoteArray.Length;" This is a way to manage the array without knowing how many elements are in it. It means that "i" will continue to count up until we have reached the end of the Dynamic Array, which is represented by the value "Length".

For each iteration of our for loop, we will spawn a rocket projectile at the location of the player. Then using our newly created projectile, we "aim" it by using the projectiles Init( ) function, which is designed to point the projectile in the direction it should go. That is done using the Normal( ) function. Normal( ) will take two vector locations and create a new vector that points from one to another. This means we can aim the projectile from the player, to the location of the Note.

```
Note location - Pawn location = projectile direction.
```

If you run the game and wait THREE point FIVE seconds, you will see the result, which is FIVE rockets firing from the player, to each Note.

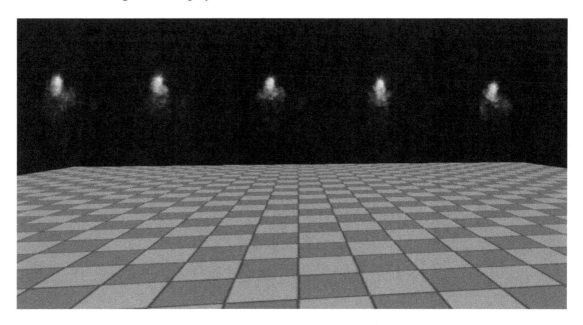

You'll notice that the rockets fire very quick, like they are all firing at once. This is because the calculations of the for loop is very quick.

The While Loop:

Another kind of loop is called the "while loop". This works in the same way as the for loop, in terms of calculating the same code over again. The difference is instead of calculating the exact number of iterations, while loops will continue to iterate as long as the condition is TRUE.

If you do not want the FIVE rockets to spawn every time you debug the game, go ahead and comment out the SetTimer( ) function in PostBeginPlay( ), in the USL_GameInfo.uc class.

Such as:

```
simulated function PostBeginPlay( )
{
   super.PostBeginPlay( );

   //SetTimer( 3.5,, 'LoopTesting' );
```

```
   // Add all the Notes to the Dynamic Array
   FindNoteActors( );
}
```

Let's setup the USL_PlayerController.uc class to work for our while loop. Create a new class bool variable:

```
// Used to control when to fire our projectile
var bool bFireProjectile;
```

Instead of having to worry about making a new input command, let's use one that already exists inside of the player controller. Add this function under our bFireProjectile bool variable:

```
// Overide the default "StartFire" function, so we can use our
// mouse button as input.
exec function StartFire( optional byte FireModeNum  )
{
   bFireProjectile = true;
}
```

You'll notice this function looks a bit different with the exec in front of it. An **exec function** is a unique way UDK to call a function during run time. These behave similar to a console command and can be called through the console window (if you're in game, press the tilde key (`), above tab, to open the console). These functions are also used because they can be called through the DefaultInput.ini config file (among other places). Since this is already setup as a default input function (by pressing LEFT or RIGHT mouse button) it will be easy for us to modify it to work the way we want it to.

Let's start to write a PlayerTick( ) function, so we are able to check when a key is pressed. In your USL_PlayerController.uc, add the following:

```
// Tick function used to check input : called once per frame.
function PlayerTick( float DeltaTime )
{

}
```

A PlayerTick( ) function is called every frame. This works just like the DrawHUD( ) function in our HUD class but is used in Player Controller classes. The same sort of concerns should be met with dealing with PlayerTick( ) as in dealing with DrawHUD( ); you do not want to overload these functions with too much, as it will cause a performance decrease. Try to call functions when they are needed, not when it is easy.

Let's introduce the while loop. Write the following inside of the PlayerTick( ) function:

```
// Tick function used to check input : called once per frame.
function PlayerTick( float DeltaTime )
{
    // Used to spawn and reference a UTProj_Rocket
    local UTProj_Rocket proj;

    // Used to reference our pawn, so we can use its location.
    local Pawn P;

    // We dont want to overrid the entire PlayerTick( ) function,
    // so lets include the previous class code.
    super.PlayerTick( DeltaTime );

    // While we have pressed our Left-Mouse button, to
    // turn bFireProjectile TRUE
    while( bFireProjectile )
    {
        // Get a reference to a local Pawn
        foreach WorldInfo.AllPawns( class'Pawn', P )
        {
            // Spawn the projectile and the pawns location,
            // given the pawns rotation.
            proj = Spawn( class'UTProj_Rocket', proj,,
                P.Location, P.Rotation );

            // Set the direction of the projectile the same as
            // the pawns
            proj.Init( Vector( P.Rotation ) );

            // Turn our bFireProjectile bool off, so we don't
            // keep firing rockets.
            bFireProjectile = false;
        }
    }
}
```

A lot of this should look familiar to you. We are using local variables to declare and reference a Projectile and a Pawn. We are also using super.PlayerTick( ) to make sure we don't completely overwrite the previously written code in the parent Player Controller. We are using a foreach iterator to reference our Pawn in order to get its location and rotation. Then we are using the Spawn( ) function to spawn our projectile and then use a reference to it, to point it in the right direction.

The one big thing going on here is the "while(bFireProjectile)". This might look odd because this doesn't look like a traditional condition statement that we have been using before. One of the cool things about using bool variables is that they have just two possible values, TRUE or FALSE. Because of this, there is a short-cut we can take when using them in conditional statements, that involve a bool.

This:

```
while( bFireProjectile )
```

Is the same as:

```
while( bFireProjectile == true )
```

And, the other variation would be:

```
while( !bFireProjectile )
```

Is the same as:

```
while( bFireProjectile == false )
```

The end result of the while statement is to call the rest of the code in the while loop when the condition is TRUE. bFireProjectiles will become true when we press our LEFT or RIGHT MOUSE button. If you run the game, by pressing the "Start Debugging" button in Visual Studio you be able to fire rockets by pressing your LEFT or RIGHT mouse button.

You will notice that you may die, as the rockets spawn from the location of the pawn, and have splash damage when they explode.

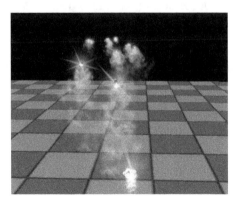

The USL_PlayerController.uc class should now look like:
```
class USL_PlayerController extends PlayerController;
```

```
// Used to control when to fire our projectile
var bool bFireProjectile;

// Override the default "StartFire" function, so we can use our
// Left or Right Mouse button as input.
exec function StartFire( optional byte FireModeNum  )
{
   bFireProjectile = true;
}

// Tick function used to check input : called once per frame.
function PlayerTick( float DeltaTime )
{
   // Used to spawn and reference a UTProj_Rocket
   local UTProj_Rocket proj;

   // Used to reference our pawn, so we can use its location.
   local Pawn P;

   // We dont want to override the entire PlayerTick( ) function, so
   // lets include the parent class code.
   super.PlayerTick( DeltaTime );

   // While we have pressed our Left-Mouse button, to
   // turn bFireProjectile TRUE
   while( bFireProjectile )
   {
      // Get a reference to a local Pawn
      foreach WorldInfo.AllPawns( class'Pawn', P )
      {
         // Spawn the projectile and the pawns location, given the
         // pawns rotation.
         proj = Spawn( class'UTProj_Rocket', proj,,
               P.Location, P.Rotation );

         // Set the direction of the projectile the same as the
         // pawns
         proj.Init( Vector( P.Rotation ) );

         // Turn our bFireProjectile bool off, so we don't keep
         // firing rockets.
         bFireProjectile = false;
      }
   }
}
```

The Do Loop:

Another way to iterate through a block of code many times is with the do loop. This is similar to the while loop, so let's modify our current setup to work as a do loop.

Create another function:

```
// Used to show how Do loops work
function OurDoLoop( )
{
    // Used to spawn and reference a UTProj_Rocket
    local UTProj_Rocket proj;

    // Used to reference our pawn, so we can use its location.
    local Pawn P;

    // Used to count our do loop
    local int i;

    // Get a reference to all of the Pawn class in our game world
    foreach WorldInfo.AllPawns( class'Pawn', P )
        {
            do
            {

            // Spawn the projectile and the pawns location, given the
            // pawns rotation.
            proj = Spawn( class'UTProj_Rocket', proj,,
                    P.Location, P.Rotation );

            // Set the direction of the projectile the same as the
            // pawns
            proj.Init( Vector( P.Rotation ) );

            // Debug so we can see all of our Projectile names
            DebugMessagePlayer( proj );

            // Turn our bFireProjectile bool off, so we don't keep
            // firing rockets.
            bFireProjectile = false;

            // Increment our counter.
            i++;
        } until ( i == 5 );
    }
}
```

Then change the StartFire( ) function so our new function will be called instead.
```
// Override the default "StartFire" function, so we can use our
```

47

```
// Left or Right Mouse button as input.
exec function StartFire( optional byte FireModeNum  )
{
   OurDoLoop( );
}
```

If you debug the game now and press ANY mouse button you will see something very similar as before. Since there is a DebugMessagePlayer( ) function call displaying all of our projectile names, you can see that each time you press a mouse button, you are indeed firing FIVE projectiles. If you were to change the last line of the do loop (until (i == 5)) to a higher number, you will start to see a longer trail behind the projectiles.

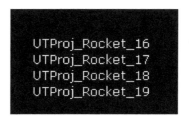

Do loops are great for iterating through blocks of code, just as a for loop or while loop, though I find myself not using them very often, as for and while loops end up covering most of what I need done. Do loops are still handy in specific situations. Don't forget about them.

The entire USL_PlayerController.uc class should look like this, including the PlayerTick( ) function. If you are having compiling issues, check your code against this:

```
class USL_PlayerController extends PlayerController;

// Used to control when to fire our projectile
var bool bFireProjectile;

// Override the default "StartFire" function, so we can use our Left
or Right Mouse button as input.
exec function StartFire( optional byte FireModeNum  )
{
   OurDoLoop( );
}

// Tick function used to check input : called once per frame.
function PlayerTick( float DeltaTime )
{
   // Used to spawn and reference a UTProj_Rocket
   local UTProj_Rocket proj;

   // Used to reference our pawn, so we can use its location.
   local Pawn P;
```

```
    // We dont want to override the entire PlayerTick( ) function,
    // so lets include the previous class code.
    super.PlayerTick( DeltaTime );

    // While we have pressed our Left-Mouse button,
    // to turn bFireProjectile TRUE
    while( bFireProjectile )
    {
        // Get a reference to a local Pawn
        foreach WorldInfo.AllPawns( class'Pawn', P )
        {
            // Spawn the projectile and the pawns location, given the
            // pawns rotation.
            proj = Spawn( class'UTProj_Rocket', proj,,
                    P.Location, P.Rotation );

            // Set the direction of the projectile the same as the
            // pawns
            proj.Init( Vector( P.Rotation ) );

            // Turn our bFireProjectile bool off, so we don't keep
            // firing rockets.
            bFireProjectile = false;
        }
    }
}

// Used to show how Do loops work
function OurDoLoop( )
{
    // Used to spawn and reference a UTProj_Rocket
    local UTProj_Rocket proj;

    // Used to reference our pawn, so we can use its location.
    local Pawn P;

    // Used to count our do loop
    local int i;

    // Get a reference to all of the Pawn class in our game world
    foreach WorldInfo.AllPawns( class'Pawn', P )
    {
            do
            {

            // Spawn the projectile and the pawns location, given the
            // pawns rotation.
            proj = Spawn( class'UTProj_Rocket', proj,,
```

```
                P.Location, P.Rotation );

            // Set the direction of the projectile the same as the
            // pawns
            proj.Init( Vector( P.Rotation ) );

            // Debug so we can see all of our Projectile names
            DebugMessagePlayer( proj );

            // Turn our bFireProjectile bool off, so we don't keep
            // firing rockets.
            bFireProjectile = false;

            // Increment our counter.
            i++;
        } until ( i == 5 );
    }
}

DefaultProperties
{
}
```

Remember that the while loop in PlayerTick( ) is not being used because we changed the way StartFire( ) works. Let us go back to using the while loop.

Remove OurDoLoop() in StartFire( ):

```
// Override the default "StartFire" function, so we can use our
// Left or Right Mouse button as input.
exec function StartFire( optional byte FireModeNum  )
{

}
```

and add:

```
// Override the default "StartFire" function, so we can use our
// Left or Right Mouse button as input.
exec function StartFire( optional byte FireModeNum  )
{
   bFireProjectile = true;
}
```

Conditional Statements:

We have touched on this already but it will be good to go into more depth on how these sorts of statements work.

The first conditional statement we will look at is the if statement.

Begin by adding a new class variable:

```
// Used to keep track of our "ammo"
var int iAmmoCount;
```

Add this to the DefaultProperties:

```
// Default ammo count
iAmmoCount = 10;
```

Add a conditional statement in the while loop so it checks for our ammo count and will also subtract ONE each time a projectile is spawned.

PlayerTick( ) should currently look like:

```
// While we have pressed our Left-Mouse button, to
// turn bFireProjectile TRUE
while( bFireProjectile )
{
   // Get a reference to a local Pawn
   foreach WorldInfo.AllPawns( class'Pawn', P )
   {
      // Spawn the projectile and the pawns location, given the pawns
      // rotation.
      proj = Spawn( class'UTProj_Rocket', proj,,
            P.Location, P.Rotation );

      // Set the direction of the projectile the same as the pawns
      proj.Init( Vector( P.Rotation ) );

      // Turn our bFireProjectile bool off, so we don't keep firing
      // rockets.
      bFireProjectile = false;

   }
}
```

Change it too this:

```
// While we have pressed our Left-Mouse button, to
```

```
//turn bFireProjectile TRUE
while( bFireProjectile )
{
    if( iAmmoCount > 0 )
    {
        // Get a reference to a local Pawn
        foreach WorldInfo.AllPawns( class'Pawn', P )
        {
            // Spawn the projectile and the pawns location, given the
            // pawns rotation.
            proj = Spawn( class'UTProj_Rocket', proj,,
                    P.Location, P.Rotation );

            // Set the direction of the projectile the same as the
            // pawns
            proj.Init( Vector( P.Rotation ) );

            // Turn our bFireProjectile bool off, so we don't keep
            //firing rockets.
            bFireProjectile = false;

            // Subtract ONE from our ammo.
            iAmmoCount--;
        }
    }
}
```

If you debug the game now, you'll notice there is nothing to tell us how much ammo we have. This is because we have nothing displaying the number on screen. Our conditional is also in a while loop and the if statement doesn't have another option you may get a run time error when you shoot TEN projectiles. Something like:

```
[0010.49] Log: Recursion limit reached...breaking UDebugger
```

In order to fix this we need to give another option from the if statement, in case it is FALSE. To do this, there needs to be an "else" in the while loop.

Add to the while loop:

```
// While we have pressed our Left-Mouse button, to
// turn bFireProjectile TRUE
while( bFireProjectile )
{

        if( iAmmoCount > 0 )
        {
```

```
              // Get a reference to a local Pawn
              foreach WorldInfo.AllPawns( class'Pawn', P )
              {
                      // Spawn the projectile and the pawns location, given
                      // the pawns rotation.
                      proj = Spawn( class'UTProj_Rocket',
                              proj,, P.Location, P.Rotation );

                      // Set the direction of the projectile the same as
                      //the pawns
                      proj.Init( Vector( P.Rotation ) );

                      // Turn our bFireProjectile bool off, so we don't
                      // keep firing rockets.
                      bFireProjectile = false;

                      // Subtract ONE from our ammo.
                      iAmmoCount--;
              }
        }
        else
        {
              // Don't want to have this to stay true after pressing the
              // mouse button to fire
              bFireProjectile = false;
        }
    }
}
```

What we did is tell the program that we want to fire if our iAmmoCount is more than ZERO.

```
if( iAmmoCount > 0 )
```

If it is TRUE, we get a reference to our Pawn, spawn a projectile, turn our fire bool to FALSE, and subtract ONE from our iAmmoCount.

If it is FALSE, there is a second condition that we attached to the if statement, which is called else. This is exactly as it sounds: If our condition is TRUE, do that, else, do this.

```
else
{
   // Don't have this to stay true after pressing the mouse button
   bFireProjectile = false;
}
```

You will NOT be able to use else on its own. It must be at the end of an if statement block. The reason that bFireProjectile is set to FALSE here is because we don't want to the while loop to be TRUE after we run out of ammo, as it would have to calculate the code after while(bFireProjectile) and waste resources.

In order to properly use an if and else statement, there is a specific format to make sure they work together. The most simple format for the if – else statement is:

```
if ( )
{
}
else
{
}
```

Also, if you use an else, that is the end of the conditional statement. You can't add an else after a previous else. Such as: if – else – else. This won't compile.

There are many different operators that you can use when using conditional statements. They are as follows:

Comparison Operators:

Equality: ==
  Compares **BOTH** values to see if they are exactly the same. If they are the same, return **TRUE**.
Approximate equality: ~=
  Compares **TWO float variables**. If they are within **0.0001** of each other, this returns **TRUE**.
Inequality: !=
  Compares both values to see if they are **different**. If so return **TRUE**.
Less Than: <
  If the **LEFT** side value is **LESS** than the **RIGHT** side value, returns **TRUE**.
Less Than or Equal To: <=
  If the **LEFT** side value is **LESS** than or **EQUAL** to the **RIGHT** side value, returns **TRUE**.
Greater Than: >
  If the **LEFT** side value is **GREATER** than the **RIGHT** side value, returns **TRUE**.
Greater Than or Equal To: >=
  If the **LEFT** side value is **GREATER** than or **EQUAL** to the **RIGHT** side value, return **TRUE**.

Logical Operators:

*And: **&&***
  If both **conditions** to the **LEFT** and **RIGHT** of this operator are **TRUE**, the entire

condition returns **TRUE**.

Or: ||

Returns **TRUE** if either of the **conditions** to the **LEFT** or **RIGHT** of this operator are **TRUE**.

If you debug the game now, you will be able to fire TEN rockets. After that, nothing will happen if you press the mouse button(s) that spawn the projectile, as the conditional statement that checks iAmmoCount will be FALSE.

Conditional statements can also serve the purpose of making sure that specific blocks of code are called if other variables or classes exist. For instance, let's say that for some reason there was no Pawn class in the world. Then, we tried to use a foreach iterator to spawn a projectile:

```
foreach WorldInfo.AllPawns( class'Pawn', P )
{
    // Spawn the projectile and the pawns location, given the pawns
    // rotation.
    proj = Spawn( class'UTProj_Rocket', proj,, P.Location, P.Rotation );

    // Set the direction of the projectile the same as the pawns
    proj.Init( Vector( P.Rotation ) );

    // Turn our bFireProjectile bool off, so we don't keep
    // firing rockets.
    bFireProjectile = false;

    // Subtract ONE from our ammo.
    iAmmoCount--;
}
```

There is a chance here that the projectile being spawned might not have a reference through "proj". Because the class declaration within the Spawn( ) function isn't checked, it is possible to have a typing error, or maybe the class gets renamed. To prevent any issue with the folowing Init( ) function, we can use a conditional statement to first make sure the projectile exists before trying to call its Init( ).

Change this code inside of your PlayerTick( ) function, to this:

```
foreach WorldInfo.AllPawns( class'Pawn', P )
{
    // Spawn the projectile and the pawns location, given the pawns
    // rotation.
    proj = Spawn( class'UTProj_Rocket', proj,,P.Location, P.Rotation );

    if ( proj != none )
```

```
    {
            // Set the direction of the projectile the same as
            // the pawns
            proj.Init( Vector( P.Rotation ) );

            // Turn our bFireProjectile bool off, so we don't keep
            // firing   rockets.
            bFireProjectile = false;

            // Subtract ONE from our ammo.
            iAmmoCount--;
    }
}
```

Let's say that the foreach iterator didn't find any Pawn class to reference. This would result in this iterator to NOT run. If there are no classes to reference within the foreach iterator, it wont do anything. This important to remember when using foreach.

Checking to see if objects are being spawned (created) is common. You will find yourself doing often, as everything you reference or create should be checked before being used; though there are always some exceptions. This makes the code a bit more tedious to write but also much more reliable and in the end. It will have less errors, especially if it is a big project and/or has many programmers working on it.

For instance, we can update this block of code even more, to this:

```
foreach WorldInfo.AllPawns( class'Pawn', P )
{
  if ( P != none )
  {
  // Spawn the projectile and the pawns location, given the
  // pawns rotation.
  proj = Spawn( class'UTProj_Rocket', proj,, P.Location, P.Rotation );

  if ( proj != none )
  {
      // Set the direction of the projectile the same as the pawns
      proj.Init( Vector( P.Rotation ) );

      // Turn our bFireProjectile bool off, so we don't keep
      // firing rockets.
      bFireProjectile = false;

      // Subtract ONE from our ammo.
      iAmmoCount--;
      }
  }
```

}

Adding this will have yet another check, to make sure the Pawn did spawn, which is redundant, as this loop wouldn't of run if it didn't find one.

There is also another practice to include a debug `Log( ) function (we have use something similar, DebugMessagePlayer( )) when something is not going the way it is supposed to; if the game can't find a reference or perhaps has an error creating a class.

Let's introduce some else statements that output log files, if either of these if statements were to fail. Add this:

```
foreach WorldInfo.AllPawns( class'Pawn', P )
{
   // Make sure a Pawn is found
   if ( P != none )
   {
   // Spawn the projectile and the pawns location, given the
   // pawns rotation.
   proj = Spawn( class'UTProj_Rocket', proj,, P.Location, P.Rotation );

         // Make sure the projectile exists
         if ( proj != none )
         {
            // Set the direction of the projectile the same
            // as the pawns
            proj.Init( Vector( P.Rotation ) );

            // Turn our bFireProjectile bool off, so we don't keep
            // firing rockets.
            bFireProjectile = false;

            // Subtract ONE from our ammo.
            iAmmoCount--;
         }
         else
         {
            `Log( "proj did not spawn" );
         }
   }
   else
   {
      `Log( "Pawn class not found" );
   }
}
```

This is one of those things that makes it hard not to be lazy. Let's use what we have done so far as an example. I know 100% of the time that there is going to he a Pawn class spawned in the world. Given that knowledge, it would be easy for me to forget the `log( ) to tell the programmer that the Pawn class is not found. But this could be an issue later on down the road as what if something changes? While it can become annoying, it is important to keep track of your code through conditional statements. It offers a more likely outcome of fewer script warnings and errors.

The next type of conditional would be **else if.** Else if is designed to go just after the original if statement (just like the else) but it gives the programmer another opportunity to check something. It also doesn't have the limitation of being used once after the initial if statement. You can have many "else if" statements after the original if statement.

Introduce some changes to the same block of code so we can do different things if the Pawn is falling or walking:

Add new local variables to the PlayerTick( ) function – make sure they are above the call to super.PlayerTick( ):

```
// Used for our "Falling" projectile for loop
local int i;

// Offset used to shoot projectiles in a cirlce
local Rotator projRotOffset;
```

Add a new class variable:

```
// Used to keep track if the pawn is falling or not
var bool bFallingCheck;
```

Change the **StartFire( ) function** to help us know when the player is falling:

```
// Override the default "StartFire" function, so we can use our
// Left or Right Mouse button as input.
exec function StartFire( optional byte FireModeNum  )
{
  // We need to reference our pawn to get its physics
  local Pawn P;

  // If we fire, change bFireProjectile, for PlayerTick( )
  bFireProjectile = true;

  // Get a reference to a pawn
  foreach WorldInfo.AllPawns( class'Pawn', P )
  {
     // If the pawns physics is falling
     if ( P.GetPhysicsName( ) == "Falling" )
```

```
        {
                // set bool to say it is falling
                bFallingCheck = true;
        }
        // If it is not falling
        else
        {
                // set bool to say it is not falling
                bFallingCheck = false;
        }
    }
}
```

And finally, update the PlayerTick( ) to handle the new conditions:

```
// While we have pressed our Left-Mouse button, to
// turn bFireProjectile TRUE
while( bFireProjectile )
{
    // while we have a positive ammo count
    if( iAmmoCount > 0 )
    {
        // Get a reference to a local Pawn
        foreach WorldInfo.AllPawns( class'Pawn', P )
        {
                // if there is a pawn and it is not falling
                if ( P != none && !bFallingCheck )
                {
                        // Spawn the projectile and the pawns location, given
                        // the pawns rotation.
                        proj = Spawn( class'UTProj_Rocket', proj,,
                                P.Location, P.Rotation );

                        if ( proj != none )
                        {
                                // Set the direction of the projectile the same
                                // as the pawns
                                proj.Init( Vector( P.Rotation ) );

                                // Turn our bFireProjectile bool off, so we
                                // don't keep firing rockets.
                                bFireProjectile = false;

                                // Subtract ONE from our ammo.
                                iAmmoCount--;

                        }
                }
```

```
                    // If there is a pawn found and it is falling
                    else if ( P != none && bFallingCheck )
                    {
                            // Set our initial offset to the same rotation as the
                            // pawn
                            projRotOffset = P.Rotation;

                            // We want to fire 15 rockets : i < 15 -> continue
                            for( i= 0; i < 15; i++ )
                            {
                                    // Update the rotation to 1/15th of 360 degrees
                                    projRotOffset += Rot( 0,4370,0 );

                                    // Spawn the projectile at the pawns location
                                    proj = Spawn( class'UTProj_Rocket', proj,,
                                            P.Location );

                                    // set the direction by the offest
                                    proj.Init( Vector( projRotOffset ) );

                            }

                            // turn off our falling check when the else if is
                            // finished -  after the for loop
                            bFallingCheck = false;
                    }
                    else
                    {
                            `Log( "Can't find Pawn" );
                    }
                }
            }
            else
            {
                // Don't want to have this stay true after pressing the mouse
                // button to fire
                bFireProjectile = false;

            }
        }
```

If you look at the StartFire( ) function you will notice a new foreach iterator to get a reference to a Pawn, as well as a if – else conditional. Though we will go into using functions later, I will say now that functions can return a variable type. In this case, we are calling GetPhysicsName( ) and checking to see if it returns a string that matches "Falling". If it does, we set our bool bFallingCheck to TRUE. If it doesn't, we set bFallingCheck to FALSE. Since bFallingCheck is a class variable we will also be able to check it within our PlayerTick( ) function.

This is how our PlayerTick( ) function works, line by line:

- While bFireProjectile is true,
- We check to see if the iAmmoCount is more than 0.
- If it is, we use a foreach iterator to reference our Pawn.
- We check to make sure if the Pawn exists and if it is NOT falling.
- If it is NOT falling, we Spawn a projectile and reference it with proj.
- If proj does not equal none (it exists).
- Point proj in the right direction.
- Turn bFireProjectiles to false, so we can fire again.
- Decrease iAmmoCount by ONE;
- Else if Pawn exists and IS falling.
- Set projRotOffset to the Pawns rotation.
- Spawn the projectile with a reference to it: proj.
- Set the direction of the projectile with the offset rotator.
- Turn bFallingCheck to false;
- Else
- Log that the Pawn is not found.

This line may be confusing because UDK handles rotations in a unique way:

```
// Update the rotation to 1/15th of 360 degrees
projRotOffset += Rot( 0,4370,0 );
```

Rot is a constant literal value. This means that it cannot be edited and will never change. There is nothing we can do to change this value in the code, during run time.

The confusing part here is the number: 4370. In Rot( ) there are THREE values in this order: Pitch, Yaw, Roll. Each of these values represent a full THREE-HUNDRED and SIXTY degrees on their respective rotation. In UDK, THREE-HUNDRED and SIXTY degrees is equal to the value of: 65536. In this instance, 4370 is equal to just under FIFTEEN degrees (the exact value is: 14.99679633867277); very close to the amount of projectiles that are planned to be shot.

If you debug the game, you will fire normal rockets (as the example(s) before) but if you jump – by pressing SPACEBAR – and then MOUSE-BUTTON, there will be a circle of projectiles that spawn around you.

The entire USL_PlayerController.uc class, for this chapter:

```
class USL_PlayerController extends PlayerController;

// Used to control when to fire our projectile
var bool bFireProjectile;

// Used to keep track of our "ammo"
var int iAmmoCount;

// Used to keep track if the pawn is falling or not
var bool bFallingCheck;

// Override the default "StartFire" function, so we can use our
// Left or Right Mouse button as input.
exec function StartFire( optional byte FireModeNum )
{
   // We need to reference our pawn to get its physics
   local Pawn P;

   // If we fire, change bFireProjectile, for PlayerTick( )
   bFireProjectile = true;

   // Get a reference to a pawn
   foreach WorldInfo.AllPawns( class'Pawn', P )
   {
      // If the pawns physics is falling
      if ( P.GetPhysicsName( ) == "Falling" )
      {
          // set bool to say it is falling
          bFallingCheck = true;
      }
      // If it is not falling
      else
```

```
        {
            // set bool to say it is not falling
            bFallingCheck = false;
        }
    }
}


// Tick function used to check input : called once per frame.
function PlayerTick( float DeltaTime )
{
    // Used to spawn and reference a UTProj_Rocket
    local UTProj_Rocket proj;

    // Used to reference our pawn, so we can use its location.
    local Pawn P;

    // Used for our "Falling" projectile for loop
    local int i;

    // Offset used to shoot projectiles in a cirlce
    local Rotator projRotOffset;

    // We dont want to overrid the entire PlayerTick( ) function, so
    // lets include the previous class code.
    super.PlayerTick( DeltaTime );

    // While we have pressed our Left-Mouse button, to
    // turn bFireProjectile TRUE
    while( bFireProjectile )
    {
        // while we have a positive ammo count
        if( iAmmoCount > 0 )
        {
        // Get a reference to a local Pawn
        foreach WorldInfo.AllPawns( class'Pawn', P )
        {
            // if there is a pawn and it is not falling
            if ( P != none && !bFallingCheck )
            {
                // Spawn the projectile and the pawns location,
                // given the pawns rotation.
                proj = Spawn( class'UTProj_Rocket', proj,,
                    P.Location, P.Rotation );

                if ( proj != none )
                {
                    // Set the direction of the projectile
                    // the same as the pawns
```

```
                        proj.Init( Vector( P.Rotation ) );

                        // Turn our bFireProjectile bool off, so
                        // we don't keep firing rockets.
                        bFireProjectile = false;

                        // Subtract ONE from our ammo.
                        iAmmoCount--;

                }
        }
        // If there is a pawn found and it is falling
        else if ( P != none && bFallingCheck )
        {
                // Set our initial offset to the same rotation
                // as the pawn
                projRotOffset = P.Rotation;

                // We want to fire 15 rockets : i < 15 ->
                // continue
                for( i= 0; i < 15; i++ )
                {
                        // Update the rotation to 1/15th of 360
                        // degrees
                        projRotOffset += Rot( 0,4370,0 );

                        // Spawn the projectile at the pawns
                        // location
                        proj = Spawn( class'UTProj_Rocket',
                                proj,, P.Location );

                        // set the direction by the offest
                        proj.Init( Vector( projRotOffset ) );

                }

                // turn off our falling check when the else if
                is finished - happens after the for loop
                bFallingCheck = false;
        }
        else
        {
                `Log( "Can't find Pawn" );

        }

        }
}
else
```

```
        {
                // Don't want to have this stay true after pressing the
                // mouse button to fire
                bFireProjectile = false;
        }
    }
}

// Used to show how Do loops work
function OurDoLoop( )
{
    // Used to spawn and reference a UTProj_Rocket
    local UTProj_Rocket proj;

    // Used to reference our pawn, so we can use its location.
    local Pawn P;

    // Used to count our do loop
    local int i;

    // Get a reference to all of the Pawn class in our game world
    foreach WorldInfo.AllPawns( class'Pawn', P )
        {
                do
                {

                // Spawn the projectile and the pawns location, given the
                // pawns rotation.
                proj = Spawn( class'UTProj_Rocket', proj,,
                    P.Location, P.Rotation );

                // Set the direction of the projectile the same as the
                // pawns
                proj.Init( Vector( P.Rotation ) );

                // Debug so we can see all of our Projectile names
                DebugMessagePlayer( proj );

                // Turn our bFireProjectile bool off, so we don't keep
                // firing rockets.
                bFireProjectile = false;

                // Increment our counter.
                i++;
        } until ( i == 5 );
    }
}

DefaultProperties
```

```
{
   // Default ammo count
   iAmmoCount = 1000;
}
```

Switch statements:

Switch statements can be used to call different code depending on the value of a positive int or a byte variable (a whole numerical value). For instance, we can use a int value to tell the statement what block of code to run. Switch statements need to be within the block of a function just like loops and conditional statements.

The format for a switch statement is as follows:

```
// EXAMPLE: Basic format for a switch statement
function SwitchStatement( )
{
   switch( VALUE_THAT_DECIDES )
   {
   case 0:
      DebugMessagePlayer( "Case 0" );
      break;
   case 1:
      DebugMessagePlayer( "Case 1" );
      break;
   }
}
```

In this example, if we wanted to run case ZERO, the VALUE_THAT_DECIDES (which is generally a int or byte variable declared earlier) would need to be ZERO. For example, if it was ONE, it would then run case ONE.

Also, an important keyword being used here is the "break" at the end of each case. This tells the game that the code should stop running that block when it reaches that location. This prevents the code from continuing down the block and running cases it should not. Knowing this, you can also take advantage of the circumstance and say, run case ZERO and ONE before breaking out of that block – though this usually does not happen as you could just make sure both are a part of ONE case.

As an example, if there was no break specifier in case ZERO, and we called case ZERO, it would run case ZERO as well as case ONE, then break in case ONE, because the specifier is there.

Now that you understand the basic format for a switch statement, let's discuss "VALUE_THAT_DECIDES". This variable is generally a int or a byte and is used to decide what case to run. Also, this variable is usually altered in the course of game play, to change what switch case to run during the "run time" of the game.

As an example, you could create a switch statement that will run different types of player camera setups, depending on what the player would like to use; such as FPS, 3rd person, top-down, and side-scroller.

Or, for what we will be doing, set up a toggle so the user can use buttons ONE through THREE to select what type of projectiles the weapon will fire.

Inside of the USL_PlayerController.uc, create a couple class variables:

```
// Used to set what projectile the weapon fires
var int iProjectileSet;
// Used to store our three projectile types
var class<UTProjectile> ProjectileType[3];
```

The iProjectileSet will decide what switch case to use as well as what projectile in our ProjectileType array to use and the ProjectileType will hold the classes we will use as a projectile when the mouse button(s) are pressed.

Add the default projectile types for the ProjectileType array. In the defaultproperties, add this:

```
// Default projectile name types
ProjectileType[0] = class'UTProj_Rocket'
ProjectileType[1] = class'UTProj_LinkPlasma'
ProjectileType[2] = class'UTProj_Grenade'
```

Inside of the PlayerTick( ) function, let's add the portion of code that will allow use to know when the player is pressing a key. Insert this under the super.PlayerTick(DeltaTime) line:

```
// Used to know when the player is pressing ONE, TWO, or THREE
if ( PlayerInput.PressedKeys.Find( 'One' ) >= 0 )
{
}
if ( PlayerInput.PressedKeys.Find( 'Two' ) >= 0 )
{
}
if ( PlayerInput.PressedKeys.Find( 'Three' ) >= 0 )
{
}
```

We are accessing the already included code from the PlayerInput (which is a part of the PlayerController class) and then using an array of possible input options stored in the PressedKeys array to "find" the keys we are looking for by using the conditional if the pressed key is GREATER than, or EQUAL to ZERO (if it is pressed), execute this block of code. Remember, since this is a part of the PlayerTick( ) function it is called every frame; it checks if the player is pressing any of these buttons every frame.

Within each of the input blocks let's set the value of the iProjectileSet so we know both what switch case to use as well as what projectile to fire.

```
// Used to know when the player is pressing ONE, TWO, or THREE
if ( PlayerInput.PressedKeys.Find( 'One' ) >= 0 )
{
   if ( iProjectileSet != 0 )
   {
      iProjectileSet = 0;
   }
}
if ( PlayerInput.PressedKeys.Find( 'Two' ) >= 0 )
{
   if ( iProjectileSet != 1 )
   {
      iProjectileSet = 1;
   }
}
if ( PlayerInput.PressedKeys.Find( 'Three' ) >= 0 )
{
   if ( iProjectileSet != 2 )
   {
      iProjectileSet = 2;
   }
}
```

The extra if statement here is to check to make sure that the iProjectileSet isn't already set which will avoid setting the value, if it has already been set to the proper value.

We will now have to change a bit of the code that has already been written and create a function for it. This will allow us to call that function with the proper information in regards to what projectile to fire, depending on what physics state the player is in.

COPY and then delete all this code in the PlayerTick( ) function:

```
// While we have pressed our Left-Mouse button, to
// turn bFireProjectile TRUE
while( bFireProjectile )
{
   // while we have a positive ammo count
   if( iAmmoCount > 0 )
   {
      // Get a reference to a local Pawn
```

```
foreach WorldInfo.AllPawns( class'Pawn', P )
{
    // if there is a pawn and it is not falling
    if ( P != none && !bFallingCheck )
    {
        // Spawn the projectile and the pawns location, given
        // the pawns rotation.
        proj = Spawn( class'UTProj_Rocket', proj,,
            P.Location, P.Rotation );

        if ( proj != none )
        {
            // Set the direction of the projectile the same
            // as the pawns
            proj.Init( Vector( P.Rotation ) );

            // Turn our bFireProjectile bool off, so we
            // don't keep firing rockets.
            bFireProjectile = false;

            // Subtract ONE from our ammo.
            iAmmoCount--;

        }
    }
    // If there is a pawn found and it is falling
    else if ( P != none && bFallingCheck )
    {
        // Set our initial offset to the same rotation as the
        // pawn
        projRotOffset = P.Rotation;

        // We want to fire 15 rockets : i < 15 -> continue
        for( i= 0; i < 15; i++ )
        {
            // Update the rotation to 1/15th of 360 degrees
            projRotOffset += Rot( 0,4370,0 );

            // Spawn the projectile and the pawns location
            proj = Spawn( class'UTProj_Rocket', proj,,
                P.Location, P.Rotation );

            // set the direction by the offest
            proj.Init( Vector( projRotOffset ) );

        }

        // turn off our falling check when the else if is
        // finished - happens after the for loop
```

```
                    bFallingCheck = false;
            }
            else
            {
                    `Log( "Can't find Pawn" );
            }
        }
    }
    else
    {
        // Don't want to have this stay true after pressing the mouse
        // button to fire
        bFireProjectile = false;
    }
}
```

Create a function using it including a integer argument called "type", such as:

```
// Used to decide what projectile to fire, during what state
function FireProjectileType( int type )
{
    // Used to reference any pawns
    local Pawn P;

    // Used to spawn and reference a projectile
    local UTProjectile proj;

    // Used to offset when we fire projecitles
    local Rotator projRotOffset;

    // Used in our for loop
    local int i;

    // While we have pressed our Left-Mouse button, to
    // turn bFireProjectile TRUE
    while( bFireProjectile )
    {
        // while we have a positive ammo count
        if( iAmmoCount > 0 )
        {
            // Get a reference to a local Pawn
            foreach WorldInfo.AllPawns( class'Pawn', P )
            {
                // if there is a pawn and it is not falling
                if ( P != none && !bFallingCheck )
                {
                    // Spawn the projectile and the pawns location,
                    // given the pawns rotation.
```

```
proj = Spawn( ProjectileType[ type ], proj,,
    P.Location, P.Rotation );

if ( proj != none )
{
    // Set the direction of the projectile
    // the same as the pawns
    proj.Init( Vector( P.Rotation ) );

    // Turn our bFireProjectile bool off, so
    // we don't keep firing rockets.
    bFireProjectile = false;

    // Subtract ONE from our ammo.
    iAmmoCount--;

    }
}
// If there is a pawn found and it is falling
else if ( P != none && bFallingCheck )
{
    // Set our initial offset to the same rotation
    // as the pawn
    projRotOffset = P.Rotation;

    // We want to fire 15 rockets : i < 15 ->
    //continue
    for( i= 0; i < 15; i++ )
    {
        // Update the rotation to 1/15th of 360
        // degrees
        projRotOffset += Rot( 0,4370,0 );

        // Spawn the projectile at the pawns
        // location
        proj = Spawn( ProjectileType[ type ],
            proj,, P.Location );

        // set the direction by the offest
        proj.Init( Vector( projRotOffset ) );

    }

    // turn off our falling check when the else if
    // is finished - happens after the for loop
    bFallingCheck = false;
}
else
{
```

```
                    `Log( "Can't find Pawn" );

                }

            }
        }
        else
        {
            // Don't want to have this stay true after pressing the
            // mouse button to fire
            bFireProjectile = false;
        }
    }
}
```

For both of the lines that begin with proj = Spawn( ) we need to change what class to choose to fire. In order to do this set them to look like:

```
// Spawn the projectile and the pawns location, given
//the pawns rotation.
proj = Spawn( ProjectileType[ type ], proj,, P.Location, P.Rotation );
```

If you remember, we are able to use a int variable as a reference to an element in an array. Also, we are able to pass a variable into a function from another function, which in this case will be the (int type) parameter.

This allows us to call this function and use the proper class depending on how the switch statement is being called; by which case.

We also need to move a few local variables from the PlayerTick( ) function to the new FireProjectileType( ) function.

Add the following to FireProjectileType( ):

```
// Used to reference any pawns
local Pawn P;

// Used to spawn and reference a projectile
local UTProjectile proj;

// Used to offset when we fire projecitles
local Rotator projRotOffset;

// Used in our for loop
local int i;
```

Since we no longer need these within the PlayerTick( ) function you can remove all four of these local variables that we just moved over to the FireProjectileTypes( ) function.

Back inside of the PlayerTick( ) function, let's introduce the switch statement. Add this:

```
// used to spawn the proper type of projectile
switch( iProjectileSet )
{
   case 0:
      FireProjectileType( 0 );
      break;
   case 1:
      FireProjectileType( 1 );
      break;
   case 2:
      FireProjectileType( 2 );
      break;
}
```

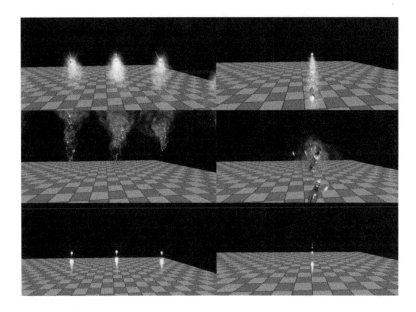

When you debug the game you should be able to use the ONE, TWO, and THREE keys to switch between what types of weapon you'll be firing for both when the Pawn is walking and falling.

Here is the entire USL_PlayerController class:

```
class USL_PlayerController extends PlayerController;

// Used to control when to fire our projectile
```

```
var bool bFireProjectile;

// Used to keep track of our "ammo"
var int iAmmoCount;

// Used to keep track if the pawn is falling or not
var bool bFallingCheck;

// Used to set what projectile the weapon fires
var int iProjectileSet;

// Used to store our three projectile types
var class<UTProjectile> ProjectileType[3];

// Override the default "StartFire" function, so we can use our
// Left or Right Mouse button as input.
exec function StartFire( optional byte FireModeNum  )
{
   // We need to reference our pawn to get its physics
   local Pawn P;

   // If we fire, change bFireProjectile, for PlayerTick( )
   bFireProjectile = true;

   // Get a reference to a pawn
   foreach WorldInfo.AllPawns( class'Pawn', P )
   {
      // If the pawns physics is falling
      if ( P.GetPhysicsName( ) == "Falling" )
      {
          // set bool to say it is falling
          bFallingCheck = true;
      }
      // If it is not falling
      else
      {
          // set bool to say it is not falling
          bFallingCheck = false;
      }
   }
}

// Tick function used to check input : called once per frame.
function PlayerTick( float DeltaTime )
{
   // We dont want to overrid the entire PlayerTick( ) function, so
   // lets include the previous class code.
   super.PlayerTick( DeltaTime );
```

```
// Used to know when the player is pressing ONE, TWO, or THREE
if ( PlayerInput.PressedKeys.Find( 'One' ) >= 0 )
{
    if ( iProjectileSet != 0 )
    {
            iProjectileSet = 0;
    }
}
if ( PlayerInput.PressedKeys.Find( 'Two' ) >= 0 )
{
    if ( iProjectileSet != 1 )
    {
            iProjectileSet = 1;
    }
}
if ( PlayerInput.PressedKeys.Find( 'Three' ) >= 0 )
{
    if ( iProjectileSet != 2 )
    {
            iProjectileSet = 2;
    }
}

// used to spawn the proper type of projectile
switch( iProjectileSet )
{
    case 0:
            FireProjectileType( 0 );
            break;
    case 1:
            FireProjectileType( 1 );
            break;
    case 2:
            FireProjectileType( 2 );
            break;
}
}

// Used to decide what projectile to fire, during what state
function FireProjectileType( int type )
{
  // Used to reference any pawns
  local Pawn P;

  // Used to spawn and reference a projectile
  local UTProjectile proj;

  // Used to offset when we fire projecitles
  local Rotator projRotOffset;
```

```
// Used in our for loop
local int i;

// While we have pressed our Left-Mouse button, to
// turn bFireProjectile TRUE
while( bFireProjectile )
{
    // while we have a positive ammo count
    if( iAmmoCount > 0 )
    {
        // Get a reference to a local Pawn
        foreach WorldInfo.AllPawns( class'Pawn', P )
        {
            // if there is a pawn and it is not falling
            if ( P != none && !bFallingCheck )
            {
                // Spawn the projectile and the pawns location,
                // given the pawns rotation.
                proj = Spawn( ProjectileType[ type ], proj,,
                    P.Location, P.Rotation );

                if ( proj != none )
                {
                    // Set the direction of the projectile
                    // the same as the pawns
                    proj.Init( Vector( P.Rotation ) );

                    // Turn our bFireProjectile bool off, so
                    // we don't keep firing rockets.
                    bFireProjectile = false;

                    // Subtract ONE from our ammo.
                    iAmmoCount--;

                }
            }
            // If there is a pawn found and it is falling
            else if ( P != none && bFallingCheck )
            {
                // Set our initial offset to the same rotation
                // as the pawn
                projRotOffset = P.Rotation;

                // We want to fire 15 rockets : i < 15 ->
                //continue
                for( i= 0; i < 15; i++ )
                {
                    // Update the rotation to 1/15th of 360
```

```
                                     // degrees
                                     projRotOffset += Rot( 0,4370,0 );

                                     // Spawn the projectile at the pawns
                                     // location
                                     proj = Spawn( ProjectileType[ type ],
                                             proj,, P.Location );

                                     // set the direction by the offest
                                     proj.Init( Vector( projRotOffset ) );

                              }

                              // turn off our falling check when the else if
                              // is finished - happens after the for loop
                              bFallingCheck = false;
                      }
                      else
                      {

                              `Log( "Can't find Pawn" );

                      }

               }
       }
       else
       {
               // Don't want to have this stay true after pressing the
               // mouse button to fire
               bFireProjectile = false;
       }
   }
}

// Used to show how Do loops work
function OurDoLoop( )
{
   // Used to spawn and reference a UTProj_Rocket
   local UTProj_Rocket proj;

   // Used to reference our pawn, so we can use its location.
   local Pawn P;

   // Used to count our do loop
   local int i;

   // Get a reference to all of the Pawn class in our game world
   foreach WorldInfo.AllPawns( class'Pawn', P )
       {
```

```
        do
        {
            // Spawn the projectile and the pawns location, given the
            //pawns rotation.
            proj = Spawn( class'UTProj_Rocket', proj,,
                  P.Location, P.Rotation );

            // Set the direction of the projectile the same as the
            // pawns
            proj.Init( Vector( P.Rotation ) );

            // Debug so we can see all of our Projectile names
            DebugMessagePlayer( proj );

            // Turn our bFireProjectile bool off, so we don't keep
            // firing rockets.
            bFireProjectile = false;

            // Increment our counter.
            i++;
        } until ( i == 5 );
    }
}

DefaultProperties
{
    // Default ammo count
    iAmmoCount = 1000;

    // Default projectile name types
    ProjectileType[0] = class'UTProj_Rocket'
    ProjectileType[1] = class'UTProj_LinkPlasma'
    ProjectileType[2] = class'UTProj_Grenade'
}
```

Hopefully by this point you have a better understanding of how we are able to work with our game classes by using variable types, loops, and switch plus condition statements. If you are still finding this a bit hard to grasp, don't worry, there is plenty of examples ahead that should help with the practice of using all of these.

Challenges:

To further educate yourself, here is a few things you can try to do, in order to get a better understanding of loops and conditionals.

1) Cycle through the Note array used in a for loop in the LoopTesting( ) function

inside of USL_GameInfo class twice. This will fire a projectile at each of the Notes once and then repeat the process again.

2) Reverse the way the projectiles fire when the "Falling" physics name is TRUE, to how it it currently works when "Falling" is FALSE. Then, change the way projectiles fire when the "Falling" physics name is FALSE, to how it is when "Falling" is TRUE.

Possible answers:

Question ONE:

(Change LoopTesting( ) inside of USL_GameInfo.uc)

```
function LoopTesting( )
{
    // Help to show us what our loops are doing by firing rockets
    local UTProj_Rocket proj;

    // Used to keep track of our loops
    local int i;

    // Used to reference the Pawn within our world
    local Pawn P;

    // Get a reference to our pawn
    foreach WorldInfo.AllPawns( class'Pawn', P )
    {
        // A for loop : cycles five times * 2
        for( i = 0; i < NoteArray.Length * 2; i++ )
        {
            // Spawn a projectile at the location and given the
            // rotation of the pawn
            proj = Spawn( class'UTProj_Rocket', P,,
                P.Location, P.Rotation );

            // If our for loop has reached the end of the NoteArray
            if ( i >= NoteArray.Length )
            {
                // Direct the projectile at the location of the Note
                // that is FIVE less than the value of i
                proj.Init( Normal( NoteArray[ i - 5 ].Location -
                    P.Location ) );

                // Debug to show us the location of where the
                // projectile going
                DebugMessagePlayer( "Second Set: " $
                    NoteArray[ i - 5 ].Location );
```

```
        }
        else
        {
            // Tell the projectile which way to go
            proj.Init( Normal( NoteArray[i].Location -
                P.Location ) );

            // Debug to show us the location of where the
            // projectile is going
            DebugMessagePlayer( "First Set: " $
                NoteArray[i].Location );
        }
    }
  }
}
```

Question two:

(Reverse the assignment for bFallingCheck in the StartFire( ) function, in USL_PlayerController.uc)

```
// Override the default "StartFire" function, so we can use our
//Left or Right Mouse button as input.
exec function StartFire( optional byte FireModeNum  )
{
   // We need to reference our pawn to get its physics
   local Pawn P;

   // If we fire, change bFireProjectile, for PlayerTick( )
   bFireProjectile = true;

   // Get a reference to a pawn
   foreach WorldInfo.AllPawns( class'Pawn', P )
   {
      // If the pawns physics is falling
      if ( P.GetPhysicsName( ) == "Falling" )
      {
          // set bool to say it is falling
          bFallingCheck = false;  // ← CHANGE this
      }
      // If it is not falling
      else
      {
          // set bool to say it is not falling
          bFallingCheck = true;   // ← CHANGE this
      }
   }
}
```

More reading:

More on the For Loop:
http://en.wikipedia.org/wiki/For_loop
http://udn.epicgames.com/Three/UnrealScriptControlStructures.html#For Loops

More on the While loop:
http://udn.epicgames.com/Three/UnrealScriptControlStructures.html#While Loops
http://en.wikipedia.org/wiki/While_loop

More on the Do loop:
http://udn.epicgames.com/Three/UnrealScriptControlStructures.html#Do Loops

More on Dynamic Arrays, in Unreal:
http://udn.epicgames.com/Three/UnrealScriptVariables.html#Dynamic Arrays

More on Recursion:
http://en.wikipedia.org/wiki/Recursion_(computer_science)

More on conditional statements:
https://en.wikipedia.org/wiki/Conditional_(computer_programming)

More on Relational Operators:
http://en.wikibooks.org/wiki/C%2B
%2B_Programming/Operators/Operator_Overloading#Relational_operators

More on Exec functions:
http://udn.epicgames.com/Three/ExecFunctions.html

More on UnrealScript Constants:
http://udn.epicgames.com/Three/UnrealScriptVariables.html#Constants

Functions and Type Casting
Chapter Four

We have been using functions in the past examples but I haven't really described how they work. In short, a function is a named section of the program that performs a specific task.

Because of the formatting of this book you may see some lines of code that don't seem right. Such as:

```
function PawnStats( out name name, out Vector location, out Rotator
    rotation, out float speed )
```

This is because the whole line won't fit across the available space of the page, not because that is how it should be formatted when writing the code. If you want to, you can write the code exactly as you see it in the book.

If you see a line of code that continues WITHOUT a space and is indented, it is because of this. You can write these lines in a single line within your IDE if you wish. Or as stated above, you can follow along exactly how it is written in the book.

As an example, the line of code above is normally written like this, within the IDE:

```
function PawnStats( out name name, out Vector location, out Rotator rotation, out float speed )
```

UDK comes with a lot of "reusable" functions, that we "the programmer" can use to alter our game. When a programming language is used and it has "reusable" functions, variables, and classes, like UDK, it is referred to as the "Application programming interface" or API.

An API is essentially a library of code that includes different functions, variables, and classes that can be adapted or overwritten. Having an API you can us is exceptionally handy, as the code has already been written. The hard part is know what is there to use.

Since the UDK library is quite big, the task of learning what you can reuse is often most of the learning process especially when you're coming from a different game engine or already know how to program with a different programming language. Once you become more adept at the practice of programming, it is highly recommended that you start to read through the "base" classes. These include but are not limited to:

- **Object.uc**
- **Actor.uc**
- **Pawn.uc**
- **PlayerController.uc**
- **GameInfo.uc**
- **HUD.uc**
- **Engine.uc**
- **Input.uc**

Another practice that I have picked up is if you are in Visual Studio and use a function, variable, or class that comes from UDK you can highlight it RIGHT-CLICK →Go to Declaration.

This will lead you to the original location of whatever you right-clicked. This is very helpful in seeing exactly what is going on when you use it. For instance, if go to the declaration of Spawn( ) its comment will show a lot of information on how it works.

```
/** Spawn an actor. Returns an actor of
 * the specified class, notof class Actor
 * (this is hardcoded in the compiler).
```

```
 * Returns Noneif the actor could not be
 * spawned (if that happens, there will be a
 * log warning indicating why)Defaults to
 * spawning at the spawner's location.
 *
 * @note: ActorTemplate is sent for replicated
 * actors and therefore its properties
 * will also be applied
 *
 * at initial creation on the client. However,
 * because of this, ActorTemplate must be a
 * static resource(an actor archetype, default
 * object, or a bStatic/bNoDelete actor in a
 * level package)or the spawned Actor cannot
 * be replicated
 */

native noexport final function coerce actor Spawn( )
```

"Native" means that the code originated in the C++ side of the engine. In its current state, UDK does not allow you to access this "engine" (C++) code. This is due to Epic not wanting UDK users to alter the actual engine programming. While this does sound restrictive, UDK is able to accomplish just about any game you can imagine.

As an example, games like Borderlands 2©, Injustice: Gods Among Us©, and BioShock© all run on the Unreal 3 Engine; the same as what UDK is based on. The difference between games like this and games possible with UDK is that these games take a HUGE amount of engine programming to create custom attributes, to where it becomes very difficult to even compare a game made with UDK to a game made with the Unreal 3 Engine. Think of UDK as a custom game that you are able to use to create your game with (which is how UDK is setup. It is a "game" written in Unreal Script that also allows you to use the editor to make extended games).

UDK is restricted but only in the way of altering how the engine works (things like rendering, lighting, custom tools, and the editor) not in what you can program when making game play.

Whenever you come across the term "native" it comes from the native code of the engine. You still use it in the same way as everything else.

When you are dealing with most of the base Unreal Script classes, such as Actor (where Spawn( ) is written) you will see a lot of specifiers in front of the function – like for Spawn( ). Here is a list of meanings for the specifiers:

- **Native**: Indicates that this class uses C++ support.

- **Noexport**: Indicates that this classes C++ declaration should NOT be included in the automatically generated C++ header file by the script compiler
- **Final**: Means that this function cannot be overwritten by child classes.
- **Coerce**: Forces the parameter to be converted to the parameters type, regardless of whether UnrealScript would normally do that, or not.

Hopefully this is the first time you have read anything and went, "... ?"

That's fine! None of this is terribly important to remember just yet, when you are extending classes and other things that we will be doing for this book. I felt that for those who may be interested to give them some insight into what some specifiers mean. Look at the advanced reading, if you want to know more.

Now that we understand that functions either created or used, are portions of the program designed to do perform a specific task, let's go into creating our own to better understand how to use them.

At this point, I recommend either saving what has been done to a different location or delete everything we have done so far and return back to having the "blank" classes we started with. As a reminder, you classes should look like this:

Game Info:

```
class USL_GameInfo extends GameInfo;

DefaultProperties
{
   HUDType = class'UnrealScriptLesson.USL_HUD'
   PlayerControllerClass=class'UnrealScriptLesson.USL_PlayerController'
   DefaultPawnClass = class'UnrealScriptLesson.USL_Pawn'
   bDelayedStart = false
}
```

Player Controller:

```
class USL_PlayerController extends PlayerController;

DefaultProperties
{
}
```

Pawn:

```
class USL_Pawn extends Pawn;
```

```
DefaultProperties
{
}
```

HUD:

```
class USL_HUD extends HUD;

// This is the HUD class "Main" draw loop. Used to draw HUD
// elements to the screen.
function DrawHUD( )
{
}

DefaultProperties
{
}
```

I know it might seem a little strange to start over but it is probably the best way to move forward, as modifying the other code to fit might not work well as we didn't understand the purpose of functions yet, which is much more flexible than the past examples.

Open up the USL_HUD.uc class and create a new function.

```
// Draws text to the screen
function DrawOurText( )
{
   // Set the position on the screen to draw text
   Canvas.SetPos( Canvas.SizeX * 0.5, Canvas.SizeY * 0.5 );

   // Set the color of the text to draw on screen
   Canvas.SetDrawColor( 255,255,255,255 );

   // Draw the text to the screen
   Canvas.DrawText( "Functions!" );
}
```

Then, add a function call to the DrawHUD( ) function, like:

```
// This is the HUD class "Main" draw loop. Used to draw HUD
// elements to the screen.
function DrawHUD( )
{
   // Calls the DrawText( ) function
   DrawOurText( );
}
```

If you debug the game now, you will see:

Nothing here should be outside of what you've seen before.

Let's do something you haven't seen before, and add a "parameter" to the DrawOurText( ) function:

```
// Draws text to the screen
function DrawOurText( string toDraw )
{
   // Set the position on the screen to draw text
   Canvas.SetPos( Canvas.SizeX * 0.5, Canvas.SizeY * 0.5 );

   // Set the color of the text to draw on screen
   Canvas.SetDrawColor( 255,255,255,255 );

   // Draw the text to the screen
   Canvas.DrawText( toDraw );
}
```

If you tried to compile now, you would get a error telling you that you have a "bad or missing expression" This is because in our DrawHUD( ) function we are trying to call a function that now requires a parameter (also called an argument). To fix that we need to pass a string into the DrawOurText( ) function as that is the type it expects:

```
// Calls the DrawText( ) function
DrawOurText( "Functions!" );
```

If you debug the game now, you will see the exact same thing as before. Let's take it another step and use a class variable. Add this:

```
// String used to draw text
var string OurString;
```

Then, in the defaultproperties, add this:

```
DefaultProperties
{
```

```
   // Default value of our string to draw on screen
   OurString = "Functions!"
}
```

You will also need to change the DrawHUD( ) function, to accommodate our variable change.

```
// Calls the DrawText( ) function
DrawOurText( OurString );
```

If you debug the game again you will see the same "Functions!" text in the middle of your screen. Here is a break down of how this is working:

- We have our class variable: OurString.
- OurString has a default value of, "Functions!"
- DrawHUD( ) calls DrawOurText( ) which accepts ONE string parameter.
- We are using OurString variable as that parameter.
- DrawOurText( ) takes the passed parameter, OurString, and uses it to draw the text to the screen through the reference of toDraw.

Let's change this up a bit to show how these sorts of functions can be useful. To start, change the OurString variable into an array that holds THREE elements:

```
// String used to draw text
var string OurString[3];
```

Then, in the default properties, set each of the array elements with a value:

```
// Default value of our string to draw on screen
OurString[0] = "Look at my "
OurString[1] = "text, using: "
OurString[2] = "Functions!"
```

Introduce two more class variables:

```
// Used to keep track of game time
var float fLocalTime;
// Keeps tabs on what string we are displaying
var int StringTally;
```

Then, lets modify the DrawHUD( ) function to draw each of OurString elements every TWO seconds.

Start by keeping track of the game time. Add this to DrawHUD( ):

```
// Keeps a tally on deltatime
fLocalTime += RenderDelta;
```

To setup our DrawOurText( ) function to work with the array, change the call to it in DrawHUD( ) to this:

```
// Draws our text to screen, using our function
DrawOurText( OurString[ StringTally ] );
```

This might look strange to you. How this works is, we are passing an array element as a argument. It is just like passing any other variable, but we are passing the variable within the array. Then, we are using a int variable, to tell what element in the array to pass into DrawOurText( ). You have seen something similar, when we did our for loops. We used "i" as the element there. This is the same idea, just with a class variable, instead of a local variable.

We now need a condition to draw each of the THREE OurString elements to display for TWO seconds each and to keep track of our StringTally int variable:

```
// If our local time is more than TWO seconds
if ( fLocalTime > 2 )
{
    // Reset local time
    fLocalTime = 0;

    // Increase the StringTally ( change the text we see on the screen )
    StringTally++;

    // If our string tally is bigger than our static array
    if ( StringTally == 3 )
    {
        // reset the value of it, so the text on screen loops
        StringTally = 0;
    }
}
```

If you debug the game now, you will see the text changing every TWO seconds.

Another way to access a variable is through a function that returns a specific variable type. These functions are called an "accessor" or a "getter". These types of functions do NOT modify the state of a variable or class, they just return the current value of it.

Let's modify the way our DrawOurText( ) function handles the OurString array by creating a function that returns the proper array element, so we don't have to directly access the array.

```
// Get the array element we want
function string GetStringArrayElement( int i )
{

}
```

This function is designed to return a string type, which is why we have the "string" specifier in front of the function name. Also, since this function is designed to return an array element we need a way to tell it which array element we are looking for, which is why there is the "int i" parameter.

In order for a function that has a type to compile, it has to return something. Modify the GetStringArrayElement( ) function to accommodate this:

```
// Get the array element we want
function string GetStringArrayElement( int i )
{
   return ( OurString[ i ] );
}
```

We need to modify the DrawHUD( ) function so we can use this GetStringArrayElement( ) function.

Change the DrawHUD( ) function:

```
// Draws our text to screen, using our function
DrawOurText( OurString[ StringTally ] );
```

to this:

```
// Draws our text to screen, using our function
DrawOurText( GetStringArrayElement( StringTally ) );
```

The big change here is that we are no long using the OurString array directly. Instead, we are using the GetStringArrayElement( ) function to give us the element we are looking for.

Why use an accessor to get our variable, instead of just using the variable itself? This allows the programmer to perform a special handling when a variable is accessed or modified. For instance, it offers the ability to control the access of the property, if the variable is set to private.

To reiterate, "private" is a specifier used by programmers that want to limit the access to the class it is declared in. This means that if we use the specifier private in USL_HUD.uc, only USL_HUD.uc can access and modify the direct property of it. So what if another class needs to access that property but we still want to restrict the direct access of it? That is exactly what these accessor functions are for. It allows the programmer to get a variable in a more "clean" way; by "clean" I mean, it is impossible to accidentally alter the value of a variable if you are using an accessor function to access it. If you are directly accessing any variable it can accidentally become altered, if mismanaged. Accessor functions are a tool to eliminate that from happening.

As an example, in the last chapter we used a function called GetPhysicsName( ) which returned a string value of the current Pawn physics state. This allowed us to compare the current physics state the Pawn is in with a known physics type.

In order for the accessor to work in tandem it has a friend called the "modfier" function, also called a "set" function; the two of the accessor and modifier functions are often called "setter" and "getter" functions. The modifier function is designed to change the value of the variable(s) within the function. Let's update our USL_HUD.uc class so we can use a modifier function:

Add a new class variable:

```
// Current string value to draw on screen
var string CurrentString;
```

Then, create a new **accessor function**, to get the **CurrentString** value:

```
// Get the value of CurrentString
function string GetCurrentString( )
{
   return ( CurrentString );
}
```

Update the DrawHUD( ) function so it will draw this instead of an element of the OurString array.

Change this:

```
// Draws our text to screen, using our function
DrawOurText( GetStringArrayElement( StringTally ) );
```

To this:

```
// Draws our text to screen, using our function
DrawOurText( GetCurrentString( ) );
```

Create an exec function so that the user is able to set the value of CurrentString:

```
// Allows the user to set the value of CurrentString
exec function SetCurrentString( string toSet )
{
   CurrentString = toSet;
}
```

If you debug the game now, you can press either the Tilde (`) or Tab key, to bring up the console. Then type: SetCurrentString YOURTEXTHERE

The HUD will update and show whatever you typed as "YOURSTRINGHERE" in the middle of the screen. Feel free to do this as much as you want.

One thing that may be confusing is the difference between the class variables being set and the parameters in the set and get functions. For instance, in the SetCurrentString( ) function there is a parameter "string toSet". This is the parameter passed into the function that is used to assign the class variable (in this case "CurrentString"). Whatever string variable that is passed into SetCurrentString( ) is what CurrentString will be assigned to.

Sometimes you'll need to return more than ONE type of variable from a function. There is a specifier for parameters that allow this. It is called **out**. Out is a specifier that allows the function to take an argument change it within that function, then at the end of the block will return the new value of it. This is handle if you have many things that you would like to do at once that involve many different types of parameters.

Let's create a function that gives us a few different stats on our pawn:

```
// Reference stats for our pawn class
function PawnStats( out name name, out Vector location, out Rotator
      rotation, out float speed )
{
   // Used to reference the pawn class
```

```
        local Pawn pawnActor;

    // Get a reference to our pawn
    foreach WorldInfo.AllPawns( class'Pawn', pawnActor )
    {
        // Assign reference to the pawns name
        name = pawnActor.Name;

        // Assign reference to the pawns location
        location = pawnActor.Location;

        // Assign reference to the pawns rotation
        rotation = pawnActor.Rotation;

        // Assign reference to the pawns speed
        speed = VSize( pawnActor.Velocity );
    }
}
```

This might be a worrisome moment as that is a lot more parameters than what you've seen so far. Remember that even though there is more of them they are behaving a lot like our previous example. You use the parameter to change a variable then at the end of that code block the modified value is returned to the variable used as the parameter.

Input variable → it gets modified → it gets returned back to the variable passed.

The difference is instead of directly modifying a class variable, like what we were doing with the previous example, this allows us to modify any variable of the same time used as a parameter.

We need some class variables to assign by using this function. Add these to the USL_HUD.uc class:

```
// Reference variables for our pawn
var name NameReference;
var Vector LocationReference;
var Rotator RotationReference;
var float SpeedReference;
```

Now lets modify the DrawHUD( ) function so we are able to see the new references on the screen.

Start by removing everything inside of it.

```
// This is the HUD class "Main" draw loop. Used to draw HUD
// elements to the screen.
```

```
function DrawHUD( )
{
}
```

Then, let's introduce a couple more parameters to our DrawOurText( ) function, so we are able to display the string variable passed to it where we want on the screen:

```
// Draws text to the screen
function DrawOurText( String toDraw, float X, float Y )
```

We also need to change the SetPos( ) function, to use these new parameters.

Change this:

```
// Set the position on the screen to draw text
Canvas.SetPos( Canvas.SizeX * 0.5, Canvas.SizeY * 0.5 );
```

To this:

```
// Set the position on the screen to draw text
Canvas.SetPos( Canvas.SizeX * X, Canvas.SizeY * Y );
```

Add to the DrawHUD( ) function so it draws our new Pawn stats to the screen:

```
// This is the HUD class "Main" draw loop. Used to draw HUD
// elements to the screen.
function DrawHUD( )
{
   // Assign a reference to our class variables
   PawnStats( NameReference, LocationReference,
      RotationReference, SpeedReference );

   // Draws our text to screen, using our function
   DrawOurText( "Pawn Name: " $
      string( NameReference ), 0.5, 0.5 );
   DrawOurText( "Pawn Location: " $
       string( LocationReference ), 0.5, 0.52  );
   DrawOurText( "Pawn Rotation: " $
      string( RotationReferece ), 0.5, 0.54  );
   DrawOurText( "Pawn Speed: " $
      string( SpeedReference ), 0.5, 0.56  );
}
```

It is generally better to only update these variables through PawnStats( ) when would need them,and not every frame. But, considering that in this example, it does show an effect if we keep it updating every frame. Try to remember that philosophy, it is far better to modify a variable or class when you need to and not all the time. But there are times when you need to update something every frame as well.

The DrawOurText( ) function has changed a bit since we first introduced it. The one big thing going on here that hasn't been discussed is the variable being passed that looks like:

```
string( NameReference )
```

This is called an **explicit type cast**. An explicit type cast is a way to convert one type of variable into another. Since the first parameter in the DrawOurText( ) function is of a type string that is the only kind of variable that can be passed into it. That means, in order to pass any other kind of variable into this function we have to use this form type cast so it is of the proper type.

The *Unreal Developers Network** has a list of all variables and what they are able to be cast into. It is as follows:

String
*The **String** data type supports being converted to the following types:*
- *Byte, Int, Float - The number held in the **String** is converted to an actual numerical value. If the value of the **String** does not contain a number, the result of the cast will be **0** 0r **0.0**, depending on the type being converted to.*
- *Bool - Converts the value of the **String** to either **TRUE** or **FALSE**. If the **String** contains either **"True"** or **"False"** (case does not matter), the text is converted directly to the equivalent **Bool** value. If neither of those values are present, the value of the **String** is first converted to a numerical value (following the rules described above) and then converted to a **Bool** value with a value of **0** converting to **FASLE** and any other value being converted to **TRUE**.*
- *Vector, Rotator - Converts a **String** holding the text form of a **Vector** or **Rotation** (three numeric values separated by commas, i.e. "0.5,23.64,18.43") to the specified target data type. For **Vector** conversions, the numeric values in the **String** will be converted to **Float** values with two decimal places of accuracy. For **Rotator** conversions, the numeric values in the **String** will be truncated, or have all decimal places removed, and converted to **Int** values.*

Bool
*The **Bool** data type supports being converted to the following types:*
- *String - Converts the **TRUE** or **FALSE** value of the **Bool** to **String** values of **"True"** or **"False"**, respectively.*
- *Byte, Int, Float - Converts the **TRUE** or **FALSE** value of the **Bool** to numerical values of **1** or **0**, respectively.*

Byte, Int, Float, Vector, Rotator

These numerical data types support being converted to the following types:

- *String - Converts the numerical value(s) to text form. In the case of a **Vector** or **Rotator**, the text form is the three numerical values (**X**, **Y**, **Z** or **Pitch**, **Yaw**, **Roll**) separated by commas.*
- *Bool - Converts the numerical value(s) to **Bool** values of **TRUE** or **FALSE**. Any non-zero value converts to **TRUE**, while a value of zero converts to **FALSE**. In the case of a **Vector** or **Rotator**, the value of each component must be zero to convert to **FALSE**. If any non-zero value is present, the result will be **TRUE**.*

Name

*The **Name** data type supports being converted to the following type:*

- *String - Converts the text value of the **Name** to a **STRING** text value.*

Vector

*The **Vector** data type supports being converted to the following type:*

- *Rotator - Converts the direction from the origin of the world to the location specified by the coordinates of the **Vector** to the **Pitch** and **Yaw** values of a **Rotator** that would correspond to that direction. The **Roll** value will always be **0**.*

Rotator

*The **Rotator** data type supports being converted to the following type:*

- *Vector - Converts the **Pitch**, **Yaw**, and **Roll** values of a **Rotator** to the coordinates of a **Vector** starting at the origin and pointing in the direction of the rotations.*

Object Reference

Object Reference data types support being converted to the following types:

- *Int - Converts the **Object Reference** to a unique **Int** value.*
- *Bool - Converts the **Object Reference** to **TRUE** if the variable holds a valid reference or **FALSE** if the value is **None**.*
- *String - Converts the **Object Reference** to text form, i.e. the **Name** property of the **Object** or **Actor** being referenced (after casting the **Name** to a **String**) or **"None"** if there is no **Object** being referenced.*
- *Object Reference - An **Object Reference** can be converted from one class to another provided the two classes are related. See Converting Object References for complete details on this type of casting.*

* http://udn.epicgames.com/Three/UnrealScriptVariables.html#Type Casting

Another form of type casting is called **implicit type casting**. Implicit type casting is used for some variable types (generally numerical variables – int, float, byte). These types are automatically converted between each other, on assignment (when you tell them to be a different type). As an example:

```
// Two numerical variable types
var int intValue;
var float floatValue;

// floatValue is assigned to 17.15 ( an acceptable value for a float )
floatValue = 17.15;

// intValue is assigned to floatValue: 17.15 ( NOT an acceptable
// value for a int )
intValue = floatValue;
```

Actual value of intValue would be SEVENTEEN as int variables can only hold WHOLE numbers and the compiler will round to the first whole number. It's not like math where it will round to the nearest whole number, it will remove anything after the decimal. As an example, if floatValue was 17.15 or 17.99 will both be 17 if assigned to an int variable.

These are often less used as it is not often you want to convert a int to a float or a float to an int. But, sometimes you may want to convert a byte to an int or an int to a byte as both of these values would be whole numbers.

In short, this is way for a programmer to send one type of variable as another as long as it follows the rules of type casting.

If you debug the game now, you should see real time information about your pawn class.

```
Pawn Name: USL_Pawn_0
Pawn Location: 85.65,-230.65,145.15
Pawn Rotation: 0,-1668,0
Pawn Speed: 599.9997
```

As well as being able to pass variables into functions, you are also able to pass classes. For instance, instead of having the local variable inside of our PawnStats( ) function, we can instead pass a Pawn class variable and used that as a reference.

In order to do this, we need to update the PawnStats( ) function parameters.

Change this:

```
// Reference stats for our pawn class
function PawnStats( out name name, out Vector location,
```

```
    out Rotator rotation, out float speed )
{
   // Used to reference the pawn class
   local Pawn pawnActor;

   // Get a reference to our pawn
   foreach WorldInfo.AllPawns( class'Pawn', pawnActor )
   {
      // Assign reference to the pawns name
      name = pawnActor.Name;

      // Assign reference to the pawns location
      location = pawnActor.Location;

      // Assign reference to the pawns rotation
      rotation = pawnActor.Rotation;

      // Assign reference to the pawns speed
      speed = VSize( pawnActor.Velocity );
   }
}
```

To this:

```
// Reference stats for our pawn class
function PawnStats( Pawn pawnActor, out name name,
      out Vector location, out Rotator rotation, out float speed )
{
   // Get a reference to our pawn
   foreach WorldInfo.AllPawns( class'Pawn', pawnActor )
   {
      // Assign reference to the pawns name
      name = pawnActor.Name;

      // Assign reference to the pawns location
      location = pawnActor.Location;

      // Assign reference to the pawns rotation
      rotation = pawnActor.Rotation;

      // Assign reference to the pawns speed
      speed = VSize( pawnActor.Velocity );
   }
}
```

You'll see not a whole lot changed. We removed the local variable and introduce a parameter of the same name and type.

Then, we need to introduce a new class variable to replace the local variable. Put it under the list of your other variables for the Pawn:

```
var Pawn PawnReference;
```

We need to update the PawnStats( ) call, within DrawHUD( ):

Change this:

```
// Assign a reference to our class variables
PawnStats( NameReference, LocationReference, RotationReference,
    SpeedReference );
```

To this:

```
// Assign a reference to our class variables
PawnStats( PawnReference, NameReference, LocationReference,
    RotationReference, SpeedReference );
```

Nothing should have changed visually if you debugged the game. This is just another example of how we can use functions to communicate with our programs variables and classes.

To recap, we have gone from using basic functions to do individual tasks. We have used parameters to make the functions more usable as any variable passed into the function can then be used in it. We talked about using functions to return a type which can be used in conditional statements as well as assign class variables with data. We discussed using "out" as a specifier which works a bit like a function that returns a type but is designed around working with more than one type and is generally used with the mind set of being able to use it with different variables – not just class variables.

The current USL_HUD.uc class looks like:

```
class USL_HUD extends HUD;

// String used to draw text
var string OurString[3];

// Current string value to draw on screen
var string CurrentString;

// Used to keep track of game time
var float fLocalTime;

// Keeps tabs on what string we are displaying
```

```
var int StringTally;

// Reference variables for our pawn
var name NameReference;
var Vector LocationReference;
var Rotator RotationReference;
var float SpeedReference;
var Pawn PawnReference;

// This is the HUD class "Main" draw loop. Used to draw HUD
// elements to the screen.
function DrawHUD( )
{
   // Assign a reference to our class variables
   PawnStats( PawnReference, NameReference, LocationReference,
      RotationReference, SpeedReference );

   // Draws our text to screen, using our function
   DrawOurText( "Pawn Name: " $
      string( NameReference ), 0.5, 0.5 );
   DrawOurText( "Pawn Location: " $
      string( LocationReference ), 0.5, 0.52  );
   DrawOurText( "Pawn Rotation: " $
      string( RotationReference ), 0.5, 0.54  );
   DrawOurText( "Pawn Speed: " $
      string( SpeedReference ), 0.5, 0.56  );
}

// Reference stats for our pawn class
function PawnStats( Pawn pawnActor, out name name,
      out Vector location, out Rotator rotation, out float speed )
{
   // Get a reference to our pawn
   foreach WorldInfo.AllPawns( class'Pawn', pawnActor )
   {
      // Assign reference to the pawns name
      name = pawnActor.Name;

      // Assign reference to the pawns location
      location = pawnActor.Location;

      // Assign reference to the pawns rotation
      rotation = pawnActor.Rotation;

      // Assign reference to the pawns speed
      speed = VSize( pawnActor.Velocity );
   }
}
```

```
// Draws text to the screen
function DrawOurText( String toDraw, float X, float Y )
{
   // Set the position on the screen to draw text
   Canvas.SetPos( Canvas.SizeX * X, Canvas.SizeY * Y );

   // Set the color of the text to draw on screen
   Canvas.SetDrawColor( 255,255,255,255 );

   // Draw the text to the screen
   Canvas.DrawText( toDraw );
}

// Allows the user to set the value of CurrentString
exec function SetCurrentString( string toSet )
{
   CurrentString = toSet;
}

// Get the value of CurrentString
function string GetCurrentString( )
{
   return ( CurrentString );
}

// Get the array element we want
function string GetStringArrayElement( int i )
{
   return ( OurString[ i ] );
}

DefaultProperties
{
   // Default value of our string to draw on screen
   OurString[0] = "Look at my "
   OurString[1] = "text, using: "
   OurString[2] = "Functions!"
}
```

Next chapter, we will talk about communicating between classes, and go into how to use functions to assign specific variables between classes.

Challenge:

1) Create a class "color" array and pass elements of that to the DrawOurText( ) function, from the DrawHUD( ) function, that will alternate color when each of the OurString array elements are displayed.

Possible answer:

```
class USL_HUD extends HUD;

// Color used for DrawOurText( )
var Color CustomColor[3];

// String used to draw text
var string OurString[3];

// Used to keep track of game time
var float fLocalTime;

// Used to keep track of what string and color to display
var int StringTally;

// This is the HUD class "Main" draw loop. Used to draw HUD
// elements to the screen.
function DrawHUD( )
{
   // keep track of game time, in seconds
   fLocalTime += RenderDelta;

   // Draw our text using OurString and CustomColor array.
   DrawOurText( OurString[ StringTally ], 0.5, 0.5,
      CustomColor[ StringTally ] );

   // If game time is more than 2.5 seconds
   if ( fLocalTime > 2.5 )
   {
      // increase the string tally, which keeps track of what
      // array element to display
      StringTally++;

      // reset the game time counter
      fLocalTime = 0;

      // If StringTally is equal to our array count
      if ( StringTally == 3 )
      {
         // Reset the StringTally count, looping the display
         StringTally = 0;
      }
   }
}

// Draws text to the screen
```

```
function DrawOurText( String toDraw, float X, float Y,
    color colorElement )
{
    // Set the position on the screen to draw text
    Canvas.SetPos( Canvas.SizeX * X, Canvas.SizeY * Y );

    // Set the color of the text to draw on screen
    Canvas.DrawColor = colorElement;

    // Draw the text to the screen
    Canvas.DrawText( toDraw );
}

defaultproperties
{
    // Custom colors to use in DrawOurText
    CustomColor[0] = ( R=255, B=34, G=114, A=255 )
    CustomColor[1] = ( R=125, B=234, G=14, A=255 )
    CustomColor[2] = ( R=20, B=122, G=96, A=255 )

    // Default value of our string to draw on screen
    OurString[0] = "Look at my "
    OurString[1] = "text, using: "
    OurString[2] = "Functions!"
}
```

More reading:

More on functions:
https://en.wikipedia.org/wiki/Functional_programming

More on API:
http://en.wikipedia.org/wiki/Application_programming_interface

More on class specifiers:
http://udn.epicgames.com/Three/UnrealScriptClasses.html

More on function parameter specifiers:
http://udn.epicgames.com/Three/UnrealScriptFunctions.html#ParameterSpecifiers

More on type casting, in UDK:
http://udn.epicgames.com/Three/UnrealScriptVariables.html#Type Casting

More on Injustice: Gods Among Us development:
http://en.wikipedia.org/wiki/Injustice:_Gods_Among_Us#Development

More on Borderlands 2 development:
http://en.wikipedia.org/wiki/Borderlands_2#Development

More on Bioshock Infinite development:
http://en.wikipedia.org/wiki/BioShock_Infinite#Development

More on Accessors and Modifiers (in C++):
http://en.wikibooks.org/wiki/C%2B
%2B_Programming/Classes/Member_Functions#Accessors_and_Modifiers_.28Setter.2FGett
er.29

Class, Struct, and Enum
Chapter Five

UDK comes with many "base" classes that you are able to extend in order to inherent the class attributes. We've been using these sorts of class, such as PlayerController, Pawn, GameInfo, HUD and so on. If you wanted, you are able to completely ignore these classes and create your own. The one restriction when using UDK is that the class you create must extend from Object. This is because in UDK Object is the "root" class that everything else comes from. As an example, if you're extending from Pawn, your class is going to inherent properties from the following classes:

- **Pawn**
- **Actor**
- **Object**

This is because the Pawn class extends Actor which in turn extends Object. And, given the rules of inheritance, the properties of each extended class will carry over to the one extending it. Remember that when extending classes, the functions and variables are going to be inherited as long as they are set to. If you remember specifiers such as "private" will limit the control of such variable(s) or function(s) to that class.

If you take the time to look over the Object class you will see that there is a lot going on in there. There are things setup for vectors, rotators, quats, input settings and controls, colors, constant variables, etc. All of these attributes are incredibly important for making games with the UDK.

One of the most important aspects of the class system is the ability for one class to send data to another. This also happens to be one of the more challenging characteristics of programming with UDK, as the methods in which to do this aren't always clear. To get a better understanding, here is the list of the "main" base classes and a recommended set of guidelines on how to use them:

GameInfo:

This **class** is responsible for all of the game related information. Things such as scoring, timing, and basic goal systems could be implemented here. This **class** is also the most strait forward to access. It is done as such:

```
MYGAMEINFO ( WorldInfo.Game );
```

As an example, if I wanted to access the USL_GameInfo.uc class, it would be done like:

```
USL_GameInfo ( WorldInfo.Game );
```

This could be used to make sure this is the Game Info class being used for the game, such as:

```
if ( USL_GameInfo( WorldInfo.Game ) != none )
{
   // USL_GameInfo class is being used, do things related to this
   // game type being accessible
}
```

Or, if you wanted variable to reference USL_GameInfo.uc:

```
myGameInfo = USL_GameInfo ( WorldInfo.Game );
```

And, if you wanted to reference a class variable that is inside of USL_GameInfo.uc:

```
myIntVar = USL_GameInfo ( WorldInfo.Game ).gameIntVar;
```

If you wanted to call a function within USL_GameInfo.uc:

```
USL_GameInfo ( WorldInfo.Game ).MyGameInfoFunction ( );
```

Accessing a game info class like this is done through **casting;** Something we talked about previously. In order to access the game info class, you need to tell the compiler what sort of class it is. Which, in this case, is done by casting the game info class into the "Game" game info variable within the WorldInfo class.

This works just like any of the other explicit type casting examples.

PlayerController:

The Player Controller class is used for the actual controls of the player, such as input. It can also be used to access the HUD class and Player Input class.

There are a couple different ways to reference a Player Controller, though there needs to be some caution here, as there can be more than one type of controller active.

```
WorldInfo.GetALocalPlayerController( );
```

The concern here is that if there is a split screen game (or a client game – non online – that has more than ONE Player Controller) this will return the first Player Controller found. It will NOT return both. The comment description for the GetALocalPlayerController( ) function, in Actor says:

```
/** Return first found LocalPlayerController. Fine for single player,
in split screen, one will be picked. */
```

Another way to reference any controller, would be to reference it through the foreach iterator. One cool thing about this is you can pick a specific class type you want to search for. So, let's say there is TWO different Player Controller classes in the game, at once, you can use this to reference ONE. Such as:

```
function TestPC( )
{
   local USL_PlayerController PC;

   foreach WorldInfo.AllControllers( class'USL_PlayerController', PC )
   {
      // Reference the USL_PlayerController through PC, here
   }
}
```

This will specifically reference any class of the type USL_PlayerController. You could, for instance, reference ALL Player Controllers by doing this:

```
function TestPC( )
{
   local PlayerController PC;

   foreach WorldInfo.AllControllers( class'PlayerController', PC )
   {
      // Reference the PlayerController through "PC", here
   }
}
```

This will reference all Player Controllers, including any that extend the Player Controller class. As you can see this sort of method can be a bit to take in but it also powerful enough that referencing different class types for different things can be done with some added logic; such as conditional statements.

Also, everything needed to be done by referencing these different classes needs to be done within the foreach loop block. If you tried to use "PC" outside of the foreach loop that is referencing the Player Controller it will reference "none". You will always need a variable to use to reference the class within the foreach iterator. If you don't have a class or local variable to reference the class with the foreach statement will be incomplete and will result in a compiling error.

Pawn:

The Pawn class is the base class for all players, characters, and other types of "active" entities in the world. They represent the physical appearance of a Controller class.

Since Pawns can make up a big majority of the interaction of the player and the world, given the use of AI, NPC's, and other types of Pawns, directly accessing any one of them would need to be setup on our "the programmer"s end. As with the example for the Player Controller, one of the options is through the foreach iterator. Such as:

```
function TestPawn( )
{
   local USL_Pawn P;

   foreach WorldInfo.AllControllers( class'USL_Pawn', P )
   {
      // Reference the USL_Pawn through P, here
   }
}
```

This has the same pros and cons of the referencing any other class. If there is more than ONE type of the same class, you will the referencing them all.

Another way to have a reference to any Pawn you would like would be to create a function within the Game Info that assigns the Pawn to a class variable within the Game Info class.

For instance, inside of your USL_GameInfo.uc class there can be a class variable:

```
// Used to reference USL_Pawn
var USL_Pawn myPawn;
```

Then, still inside of the USL_GameInfo.uc class, you can create a modifier function to set this variable when the USL_Pawn is created:

```
// Used to set a reference sure USL_Pawn
function SetUSLPawn( USL_Pawn P )
{
   myPawn = P;
}
```

Within the USL_Pawn.uc class, you can setup PostBeginPlay( ) to call and set this function.

```
// Called just after this class is created
simulated function PostBeginPlay( )
{
   super.PostBeginPlay( );

   // Set a reference to this pawn within the USL_GameInfo
   USL_GameInfo( WorldInfo.Game ).SetUSLPawn( self );
}
```

"Self" is a specifier that can be used to declare itself as a class variable. This is also a way to avoid creating another reference, as it is possible to run a foreach iterator to reference the same class that it is in, then run the SetUSLPawn( ) function within that. But, using self is just a way to make sure you are sending not only the desired class you want but also a way to avoid using more code to accomplish the same result.

The purpose here would be to pass the class being created as an argument for the SetUSLPawn( ) function, within the GameInfo class, so you have a reference to it.

HUD:

The HUD (Heads Up Display) is used to display information about the game state to the player during game play. Things like player health, ammo count, and mission objectives.

The HUD class is usually referenced through the Player Controller with the variable "myHUD". As an example, let's say that you have referenced the Player Controller through GetALocalPlayerController( ) function.

A reference to the HUD class associated with your Player Controller would look like:

```
//EXAMPLE
function TestHUD( )
{
   local HUD H;

   // Can now use H to reference the HUD class
```

```
   H = WorldInfo.GetALocalPlayerController( ).myHUD;
}
```

"myHUD" is a variable that is a part of the base Player Controller class and is there so you don't have to create your own set of variables and functions to access it. If you wanted to access a different HUD class that is not attached to your Player Controller but still a part of the WorldInfo you can (again) create a modifier function in GameInfo to reference it through a variable. Or you can do something we haven't done yet and actually create the class during run time, then have a reference to it that way.

As a refresher, create a new HUD class variable within USL_GameInfo.uc:

```
//EXAMPLE
// Used to reference the USL_HUD
var USL_HUD USLHUD;
```

Then, create a function in the GameInfo to assign a reference to the HUD class:

```
//EXAMPLE
// Used to set a reference to the USL_HUD
function SetUSLHUD( USL_HUD H )
{
   USLHUD = H;
}
```

Within the USL_HUD.uc class, have the PostBeginPlay( ) function call the SetUSLHUD( ) function:

```
//EXAMPLE
// Called just after this class is created
simulated function PostBeginPlay( )
{
   super.PostBeginPlay( );

   // Assign a reference to this USL_HUD class in USL_GameInfo
   USL_GameInfo( WorldInfo.Game ).SetUSLHUD( self );
}
```

Another option is to set up a way to get a reference through the Spawn( ) function:

```
//EXAMPLE
function TestHUD( )
{
   local USL_HUD H;

   // Spawn the class USL_HUD and reference it with H.
```

```
   H = Spawn ( class'USL_HUD', self );
}
```

Given the rules of scope, the reference to this HUD would work during the time this function is being called. If you remember, the program runs line by line and at the end of a function block every reference within that scope is deleted (this means that the reference would be deleted but the class would still exist in the game world). If you wanted to have a more usable reference, create a class variable to reference the USL_HUD.uc being spawned:

```
//EXAMPLE
// Used to reference the USL_HUD
var USL_HUD H;
```

And then:

```
//EXAMPLE
function TestHUD ( )
{
   // Spawn the class USL_HUD and reference it with H.
   H = Spawn ( class'USL_HUD', self );
}
```

You would have to call this function in order for it to spawn, which can be done at your discretion. (We've been using the PostBeginPlay( ) function but creating or referencing classes doesn't have to have to happen right after another class is created, it can be done whenever you want it to be done).

As a warning, let's say you accidentally used this TestHUD( ) function twice. That would create TWO USL_HUD classes but the second time you ran it, it would overwrite the first "H" reference with the second class spawn. As a precaution, you could do something like:

```
//EXAMPLE
function TestHUD ( )
{
   // If there is NO reference to USL_HUD
   if( H == none )
   {
      // Spawn the class USL_HUD and reference it with H.
      H = Spawn ( class'USL_HUD', self );
   }
}
```

This would make sure that if the reference already exists, it won't allow you to spawn or reference any more USL_HUD classes.

Now that you know now to reference some of the common class types. Let's go over referencing from the Object class.

Create a new class, named USL_Object.uc. To do so, create a new .uc file by RIGHT-CLICKING the classes folder inside of the UnrealScripLesson folder. This is inside of the Solution Explorer in Visual Studio, then select Add and then New Item.

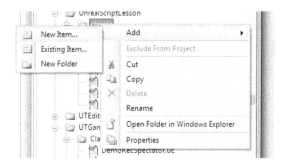

Name it USL_Object.uc and the class should look like:

```
class USL_Object extends Object;

DefaultProperties
{
}
```

Back in the USL_GameInfo.uc class, add:

```
function TestObject( )
{
   local USL_Object O;

   // Creates a new USL_Object
   O = new class'USL_Object';
}
```

This is very much like using Spawn( ) though it doesn't have the same sort of assignments (such as who is in charge the class being spawned, or where it will spawn in the world). "O" would then be the reference to the newly created USL_Object class just like when we used Spawn( ).

Let us say that the USL_Object class had a function that you wanted to access through your reference in USL_GameInfo.

Add a function in USL_Object such as:

```
function ObjTestFunction( )
```

```
{
   // Directly reference DebugMessagePlayer( ) from the world info
   class'WorldInfo'.static.GetWorldInfo( ).
         DebugMessagePlayer( "Non Static Function" );
}
```
You could call this function in **USL_GameInfo.uc** like:

```
// Creates a reference to USL_Object
exec function TestFunction( )
{
   local USL_Object O;

   O = new class'USL_Object';

   O.ObjTestFunction( );
}
```

You do not always have to have a reference for a class like we have been doing so far. If you want, you can write a "static" function within any class and have the ability to directly access that function without having a reference to the class it's within.

A "Static" function is a function that can be called without having a reference to an object of the class (one created). There are a few rules when using "static". You CAN access other static functions and default values of variables but you CANNOT access non-static functions as they cannot be called without a reference to an instance of a class object. In order to reference a static function, there has to be one created.

Add this to the inside of USL_Object.uc:

```
function static StaticTestFunction( )
{
   class'WorldInfo'.static.GetWorldInfo( ).
      DebugMessagePlayer( "Static Function" );
}
```

Back in USL_GameInfo.uc, you can directly call this function, without a reference, by doing:

```
// Uses the 'Static' specifier to ignore reference
// and directly call StaticTestFunction( )
exec function TestStaticFunction( )
{
   class'USL_Object'.static.StaticTestFunction( );
}
```

As a reminder, if you do not have a reference to an Object class and you're trying to call a function that is NOT static you will not be able to call or access it; you MUST have a reference to the Object class if you want to call any function that is non-static.

Structs:

Structs are a way to group variables together. We have also been using some structs already. Things like Vector, Color, and Rotator are all structs. You'll notice, that these "groupings" tend to relate to a singular type. For instance, a Vector is a reference to world location which needs to reference float variables, X,Y, and Z. These three values represent world coordinates. Instead of having to introduce X, Y, and Z over and over, you can reference them from a Vector. This is also the same for Rototor which reference Yaw, Pitch, and Roll. As well as Color, which references Red, Green, Blue, and Alpha.

As an example, let's say that we wanted to group our Pawns stats within a struct we could do that by adding the following to USL_Pawn.uc:

Let's say that we have a grenade projectile type that gets used by two different kind of AI. One AI is small and the other is big. We could want to delegate a difference between their ability for how far they can throw the grenade projectile. In order to do this, we could have a struct that has two variable members "short" and "far".

```
struct ThrowDistance
{
    var float Short, Far;
};
```

Then, given a set of instructions in the rest of the code, when a "small" AI throws a grenade we can tell it to throw it "Short" and if it is "Far" we can have it throw the grenade far. Once a struct is defined, you can also create a variable of that struct. Such as:

```
// Used to set values for throw distance
var ThrowDistance MyThrowDistance;
```

Then, within the Default Properties, you can assign your default values for both Short and Far:

```
MyThrowDistance = ( Short = 500, Far = 1250 )
```

We can use MyThrowDistance.Short or MyThrowDistance.Far as a value, when assigning what distance the Pawn should be able throw.

Another example would be if we needed to say debug a list of information about the game. We could create a "GameInfoMessage" struct, full of game related information:

```
struct GameInfoMessage
```

```
{
    var string PlayerName;
    var int PlayerHealth, PlayerAmmo;
    var float PlayerSpeed;
    var Vector PlayerLocation;
    var Rotator PlayerRotation;
    var Pawn Player;
};
```

Then, we could create a GameInfoMessage variable, and assign the proper references to each of these variables and access them as we did before, with the ThrowDistance struct.

Structs are powerful and useful additions for keeping track when dealing with groups of variables. Also, structs often sit in lower level classes and are accessed and used in the higher level classes as variables; such as what I had mentioned earlier: Color, Vector, Rotator, and so on.

Enums:

Enums (Enumerations) are a way to declare a name to an element in a set. Each element of an Enum is actually just a number with a name assigned to it. For instance, a simple Enum list looks like:

```
//EXAMPLE: Used to keep track of colors
enum TextColor
{
    TC_RED,
    TC_BLUE,
    TC_PURPLE,
};
```

Just like structs, enums can be declared as variables and each variable can have a set of default properties that will assign the desired value, though we won't be needing a variable for the enum. We can use it directly for this example.

Since the values within the TextColor enum are represented by a number, we can use them inside of a Color array. We are able to choose the color by a name, instead of a abstract number.

Modify the CustomColor Color array from this:

```
// Color used for DrawOurText( )
var Color CustomColor[3];
```

To this:

```
// Color used for DrawOurText( )
var Color CustomColor[TextColor];
```

It is important to have the enum TextColor BEFORE the declaration of the CustomColor array. If you happen to have it after, you will get a compile error telling you that you have a "bad or missing array size". This is because when the compiler runs through the code, it runs line by line. It will try to use TextColor enum before it is declared and tell you that it's missing.

We need to update the Default Properties to match the name of the colors.

Change this:

```
// Custom colors to use in DrawOurText
CustomColor[0] = ( R=255, B=34, G=114, A=255 )
CustomColor[1] = ( R=125, B=234, G=14, A=255 )
CustomColor[2] = ( R=20, B=122, G=96, A=255 )
```

To this:

```
// Custom colors to use in DrawOurText
CustomColor[0] = ( R=255, B=0, G=0, A=255 )
CustomColor[1] = ( R=0, B=255, G=0, A=255 )
CustomColor[2] = ( R=175, B=255, G=0, A=255 )
```

Then, clean out the **DrawHUD( )** function so it looks like:

```
// This is the HUD class "Main" draw loop. Used to draw HUD
// elements to the screen.
function DrawHUD( )
{

}
```

Then, add this:

```
// This is the HUD class "Main" draw loop. Used to draw HUD
// elements to the screen.
function DrawHUD( )
{
   DrawOurText( "RED", 0.5, 0.5, CustomColor[ TC_RED ] );
   DrawOurText( "BLUE", 0.5, 0.52, CustomColor[ TC_BLUE ] );
   DrawOurText( "PURPLE", 0.5, 0.54, CustomColor[ TC_PURPLE ] );
}
```

If you debug the game now, you should see:

This follows the same sort of example as before. When we were using the stringTally int variable to change colors but this way gives us a lot more control and it is much easier to read. As something as abstract as "stringTally" may be difficult for a person to follow along, if they didn't write the program or when the person who did write it comes back to it after a break.

Using the enum list will give you the ability to make your code easier to follow.

Challenges:

To further educate yourself, here is a few things you can try to do, in order to get a better understanding of classes, structs, and enums.

1) Create functions in the USL_GameInfo.uc class to set a reference to the USL_PlayerController, USL_Pawn, and USL_HUD. Then within each of these classes, call these functions during the PostBeginPlayer( ) function for each.
2) Create a static function within the USL_Object class that RETURNS a string value, to display to the HUD. Use the DrawHUD( ) function inside of the USL_HUD class to call it.

Possible Answers:

Number ONE:

USL_GameInfo set **functions (modifiers)** and **class variables:**

```
// Used to reference USL_Pawn
var USL_Pawn USLPawn;

// Used to reference the USL_HUD
var USL_HUD USLHUD;

// Used to reference the USL_PlayerController
var USL_PlayerController USLPlayerController;
```

```
// Used to set a reference to the USL_PlayerController
function SetUSLPlayerController( USL_PlayerController PC )
{
   USLPlayerController = PC;
}

// Used to set a reference to the USL_HUD
function SetUSLHUD( USL_HUD H )
{
   USLHUD = H;
}

// Used to set a reference sure USL_Pawn
function SetUSLPawn( USL_Pawn P )
{
   USLPawn = P;
}
```

Remember, you can be more general with the functions class arguments, as well as the class variables. This will work as well:

```
// Used to reference USL_Pawn
var Pawn USLPawn;

// Used to reference the USL_HUD
var HUD USLHUD;

// Used to reference the USL_PlayerController
var PlayerController USLPlayerController;

// Used to set a reference to the USL_PlayerController
function SetUSLPlayerController( PlayerController PC )
{
   USLPlayerController = PC;
}

// Used to set a reference to the USL_HUD
function SetUSLHUD( HUD H )
{
   USLHUD = H;
}

// Used to set a reference sure USL_Pawn
function SetUSLPawn( Pawn P )
{
   USLPawn = P;
}
```

PostBeginPlay( ) functions:

USL_Pawn:

```
simulated function PostBeginPlay( )
{
   super.PostBeginPlay( );

   // Sets a reference in the USL_GameInfo to this Pawn class
   USL_GameInfo( WorldInfo.Game ).SetUSLPawn( self );
}
```

USL_HUD:

```
   simulated function PostBeginPlay( )
{
   super.PostBeginPlay( );

   // Sets a reference in the USL_GameInfo to this HUD class
   USL_GameInfo( WorldInfo.Game ).SetUSLHUD( self );
}
```

USL_PlayerController:

```
simulated function PostBeginPlay( )
{
   super.PostBeginPlay( );

   // Sets a reference in the USL_GameInfo to this PlayerController
   // class
   USL_GameInfo( WorldInfo.Game ).SetUSLPlayerController( self );
}
```

To test, create this exec function within the USL_GameInfo class:

```
// Used to see our reference to Pawn, PlayerController, and HUD
exec function SeeReferences( )
{
   DebugMessagePlayer( "Pawn: " $ USLPawn );
   DebugMessagePlayer( "PlayerController: " $ USLPlayerController ) ;
   DebugMessagePlayer( "HUD: " $ USLHUD );
}
```

Debug the game and type in the console window: SeeReferences

You should see this:

```
>>> seereferences <<<
Pawn: USL_Pawn_0
PlayerController: USL_PlayerController_0
HUD: USL_HUD_0
```

Number TWO:

Inside of **USL_Object.uc**:

```
// Example to return exactly what string is sent into it.
// A practice in using static functions :: NOT a practical function
function static string DisplayText( string S )
{
   return S;
}
```

Within the USL_HUD:

```
// This is the HUD class "Main" draw loop. Used to draw HUD
// elements to the screen.
function DrawHUD( )
{
     DrawOurText( class'USL_Object'.static.
     DisplayText( "From a static FUNction" ), 0.5, 0.5,
     CustomColor[ TC_RED ] );
}
```

Additional Reading:

More on the Player Controller:
http://udn.epicgames.com/Three/CharactersTechnicalGuide.html#Player Controller

More on the Game Info:
http://udn.epicgames.com/Three/GametypeTechnicalGuide.html#GameInfo Class

More on the Pawn class:
http://udn.epicgames.com/Three/CharactersTechnicalGuide.html#Pawn

More on function specifiers:
http://udn.epicgames.com/Three/UnrealScriptFunctions.html#Function Specifiers

More on Enums:
http://udn.epicgames.com/Three/UnrealScriptVariables.html#Enumerations
http://en.wikipedia.org/wiki/Enumeration

More on Structs:
http://udn.epicgames.com/Three/UnrealScriptVariables.html#Structs
http://udn.epicgames.com/Three/UnrealScriptDefaultProperties.html#Struct Defaults
http://en.wikipedia.org/wiki/Struct_(C_programming_language)

More general knowledge on UnrealScript:
http://udn.epicgames.com/Three/UnrealScriptFoundations.html#UnrealScript Foundation Concepts

More on Actors vs. Objects:
http://udn.epicgames.com/Three/UnrealScriptFoundations.html#Scripts and Classes vs Objects and Actors

More on Structs in UDK:
http://udn.epicgames.com/Three/UnrealScriptStructs.html
http://udn.epicgames.com/Three/UnrealScriptReference.html

Creating An Example Game Introduction

Chapter Six

Now is the time for us to create a fully functional game! It will include a Game Info, Pawn, Player Controller, HUD, Weapon, Projectile, a Kismet Action Sequence, and an AI class. Each class will be broken up into its own chapter. This chapter will be about setting up our classes so that we are able to begin working; which should happen fairly quickly, as we have already done this before.

As a precaution, I will be naming my classes as I normally would. You do NOT have to follow my naming exactly, though if you do not, you may risk making mistakes and losing your place. I recommend that if you are a beginner to follow my naming. This will help avoid the headache of trying to figure out where your naming went wrong.

We are going to be using the assets that come with the UDK. Instead of using the Unreal Tournament characters ("Liam" and the "Iron Guard"), we will instead be using the Jazz Jackrabbit character and associated enemy characters. This will give us a level already built as well as more options when it comes to how the enemies will work.

To begin, we will be doing what we did with the USL_ classes.

Open up Visual Studio and RIGHT-CLICK on the project file, select Add and then New Folder.

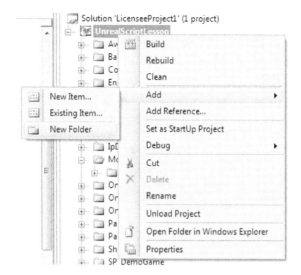

Name this folder: USLExampleGame

RIGHT-CLICK on the USLExampleGame folder and again, Add and then New Folder.

Name this folder: classes

After that, go to My Computer and then to your UDK install directory. Open the UDKGame folder and then the Config folder. Inside of this open up the DefaultEngine.ini file. Find the portion that starts with: [UnrealEd.EditorGame]

At the bottom of that list, add: +EditPackages=USLExampleGame

If you want, you can overwrite the previous UnrealScriptLesson game from the previous chapters.

Since I replaced mine, it looks like:

```
[UnrealEd.EditorEngine]
+EditPackages=UTGame
+EditPackages=UTGameContent
+EditPackages=USLExampleGame
```

Make sure you keep both UTGame and UTGameContent.

Save the DefaultEngine.ini file and then close it. Go back to Visual Studio.

RIGHT-CLICK on the classes folder and add the following classes, as we did with New Folder but this time, select New Item. After selecting New Item, make sure you have the Unreal Script file template selected.

UnrealScript
File

Name them the following:

> **EG_GameInfo**
> **EG_DropActor**
> **EG_Pawn**
> **EG_PlayerController**
> **EG_HUD**
> **EG_Weapon**
> **EG_Projectile**
> **EG_AIController**
> **EG_AIPawn**
> **SeqAct_EGAISpawner**

When you're done, the USLExampleGame, classes folder should look like the image below:

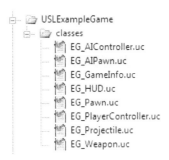

We need to now set these classes up to extend the correct classes, as well as make sure our Game Info class will use them properly.

To begin, let's start with the EG_GameInfo:

```
class EG_GameInfo extends GameInfo;
```

124

```
DefaultProperties
{
   HUDType = class'USLExampleGame.EG_HUD'
   PlayerControllerClass = class'USLExampleGame.EG_PlayerController'
   DefaultPawnClass = class'USLExampleGame.EG_Pawn'
   bDelayedStart = false
}
```

The rest of the classes are going to be changing the extension from Object to the proper class it should extend. As follows:

EG_DropActor:

```
class EG_DropActor extends Actor;

DefaultProperties
{
}
```

EG_Projectile:

```
class EG_Projectile extends Projectile;

DefaultProperties
{
}
```

EG_PlayerController:

```
class EG_PlayerController extends PlayerController;

DefaultProperties
{
}
```

EG_Pawn:

```
class EG_Pawn extends Pawn;

DefaultProperties
{
}
```

EG_HUD:

```
class EG_HUD extends HUD;
```

```
DefaultProperties
{
}
```

EG_AIPawn:

```
class EG_AIPawn extends Pawn;
```

```
DefaultProperties
{
}
```

EG_Weapon:

```
class EG_Weapon extends Actor;
```

```
DefaultProperties
{
}
```

EG_AIController:

```
class EG_AIController extends Controller;
```

```
DefaultProperties
{
}
```

SeqAct_EGAISpawner:

```
class SeqAct_EGAISpawner extends SequenceAction;
```

```
DefaultProperties
{
}
```

We will also need to update our Game Info and map name inside of Visual Studio, so when we debug the game, we are using the proper game info and map.

RIGHT-CLICK on the project file, inside of the Solution Explorer, go to Properties.

Change the Load map at startup to: KismetTutorial_Start.udk
Change the Start with specified game type to: USLExampleGame.EG_GameInfo

✓ Load map at startup:	KismetTutorial_Start.udk
✓ Start with specified game type:	USLExampleGame.EG_GameInfo

Save all of the Visual Studio files by pressing the Save All button.

Close and restart Visual Studio.

If you debug the game now, you should be able to walk around just you're used to but now, you'll be in a different level. A much more pretty one.

You'll notice that some of the trees wont look right, as well as in the building. Jazz Jackrabbit is meant to be played as a top-down style game; something we will be ignoring, even with the art hiccups.

That's it for our initial class setup. Next chapter, we will begin to setup our EG_Pawn class, to have our first physical representation of a character.

If you desire, the finished source code for the Example Game can be found at:

http://tinyurl.com/USLExampleGame

Creating An Example Game Pawn Class

Chapter Seven

As talked about in the classes chapter, the Pawn class is the physical representation in the world of a character. Such as monsters, NPCs, and so on. For our game, we will be using the Jazz Jackrabbit character model as our player character Pawn.

In order for the game to understand what Skeletal Mesh will represent the Pawn, we need to setup a Skeletal Mesh Actor Component.

Add the following in the DefaultProperties inside of the EG_Pawn class. Again, if you are following along, you do NOT have to type all the comments. They are there to help you understand what each line of code is doing.

```
DefaultProperties
{
   Begin Object Class=SkeletalMeshComponent Name=JazzPlayerPawn
      // Skeletal Mesh location to use for this component
      SkeletalMesh=SkeletalMesh'KismetGame_Assets.Anims.SK_Jazz'
      // AnimTreeTemplate that ( should ) match(s) the SkeletalMesh
      AnimTreeTemplate=AnimTree'KismetGame_Assets.Anims.Jazz_AnimTree'
      // AnimSets array list
      AnimSets( 0 )=AnimSet'KismetGame_Assets.Anims.SK_Jazz_Anims'
      // Adjustment for pawn location
      Translation=( Z=-20 )
      // Size of skeletal mesh based on its original size
      Scale=1.00
      // Everything but the owner can see this actor.
```

```
bOwnerNoSee=false
// Whether to cast any shadows or not
CastShadow=true
// Should this block rigid body phyics
BlockRigidBody=TRUE
// If true, update skeleton/attachments even when our Owner
// has not been rendered recently
bUpdateSkelWhenNotRendered=false
// If true, do not apply any SkelControls when owner has
// not been rendered recently.
bIgnoreControllersWhenNotRendered=TRUE
// If we are running physics, should we update bFixed bones
// based on the animation bone positions.
bUpdateKinematicBonesFromAnimation=true
// Controls whether the primitive should cast shadows in the
// case of non precomputed shadowing
bCastDynamicShadow=true
// Enum indicating what type of object this should be
// considered for rigid body collision.
RBChannel=RBCC_Untitled3
// Types of objects that this physics objects will collide with.
RBCollideWithChannels=( Untitled3=true )
// The lighting environment to take the primitive's
// lighting from.
LightEnvironment=LightEnvironment.
// if set, components that are attached to us have their
// bOwnerNoSee and bOnlyOwnerSee properties overridden by ours
bOverrideAttachmentOwnerVisibility=true
// If TRUE, this primitive accepts dynamic decals spawned during
// gameplay.
bAcceptsDynamicDecals=FALSE
// Indicates whether this SkeletalMeshComponent should have a
// physics engine representation of its state.
bHasPhysicsAssetInstance=true
// The ticking group this component belongs to
TickGroup=TG_PreAsyncWork
// If non-zero, skeletal mesh component will not update
//kinematic bones and bone springs when distance factor
// is greater than this (or has not been rendered for a while).
// This also turns off BlockRigidBody, so you do
// not get collisions with 'left behind' ragdoll setups.
MinDistFactorForKinematicUpdate=0.2
//If true, DistanceFactor for this SkeletalMeshComponent will be
// added to global chart.
bChartDistanceFactor=true
// Used for creating one-way physics interactions (via
// constraints or contacts) Groups with lower
// RBDominanceGroup
// push around higher values in a 'one way' fashion. Must be
```

```
      // less than 32.
      RBDominanceGroup=20
      // If TRUE, dynamically lit translucency on this primitive will
      // render in one pass,
      bUseOnePassLightingOnTranslucency=TRUE
      // If true, use per-bone motion blur on this skeletal mesh.
      bPerBoneMotionBlur=true
   End Object
   // Add to the components array
   Components.Add( JazzPlayerPawn )
}
```

This is something that we did not touch on during the previous chapters. Actor Components provide an easily accessible interface that allows settings for rendering and collision (among other things).

There are a few important things to notice here. First, the component starts with "begin object". If you are creating a class who has a parent class that does NOT have a class definition of a Actor Component type, you also want to declare one, like we did here with "class=SkeletalMeshComponent". If the parent class already has one created, you can still modify it with "begin object" and then "Name= " - omitting the "class=__".

As an example, if the parent class does NOT have a Actor Component of the type you want to use, it would be declared like:

```
   begin object class=CLASSCOMPONENT name=MYCLASSCOMPNAME
      DefaultSettings=SettingValue
      DefaultSettings=SettingValue
   end object
   Components.Add( MYCLASSCOMPNAME )
```

If you wanted to access a Actor Component from the parent class (meaning the parent class already has the one you want to use), it would look like:

```
   begin object name=MYCLASSCOMPNAME
      DefaultSettings=
      DefaultSettings=
   end object
   Components.Add( MYCLASSCOMPNAME )
```

If the comments are making this confusing, here is the same code without comments:

```
DefaultProperties
{
   Begin Object Class=SkeletalMeshComponent Name=JazzPlayerPawn
      SkeletalMesh=SkeletalMesh'KismetGame_Assets.Anims.SK_Jazz'
```

```
        AnimTreeTemplate=AnimTree'KismetGame_Assets.Anims.Jazz_AnimTree'
        AnimSets( 0 )=AnimSet'KismetGame_Assets.Anims.SK_Jazz_Anims'
        Translation=( Z=-20 )
        Scale=1.00
        bOwnerNoSee=false
        CastShadow=true
        BlockRigidBody=TRUE
        bUpdateSkelWhenNotRendered=false
        bIgnoreControllersWhenNotRendered=TRUE
        bUpdateKinematicBonesFromAnimation=true
        bCastDynamicShadow=true
        RBChannel=RBCC_Untitled3
        RBCollideWithChannels=( Untitled3=true )
        LightEnvironment=MyLightEnvironment
        bOverrideAttachmentOwnerVisibility=true
        bAcceptsDynamicDecals=FALSE
        bHasPhysicsAssetInstance=true
        TickGroup=TG_PreAsyncWork
        MinDistFactorForKinematicUpdate=0.2
        bChartDistanceFactor=true
        RBDominanceGroup=20
        bUseOnePassLightingOnTranslucency=TRUE
        bPerBoneMotionBlur=true
    End Object
    Components.Add( JazzPlayerPawn )
}
```

Then, we need to setup the actual DynamicLightEnvironmentComponent. This is another Actor Component inside of the DefaultProperties. Add this ABOVE the SkeletalMeshComponent:

```
Begin Object Class=DynamicLightEnvironmentComponent Name=LightEnvironment
    // Whether a SH light should be used to synthesize all light not
    // accounted for by the synthesized    directional light.
    bSynthesizeSHLight=TRUE
    // Whether this light environment is being applied to a
    // character
    bIsCharacterLightEnvironment=TRUE
    // Whether to use cheap on/off shadowing from the environment or
    // allow a dynamic preshadow.
    bUseBooleanEnvironmentShadowing=FALSE
    // Whether the light environment is used or treated the same as
    //a LightEnvironment=NULL reference.
    bEnabled=TRUE
End Object
Components.Add(LightEnvironment)
```

If you debug the game now, you will see the Jazz Jackrabbit model but our camera will be inside of its head.

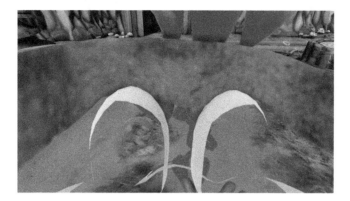

This is because the base Pawn class we extend from defaults its camera position as a first person shooter would. Before we fix that, let's add a collision Actor Component as well as introduce some more default settings for our Pawn class.

Add the collision Actor Component to the END of the DefaultProperties:

```
Begin Object Name=CollisionCylinder
    CollisionRadius=+0021.000000
    CollisionHeight=+0044.000000
End Object
CylinderComponent=CollisionCylinder
```

As I had mentioned before, if the parent class already has a declaration of a Actor Component you can modify it through "Begin Object Name= ". That is what is going on with this collision component. Since Actor (which Pawn extends from) already has an Actor Component setup under the name "CollisionCylinder" we are able to access and then modify it through that name.

The CollisionRadius and CollisionHeight are representations of Unreal Units (roughly ONE CM each if compared to real world measurements) that will put a cylinder around our player Pawn, allowing it to interact with the objects in the world.

The term "collision" doesn't always mean bump into or block. We are able to use this when the Pawn is hit by projectiles or walks through a Trigger Volume – not just when it hits a wall or Static Mesh (something solid).

To introduce more Pawn related default attributes, add the following to the TOP of the

DefaultProperties:

```
// pct. of running speed that walking speed is
WalkingPct=+0.4
// pct. of running speed that crouched walking speed is
CrouchedPct=+0.4
// Base eye height above collision center.
BaseEyeHeight=38.0
// urrent eye height, adjusted for bobbing and stairs.
EyeHeight=38.0
// Movement speed on the ground
GroundSpeed=440.0
// Movement speed in the air
AirSpeed=440.0
// Movement speed when in "water"
WaterSpeed=220.0
// max acceleration rate
AccelRate=2048.0
// Jump height
JumpZ=322.0
// Minimum z value for floor normal (if less, not a walkable floor for
// this pawn)
WalkableFloorZ=0.78
```

These settings will override the base Pawn class to be better fitting for our Pawn.

In order to have a reference to the SkeletalMeshComponent, we need to create a class variable.

Add this to the class variable list:

```
// Used to reference our SkeletalMeshComponent
var SkeletalMeshComponent JazzMesh;
```

Having this reference will give us access to sockets (determined locations on the SkeletalMesh) as well as some other useful things, like bone locations. By default the Pawn class already has this setup but I generally like to have my own reference to the SkeletalMeshComponent.

Now we are going to setup the art assets to work with the camera.

We first need to setup a location for our camera to reference. A socket is designed to do just that, by setting a location that you can place within the AnimSet Editor so you can then reference through the SkeletalMeshComponent reference in code.

In order to do this, you need to open up the UDK editor. Then within the Content Browser, navigate inside of the packages. Open up: UDKGame – Content – Mobile – Misc – KismetGame_Assets – Anims.

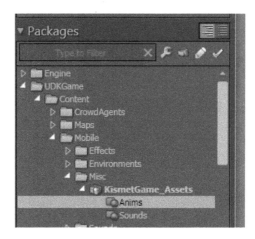

Then, with the "Anims" category selected. Select the SK_Jazz SkeletalMesh:

With it selected, double-click it. It will then open up the AnimSet Editor.

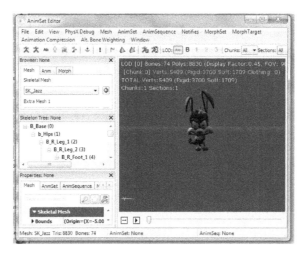

To add the Socket we need, press the Socket Manager button.

New Socket Within this window, you will see TWO sockets already created. Weapon_L and Weapon_R. Do NOT edit these. Instead, press "New Socket".

For "Bone Name", use the default, "B_Base" and hit OK.

Name the Socket: CamLoc

Press Enter or hit OK.

You will now see a new Socket in the view port window name CamLoc, with a widget of blue, green, and red lines (which represent X, Y, and Z space).

Instead of trying to move the Socket around to match what I do, enter the following into the Relative Location drop-down:

   X = -68
   Y = -133
   Z = -212

And, for Relative Rotation drop-down:

   Roll = 0.00
   Pitch = 86.00
   Yaw = 90.00

▼ Relative Location	(X=-68.000000
X	-68.000000
Y	-133.000000
Z	-212.000000
▼ Relative Rotation	(Pitch=86.00°,)
Roll	0.00°
Pitch	86.00°
Yaw	90.00°

Hit OK and close out of the AnimSet Editor and go back to the Content Browser. Select the SK_Jazz mesh again and RIGHT-CLICK – Save. This might take a minute but it is important as we want to make sure the new Socket is accessible through the code.

Once saved, close the editor and go back to our EG_Pawn class. We need to add the function that will manage getting the Socket location and use that to set our camera. Add the follow function:

```
// Controls the pawn camera location and FOV ( Field of view )
// per frame
simulated function bool CalcCamera( float fDeltaTime,
   out vector out_CamLoc, out rotator out_CamRot, out float out_FOV )
{
   // Used to reference the CamLoc socket location and rotation
   local Vector camLoc;
   local Rotator camRot;

   // Using our JazzMesh reference to the SkeletalMeshComponent,
   // get the location and rotation of the CamLoc socket
   JazzMesh.GetSocketWorldLocationAndRotation( 'CamLoc', camLoc,
        camRot );

   // Want to make sure we have a location to set
   if ( camLoc != vect( 0,0,0 ) )
   {
      // Set our camera to the location of the socket.
      out_CamLoc = camLoc;
      out_CamRot = camRot;
   }

   // Don't need any conditions, return true always.
   return true;
}
```

This is not the most advanced camera setup (in fact it's about as easy as it gets), but it will be functional. Plus, for the purposes of a beginner book, this should be right in line with what you'll understand.

This function, CalcCamera( ), comes from the Actor class and allows us to use an existing game camera for our Pawn. For more advanced games, there is a Camera class that you can use that offers more ability to manipulate how it is used. However, this method of using a Socket will work just fine for us.

GetSocketWorldLocationAndRotation( ) is designed to do as it's named. It returns the Vector and Rotator value of a Socket. Since CalcCamera( ) is called every frame, this function and subsequent location or rotation is updated every frame, which is a great tool to have when placing the location or rotation of something like the camera. As a side note, the rotation value is OPTIONAL.

If you debug the game now, you should see this:

You can run around and your camera should follow the Yaw rotation of the Pawn mesh.

Add a class variable for the Pawns health:

```
// Used to keep track of the Pawns health
var private float fHealth;
```

Then, within the DefaultProperties:

```
// default value for Pawn health
fHealth = 100
```

Then, we need to create an accessor and modifier so we can both get and set the fHealth value. Add the following functions:

```
// Gets the value of fHealth
function float GetPawnHealth( )
{
   return fHealth;
}

// Sets the value of fHealth
function SetPawnHealth( float damage )
{
   // Make sure the Pawns health is above ZERO but less than 100
   if ( GetPawnHealth( ) >= 0 && GetPawnHealth( ) <= 100 )
   {
       fHealth += damage;
   }

   // Make sure health didnt go over 100
   if ( fHealth > 100 )
   {
```

```
      fHealth = 100;
   }
}
```

Both of these functions should look familiar to you from the Functions chapter. The GetPawnHealth( ) function returns a float type with the current value of fHealth; The SetPawnHealth( ) function is designed to check to make sure the Pawns health is above ZERO and less than ONE-HUNDRED then add the amount passed into it through the "float damage" parameter. If the value passed into the function is negative it will be subtracted from the fHealth value. Also, if the fHealth value ends up being more than ONE-HUNDRED set it back to ONE-HUNDRED.

We have not setup our GameInfo accessors and modifiers yet but lets go ahead and prepare early by setting up the proper call to one of them via the PostBeginPlay( ) function within this EG_Pawn class. Add the follow function and function call to the soon to be GameInfo modifier:

```
// Called just after this class is created
simulated function PostBeginPlay( )
{
   super.PostBeginPlay( );

   // Sets a reference to this class in our EG_GameInfo
   EG_GameInfo( WorldInfo.Game ).SetPlayerPawn( self );

   // Creates and attaches weapon to pawn
   CreateWeapon( );
}
```

As before with the PostBeginPlay( ) function, we can use the concept of this being called just after the class is created to assign variables. In this case, we are calling two yet unwritten functions. SetPlayerPawn( ) sets a reference to this class in the EG_GameInfo class. Also, we are calling CreateWeapon( ),which will be designed to both spawn and attach a weapon to the Pawn mesh.

Since we only want to spawn ONE weapon, we will have to first check that there are no other weapons spawned in the world. Create this function to check that:

```
// Check to see if there are any weapons in the world
function bool CheckWeapons( )
{
   local EG_Weapon W;

   // If there are any weapons in the world, return false.
   foreach WorldInfo.AllActors( class'EG_Weapon', W )
   {
```

```
            return false;
        }

        // If there is NO weapon the world
        return true;
    }
```

We are using a foreach iterator that if it finds any weapons in the world, it will return FALSE. If it does NOT find any, it return TRUE. This allows us to check before we spawn a weapon.

We also need to create a function that will both spawn and attach our Weapon class to the Pawn.

```
// Spawns and attaches a weapon to the Pawn
function CreateWeapon( )
{
    // So we can reference our weapon after spawn
    local EG_Weapon W;

    // If there are NO weapons in the world already
    if ( CheckWeapons ( ) )
    {
        // Spawns a new weapon
        W = Spawn( class'EG_Weapon', self );

        if ( W != none )
        {
            // A EG_Weapon function to set the proper attribute to
            // where it should spawn and attach
            W.InitWeapon( JazzMesh, self, 'Weapon_R', 'B_R_Weapon' );
        }
    }
}
```

Our CreateWeapon( ) function is designed to check to see if there are any weapons already in the world and if there are NOT to spawn one. There is also the InitWeapon( ) function we are called (that we have yet to write) that will be designed to spawn and move the weapon to the correct Socket location and then attach the weapon to a bone. We will get into the specifics of this during the next chapter.

In order for our yet unwritten InitWeapon( ) function to work we need to pass the SkeletalMeshComponent, our class (self), the name of the Socket to spawn the Weapon at, and finally the name of the bone to attach the Weapon to.

At this point, we have a visible player Pawn that we can control with the W, A, S, D and mouse input. Our camera is setup as a simple third-person shooter and we have the ability to modify and access the Pawns health value.

In the next chapter, we will be working on setting up the EG_Weapon class.

This is what the entire EG_Pawn class should look like:

```
class EG_Pawn extends Pawn;

// Used to reference our light environment component from
// the components array
var DynamicLightEnvironmentComponent MyLightEnvironment;

// Used to reference our SkeletalMeshComponent
var SkeletalMeshComponent JazzMesh;

// Used to keep track of the Pawns health
var private float fHealth;

// Called just after this class is created
simulated function PostBeginPlay( )
{
   super.PostBeginPlay( );

   // Sets a reference to this class in our EG_GameInfo
   EG_GameInfo( WorldInfo.Game ).SetPlayerPawn( self );

   // Creates and attaches weapon to pawn
   CreateWeapon( );
}

// Controls the pawn camera location and FOV ( Field of view )
// per frame
simulated function bool CalcCamera( float fDeltaTime, out vector
     out_CamLoc, out rotator out_CamRot, out float out_FOV )
{
   // Used to reference the CamLoc socket location and rotation
   local Vector camLoc;
   local Rotator camRot;

   // Using our JazzMesh reference to the SkeletalMeshComponent,
   // get the location and rotation of the CamLoc socket
   JazzMesh.GetSocketWorldLocationAndRotation( 'CamLoc', camLoc,
      camRot );

   // Want to make sure we have a location to set
   if ( camLoc != vect( 0,0,0 ) )
   {
```

```
      // Set our camera to the location of the socket.
      out_CamLoc = camLoc;
      out_CamRot = camRot;
   }

   // Don't need any conditions, return true always.
   return true;
}

// Gets the value of fHealth
function float GetPawnHealth( )
{
   return fHealth;
}

// Sets the value of fHealth
function SetPawnHealth( float damage )
{
   // Make sure the Pawns health is above ZERO but less than 100
   if ( GetPawnHealth( ) >= 0 && GetPawnHealth( ) <= 100 )
   {
      fHealth += damage;
   }

   // Make sure health didnt go over 100
   if ( fHealth > 100 )
   {
      fHealth = 100;
   }
}

// Check to see if there are any weapons in the world
function bool CheckWeapons( )
{
   local EG_Weapon W;

   // If there are any weapons in the world, return false.
   foreach WorldInfo.AllActors( class'EG_Weapon', W )
   {
      return false;
   }

   // If there is NO weapon the world
   return true;
}

// Spawns and attaches a weapon to the Pawn
function CreateWeapon( )
{
```

```
    // So we can reference our weapon after spawn
    local EG_Weapon W;

    // If there are NO weapons in the world already
    if ( CheckWeapons ( ) )
    {
        // Spawns a new weapon
        W = Spawn( class'EG_Weapon', self );

        if ( W != none )
        {
            // A EG_Weapon function to set the proper attribute to
            // where it should spawn and attach
            W.InitWeapon( JazzMesh, self, 'Weapon_R', 'B_R_Weapon' );
        }
    }
}


DefaultProperties
{
    // default value for Pawn health
    fHealth = 100.000f
    // pct. of running speed that walking speed is
    WalkingPct=+0.4
    // pct. of running speed that crouched walking speed is
    CrouchedPct=+0.4
    // Base eye height above collision center.
    BaseEyeHeight=38.0
    // urrent eye height, adjusted for bobbing and stairs.
    EyeHeight=38.0
    // Movement speed on the ground
    GroundSpeed=440.0
    // Movement speed in the air
    AirSpeed=440.0
    // Movement speed when in "water"
    WaterSpeed=220.0
    // max acceleration rate
    AccelRate=2048.0
    // Jump height
    JumpZ=322.0
    // Minimum z value for floor normal (if less, not a walkable floor
    // for this pawn)
    WalkableFloorZ=0.78

    Begin Object Class=DynamicLightEnvironmentComponent
            Name=LightEnvironment
        // Whether a SH light should be used to synthesize all light not
        //accounted for by the synthesized directional light.
        bSynthesizeSHLight=TRUE
```

```
      // Whether this light environment is being applied to a
      // character
      bIsCharacterLightEnvironment=TRUE
      // Whether to use cheap on/off shadowing from the environment or
      // allow a dynamic preshadow.
      bUseBooleanEnvironmentShadowing=FALSE
      // Whether the light environment is used or treated the same as
      // a LightEnvironment=NULL reference.
      bEnabled=TRUE
End Object
Components.Add(LightEnvironment)
MyLightEnvironment=LightEnvironment

Begin Object Class=SkeletalMeshComponent Name=JazzPlayerPawn
      // Skeletal Mesh location to use for this component
      SkeletalMesh=SkeletalMesh'KismetGame_Assets.Anims.SK_Jazz'
      // AnimTreeTemplate that ( should ) match(s) the SkeletalMesh
      AnimTreeTemplate=AnimTree'KismetGame_Assets.Anims.Jazz_AnimTree'
      // AnimSets array list
      AnimSets( 0 )=AnimSet'KismetGame_Assets.Anims.SK_Jazz_Anims'
      // Adjustment for pawn location
      Translation=( Z=-20 )
      // Size of skeletal mesh based on its original size
      Scale=1.00

      // Everything but the owner can see this actor.
      bOwnerNoSee=false
      // Whether to cast any shadows or not
      CastShadow=true
      // Should this block rigid body phyics
      BlockRigidBody=TRUE
      // If true, update skeleton/attachments even when our Owner has
      // not been rendered recently
      bUpdateSkelWhenNotRendered=false
      // If true, do not apply any SkelControls when owner has not
      // been rendered recently.
      bIgnoreControllersWhenNotRendered=TRUE
      // If we are running physics, should we update bFixed bones
      // based on the animation bone positions.
      bUpdateKinematicBonesFromAnimation=true
      // Controls whether the primitive should cast shadows in
      // the case of non precomputed shadowing
      bCastDynamicShadow=true
      // Enum indicating what type of object this should be
      // considered for rigid body collision.
      RBChannel=RBCC_Untitled3
      // Types of objects that this physics objects will collide with.
      RBCollideWithChannels=( Untitled3=true )
      // The lighting environment to take the primitive's
```

```
        // lighting from.
        LightEnvironment=LightEnvironment
        // if set, components that are attached to us have their
        // bOwnerNoSee and bOnlyOwnerSee properties overridden by ours
        bOverrideAttachmentOwnerVisibility=true
        // If TRUE, this primitive accepts dynamic decals spawned
        // during gameplay.
        bAcceptsDynamicDecals=FALSE
        // Indicates whether this SkeletalMeshComponent should
        // have a physics engine representation of its state.
        bHasPhysicsAssetInstance=true
        // The ticking group this component belongs to
        TickGroup=TG_PreAsyncWork
        // If non-zero, skeletal mesh component will not update
        // kinematic bones and bone springs when distance factor
        // is greater than this (or has not been rendered for a while).
        // This also turns off BlockRigidBody, so you do
        // not get collisions with 'left behind' ragdoll setups.
        MinDistFactorForKinematicUpdate=0.2
        //If true, DistanceFactor for this SkeletalMeshComponent will be
        // added to global chart.
        bChartDistanceFactor=true
        // Used for creating one-way physics interactions (via
        // constraints or contacts) Groups with lower RBDominanceGroup
        // push around higher values in a 'one way' fashion. Must be
        // less than 32.
        RBDominanceGroup=20
        // If TRUE, dynamically lit translucency on this primitive will
        // render in one pass,
        bUseOnePassLightingOnTranslucency=TRUE
        // If true, use per-bone motion blur on this skeletal mesh.
        bPerBoneMotionBlur=true
    End Object
    // Add to the components array
    Components.Add( JazzPlayerPawn )
    // Assigns our reference to the SkeletalMeshComponent
    JazzMesh = JazzPlayerPawn

    Begin Object Name=CollisionCylinder
        CollisionRadius=+0035.000000
        CollisionHeight=+0044.000000
    End Object
    CylinderComponent=CollisionCylinder
}
```

Additional Reading:

More on the Pawn class:
http://udn.epicgames.com/Three/CharactersTechnicalGuide.html#Pawn

More on creating a basic game:
http://udn.epicgames.com/Three/BasicGameQuickStart.html

More on cameras in UDK:
http://udn.epicgames.com/Three/CameraTechnicalGuide.html

Creating An Example Game Weapon Class

Chapter Eight

You'll notice that our Weapon class is extending Actor. Since our Pawn will only have access to ONE weapon, there is really no need to extend the "Weapon" class. The Weapon class is designed around a inventory class which handles things like weapon swapping and allowing the player to hold many weapons. Using the Actor class this way we will be able to create the functionality we need without worrying about any of the more complicated code that may hinder our overall goal.

The purpose of our weapon will be able to place it in the Pawns hand, spawn a projectile that fires from the muzzle socket forward, and rely on ammo. We will also use a Particle System to create a muzzle flash when we fire.

Let's start by creating our SkeletalMeshComponent, which will represent the weapons physical appearance in the world. Add the following to the DefaultProperties inside of the EG_Weapon.uc class:

```
DefaultProperties
{
   // Creates the physical appearance of this weapon
   begin object class=SkeletalMeshComponent name=JazzGun
      SkeletalMesh=SkeletalMesh'KismetGame_Assets.Anims.SK_JazzGun'
      LightEnvironment=LightEnv
   end object
```

```
   Components.Add( JazzGun )
   GunMesh = JazzGun
}
```

We also want to create the DynamicLightEnvironmentComponent, to make sure the weapon has correct lighting when in the world. Add this ABOVE the SkeletalMeshComponent:

```
// Creates a dynamic light environment component
begin object class=DynamicLightEnvironmentComponent name=LightEnv
   bEnabled = true
end object
Components.Add( LightEnv )
```

We need to create a class variable so we can reference the Skeletal Mesh component. Add the following variable to the class:

```
// Reference the gun mesh
var SkeletalMeshComponent GunMesh;
```

The purpose of the two Actor Components and the reference variable is so the Skeletal Mesh is lit and so we have a reference to the Skeletal Mesh being used, which is needed to attach it to the Weapon_R Socket on the Pawn.

I mentioned in the last chapter that we will have a InitWeapon( ) function that will allow us to attach the weapon to the correct location. Let's create that function now:

```
// Used to move, rotate, and attach weapon to the player pawn
function InitWeapon( SkeletalMeshComponent Comp, Pawn P,
      name socketName, name boneName )
{
   // Used to reference the location and rotation of 'Weapon_R' socket
   local Vector weaponLoc;
   local Rotator weaponRot;

   // Gets the location and rotation of socket
   Comp.GetSocketWorldLocationAndRotation( socketName,
      weaponLoc, weaponRot );

   // If the weaponLoc has a value
   if( weaponLoc != Vect( 0,0,0 ) )
   {
      // Moves the weapon to the location of the socket
      self.SetLocation( weaponLoc );

         // If the weaponRot has a value
         if ( weaponRot != Rot( 0,0,0 ) )
         {
```

```
                    // Rotates the weapon to the rotation of the socket
                    self.SetRotation( weaponRot );
                }

            // Attaches the weapon to the 'B_R_Weapon' bone in the
            // pawns hand
            self.SetBase( P,, Comp, boneName );
        }

        // Set a reference to this weapon within the Game Info
        EG_GameInfo( WorldInfo.Game ).SetWeapon( self );
}
```

We are using a lot of functions here that come from the UDK code. The first being GetSocketWorldLocationAndRotation( ). This function is available through the SkeletalMeshComponent class that will return the location and rotation of the socket name passed into the function. As warning, this function will always run, even if it doesn't find the correct socket. The result of not finding any socket with the name given will be that the return Vector and Rotator will be ZERO, ZERO, ZERO (0,0,0).

We then check that the weaponLoc variable has a value other than ZERO, ZERO, ZERO (0,0,0), meaning it was assigned something. Then, if it does have a value, we set the weapon to weaponLoc.

After that, we check to make sure weaponRot has a value, just like weaponLoc. If it does, we change the rotation of the weapon to match it.

Use the SetBase( ) function to "attach" the weapon to the bone in the hand of the Pawn.

These are Actor based functions that we use here. This is what they do:

- SetLocation( ) will set the desired location of an actor.
- SetRotation( ) will set the desired rotation of an actor.
- SetBase( ) will attach the actor to another actor, with the option of a bone name for that location.

As we don't need an inventory to manage something as simple as having ONE weapon, we are instead going to allow the Game Info class to reference the weapon through the SetWeaponClass( ) function. This allows us to reference the class and shoot the weapon through the Game Info from the Player Controller.

Note: This is not normally how the weapon is handled. It usually has a Inventory Manager class that allows you to manage many different weapons. That is overkill for this example. Create a float variable for ammo, a bool to know when to fire, a float for the weapons fire rate, and a float so we can keep track of seconds (relative to DeltaTime), which we use when firing the weapon.

Add these class variables:

```
// Used to keep track of game time, relative to FPS
var float fLocalTime;

// Used to keep track of Ammo for this weapon
var float iAmmo;

// Used to know when we can fire projectiles ( fire rate )
var float fFireRate;

// Used to know if we can fire the weapon
var bool bCanFire;
```

In the DefaultProperties, we need to give a default ammo count and fire rate. So we start with more than ZERO and have a default time for how fast to fire. Add this to the DefaultProperties:

```
// Default value for iAmmo
iAmmo = 100

// Default fire rate
fFireRate = 0.15
```

The first step to making our weapon fire is to setup the Tick( ) function to work properly so we are both able to keep track of time passing as well as connected conditional statements. Add the follow function to the class:

```
// Called every frame while this class exists
function Tick( float DeltaTime )
{
   // The value of fLocalTime is equal to itself PLUS delta
   // time ( keeps track in terms of seconds )
   // If DeltaTime equal to 1, ONE second has passed
   fLocalTime += DeltaTime;

   // If the weapon can fire
   if( bCanFire )
   {
      // If the local time is more than our fire rate
      if ( fLocalTime > fFireRate )
      {
          // Fires the weapon
          FireJazzWeapon( );
```

```
                // Reset the fLocalTime to "reset" the shot timer
                fLocalTime = 0;
            }
        }
}
```

Tick( ) is a function that is called every frame; just like DrawHUD( ) function in the HUD class and PlayerTick( ) function in the Player Controller class.

Inside of our Tick( ) function we are making sure that we can fire. If we can, we use our fLocalTime variable to take on the value of DeltaTime every frame. Once the value of fLocalTime is GREATER than our fFireRate time, we fire the projectile, spawn the muzzle flash, and calculate ammo changes.

Before we write the FireJazzWeapon( ) function we need a reference to a Particle System to spawn as the muzzle flash. Add this class variable:

```
// Used to reference the Muzzle flash particle system
var ParticleSystem muzzleFlash;
```

Then, in the DefaultProperties add:

```
// Used to access the Particle System for our muzzle flash
muzzleFlash=
    ParticleSystem'KismetGame_Assets.Projectile.P_BlasterMuzzle_02'
```

Let's create a function to fire the weapon:

```
// Fire a projectile from our weapon
private function FireJazzWeapon( )
{
    // Reference the location of our muzzle socket
    local Vector muzzleLoc;

    // Reference to the proj spawned
    local Projectile proj;

    // Get the location of the socket on the GunMesh ( Muzzle )
    GunMesh.GetSocketWorldLocationAndRotation( 'Muzzle', muzzleLoc );

    // As long as we have a location to fire from
    if( muzzleLoc != Vect( 0,0,0 ) && iAmmo > 0 )
    {
        // spawn our projectile at the muzzleLoc
        proj = Spawn( class'EG_Projectile', self,, muzzleLoc,
            EG_GameInfo( WorldInfo.Game ).GetPlayerPawn( ).Rotation );
```

```
    if ( proj != none )
    {
            // Give the projecitle a direction
            proj.Init( Vector( EG_GameInfo( WorldInfo.Game ).
                GetPlayerPawn( ).Rotation ) );

            // subtract ONE from the ammo count
            SetAmmoCount( -1 );

            // Spawns the muzzle flash emitter
            SpawnMuzzleFlash( );
    }
    else
    {
            `log( "Projectile not spawning!" );
    }
}
else
{
    OutOfAmmo( );
}
}
```

The reason this function is private is that we do not want any other classes accessing it, as we should only be executing it from the Tick( ) function. The function itself shouldn't look too complicated to you. We are doing something similar as when we set the weapon location and rotation. This time though, we are not getting the 'Muzzle' rotation; some functions don't always require a argument and will be labled with the specifier "optional", such as "option vector outLoc".

As long as muzzleLoc as a value other than default, we spawn a projectile at its location. Then, using another predefined function called: Init( ), from the Projectile class, we set the direction of the projectile. Which will be down the X axis.

We also want to warn the player when they are out of ammo, with a message on the screen. In order to do this, add the following function:

```
// displays text via the HUD that there is no more ammo
function OutOfAmmo( )
{
    if( EG_HUD( EG_GameInfo(WorldInfo.Game ).
        GetPlayerController( ).myHUD ) != none )
    {
        EG_HUD( EG_GameInfo(WorldInfo.Game ).
            GetPlayerController( ).myHUD ).bOutOfAmmo = true;
    }
```

}

This is checking to make sure a HUD class exists. Then we cast the existing HUD class into our EG_HUD class to get a reference to it and then we turn the yet unwritten variable "bOutOfAmmo" to TRUE.

The cast here can be confusing. What is going on is that because we need to access the variable through the EG_HUD class, we need to reference it first. In the if statement, we check to make sure EG_HUD exists by asking if "myHUD" from Player Controller is of the class type "EG_HUD". Once we know that is TRUE, we can do the same cast and then access the "bOutOfAmmo" bool value, which will be in charge of showing the "out of ammo" message when we get to the HUD class.

We call a function we haven't written yet, which will be designed to subtract ONE from the iAmmo count.

Before we write the SetAmmoCount( ) function, write a GetAmmoCount( ) function first. As such:

```
// Returns the value of iAmmo
function float GetAmmoCount( )
{
   return iAmmo;
}
```

Add the SetAmmoCount( ) function now:

```
// Used to subtract a value from iAmmo
function SetAmmoCount( float amount )
{
   // if we have ammo
   if ( GetAmmoCount( ) <= 100 && GetAmmoCount( ) >= 0 )
   {
      iAmmo += amount;

      // Make sure iAmmo cant be more than 100
      if( iAmmo > 100 )
      {
         iAmmo = 100;
      }
   }
}
```

This function allows us to change the amount of ammo the weapon currently holds. If the "amount" passed into the function is a positive number, it INCREASE the amount of ammo the weapon holds. If the amount passed into the function is a negative (such as when we fire our weapon) the amount will decrease. The condition is to check to make sure we don't go over the amount of ONE-HUNDRED, or below ZERO.

We also check to see if iAmmo went over ONE-HUNDRED. This is because the first conditional has the chance of adding more than ONE-HUNDRED to iAmmo, as the condition will be TRUE if you already have ONE-HUNDRED ammo.

Let's write the SpawnMuzzleFlash( ) function.

```
// Spawn the muzzle flash particle system
private function SpawnMuzzleFlash( )
{
   // Spawns an emitter and attaches it to the 'Muzzle' socket
   WorldInfo.MyEmitterPool.SpawnEmitterMeshAttachment
      ( muzzleFlash, GunMesh, 'Muzzle', true );
}
```

This function is relying on the SpawnEmitterMeshComponent( ) function that is internally stored within the World Infos "MyEmitterPool". This allows us to spawn an emitter (Particle System) without worrying about creating any function that would do the same thing.

This is another example of allowing the code within UDK to aid us. It also allows us to write less code but get the same results.

The last thing we need to do is add an accessor and modifer for the fFireRate so we can later increase or decrease the time it takes to shoot the weapon.

```
// Returns the value of fFireRate
function float GetFireRate( )
{
   return fFireRate;
}

// Sets the fFireRate
function SetFireRate( float rate )
{
   // If the value passed into this function is greater than 0.05
   if ( rate > 0.05 )
   {
      fFireRate = rate;
   }
   else
   {
      // Lowest possible fire rate
      fFireRate = 0.05;
```

```
        }
}
```

These TWO functions are just like the other "set" and "get" functions we've been writing. One important aspect of the SetFireRate( ) function is the condition that if the value passed into it is lower than ZERO point ZERO FIVE (0.05) then the value will be set to ZERO point ZERO FIVE (0.05); which is a "hidden" ground to which the value can be set. This prevents the gun from firing any faster than this. This also helps performance, as if the fFireRate was say set to ZERO then we would get some warnings about spawning too many particle systems in the scene. It would also just be silly, damage wise.

The entire EG_Weapon class should look like:

```
class EG_Weapon extends Actor;

// Reference the gun mesh
var SkeletalMeshComponent GunMesh;

// Reference to the light environment component
var DynamicLightEnvironmentComponent MyLightEnvironment;

// Used to keep track of game time, relative to FPS
var float fLocalTime;

// Used to keep track of Ammo for this weapon
var float iAmmo;

// Used to know when we can fire projectiles ( fire rate )
var float fFireRate;

// Used to know if we can fire the weapon
var bool bCanFire;

// Used to reference the Muzzle flash particle system
var ParticleSystem muzzleFlash;

// Used to move, rotate, and attach weapon to the player pawn
function InitWeapon( SkeletalMeshComponent Comp, Pawn P, name
      socketName, name boneName )
{
   // Used to reference the location and rotation of 'Weapon_R' socket
   local Vector weaponLoc;
   local Rotator weaponRot;

   // Gets the location and rotation of socket
   Comp.GetSocketWorldLocationAndRotation( socketName,
       weaponLoc, weaponRot );
```

```
    // If the weaponLoc has a value
    if( weaponLoc != Vect( 0,0,0 ) )
    {
        // Moves the weapon to the location of the socket
        self.SetLocation( weaponLoc );

            // If the weaponRot has a value
            if ( weaponRot != Rot( 0,0,0 ) )
            {
                // Rotates the weapon to the rotation of the socket
                self.SetRotation( weaponRot );
            }

        // Attaches the weapon to the 'B_R_Weapon' bone in the
        // pawns hand
        self.SetBase( P,, Comp, boneName );
    }

    // Set a reference to this weapon within the Game Info
    EG_GameInfo( WorldInfo.Game ).SetWeaponClass( self );
}

// Called every frame while this class exists
function Tick( float DeltaTime )
{
    // The value of fLocalTime is equal to itself PLUS delta time
( keeps track in terms of seconds )
    // If DeltaTime equal to 1, ONE second has passed
    fLocalTime += DeltaTime;

    // If the weapon can fire
    if( bCanFire )
    {
        // If the local time is more than our fire rate
        if ( fLocalTime > fFireRate )
        {
            // Fires the weapon
            FireJazzWeapon( );

            // Reset the fLocalTime to "reset" the shot timer
            fLocalTime = 0;
        }
    }
}

// Fire a projectile from our weapon
private function FireJazzWeapon( )
{
```

```
    // Reference the location of our muzzle socket
    local Vector muzzleLoc;

    // Reference to the proj spawned
    local Projectile proj;

    // Get the location of the socket on the GunMesh ( Muzzle )
    GunMesh.GetSocketWorldLocationAndRotation( 'Muzzle', muzzleLoc );

    // As long as we have a location to fire from
    if( muzzleLoc != Vect( 0,0,0 ) && iAmmo > 0 )
    {
        // spawn our projectile at the muzzleLoc
        proj = Spawn( class'EG_Projectile', self,, muzzleLoc,
            EG_GameInfo( WorldInfo.Game ).GetPlayerPawn( ).Rotation );

        if ( proj != none )
        {
            // Give the projecitle a direction
            proj.Init( Vector( EG_GameInfo( WorldInfo.Game ).
                GetPlayerPawn( ).Rotation ) );

            // subtract ONE from the ammo count
            SetAmmoCount( -1 );

            // Spawns the muzzle flash emitter
            SpawnMuzzleFlash( );
        }
        else
        {
            `log( "Projectile not spawning!" );
        }
    }
    else
    {
        OutOfAmmo( );
    }
}

// displays text via the HUD that there is no more ammo
function OutOfAmmo( )
{
    if( EG_GameInfo( WorldInfo.Game ).
        GetPlayerController( ).myHUD != none )
    {
        EG_HUD( EG_GameInfo( WorldInfo.Game ).
            GetPlayerController( ).myHUD ).bOutOfAmmo = true;
    }
}
```

```
// Returns the value of iAmmo
function float GetAmmoCount( )
{
   return iAmmo;
}

// Used to subtract a value from iAmmo
function SetAmmoCount( float amount )
{
   // if we have ammo
   if ( GetAmmoCount( ) <= 100 && GetAmmoCount( ) >= 0 )
   {
      iAmmo += amount;

      // Make sure iAmmo cant be more than 100
      if( iAmmo > 100 )
      {
            iAmmo = 100;
      }
   }
}

// Returns the value of fFireRate
function float GetFireRate( )
{
   return fFireRate;
}

// Sets the fFireRate
function SetFireRate( float rate )
{
   // If the value passed into this function is greater than 0.05
   if ( rate > 0.05 )
   {
      fFireRate = rate;
   }
   else
   {
      // Lowest possible fire rate
      fFireRate = 0.05;
   }
}

// Spawn the muzzle flash particle system
private function SpawnMuzzleFlash( )
{
   // Spawns an emitter and attaches it to the 'Muzzle' socket
   WorldInfo.MyEmitterPool.SpawnEmitterMeshAttachment
```

```
        ( muzzleFlash, GunMesh, 'Muzzle', true );
}

DefaultProperties
{
    // Used to access the Particle System for our muzzle flash
    muzzleFlash =
        ParticleSystem'KismetGame_Assets.Projectile.P_BlasterMuzzle_02'

    // Default value for iAmmo
    iAmmo = 100

    // Default fire rate
    fFireRate = 0.15

    // Creates a dynamic light environment component
    begin object class=DynamicLightEnvironmentComponent name=LightEnv
        bEnabled = true
    end object
    Components.Add( LightEnv )
    MyLightEnvironment = LightEnv

    // Creates the physical appearence of this weapon
    begin object class=SkeletalMeshComponent name=JazzGun
        SkeletalMesh=SkeletalMesh'KismetGame_Assets.Anims.SK_JazzGun'
        LightEnvironment=LightEnv
    end object
    Components.Add( JazzGun )
    GunMesh = JazzGun
}
```

Our weapon class quite simple though it touches on some key aspects of how to create a custom weapon. We are using DeltaTime to keep track of game seconds, which allow us to fire a projectile from the MuzzleFlash Socket in front of the player Pawn. We are using a Particle System to resemble the muzzle flash which will be spawned every time a projectile is fired. We also setup the iAmmo as well as its accessor and modifier function so we can add or subtract ammo depending on specific events (such as firing the weapon or picking up an ammo drop). There is a fFireRate variable with its accessor and modifier that will allow us to modify how fast the weapon can shoot.

Overall this class should give you some insight on how a basic weapon works as well as give you some ideas on how a more complicated weapon could work.

Next chapter will be on the Projectile, so we can fire our weapon and setup the functionality to do damage to whatever enemy the Projectile hits.

Creating An Example Game Projectile Class

Chapter Nine

The purpose of the projectile class is to have a physical representation of an object flying through the world. In our case, the projectile will spawn from the tip of the gun mesh our Pawn is using and fly forward, in relation to the rotation of the Pawn. When our projectile hits something it will be destroyed and then spawn another Particle System to show that it has hit something. We will also delegate what the projectile should do if it hits an enemy AI Pawn, a wall, or a Static Mesh.

Add a few class variables. One for the projectile acceleration, one for the Particle System that represents the Projectile, a Particle System for when the Projectile hits something, a reference to the Particle System Component after it has be spawned, and the amount of damage the Projectile will do if it hits an enemy.

```
// Used for the projectiles acceleration
var float AccelerationRate;

// The visual appearance of the projectile in flight
var ParticleSystem ProjectileFireParticleSystem;

// The visual appearance of the projectile after hitting something
```

```
var ParticleSystem ProjectileHitParticleSystem;

// Used to reference the component that is attached to this
// class ( the particle system )
var ParticleSystemComponent ProjectileEffects;

// Used to reference Sound Cues, to play when firing and
// when projectile hits
var SoundCue ProjectileFireSound;
var SoundCue ProjectileHitSound;

// Used to damage enemies
var float damageAmount;
```

AccelerationRate will be the set for how quickly the projectile is set to speed. This will be done later on in the Init( ) function along with setting velocity and rotation.

The two ParticleSystem variables are for display purposes. It is completely possible to have a projectile fly through the world without showing anything but that kind of defeats the purpose of having a "slow" (in comparison to instant hit) move projectiles. In order to display these projectiles, we first need to have a reference to the art within our content browser.

We also need to reference the Particle System after it has been spawned in order to attach it to the class (so it moves along with the projectile class itself). I know this sounds a bit weird but remember that the Projectile class itself is NOT a visual thing. It is data doing what we tell it to. Part of that is telling it what to look like, which takes a separate class; the Particle System.

There is also TWO references to SoundCues which will be used when the Projectile is fired and when the Projectile hits something.

Add a PostBeginPlay( ) function to spawn our visual Particle System just after this Projectile class is created:

```
// Called before this class is created
simulated function PostBeginPlay( )
{
   super.PostBeginPlay( );

   // Spawn the projectile particle system
   SpawnProjectileFireParticleSystem( );
}
```

We are using the PostBeginPlay( ) function to execute our yet unwritten SpawnProjectileFireParticleSystem( ) function because we don't want much delay between when the class is created to when the projectile has an appearance. This function makes it easy for us to do that. Another possibility would be to put this into our Init( ) function (as that is called just after our Projectile class is spawned within our EG_Weapon class) but that might be more confusing for another programmer to read down the line.

Let's write the SpawnProjectileFireParticleSystem( ) function now:

```
// Spawns and attaches the particle system to this class
private function SpawnProjectileFireParticleSystem( )
{
  // Spawn the particle system, using the fire particle system
  ProjectileEffects = WorldInfo.MyEmitterPool.
    SpawnEmitterCustomLifetime( ProjectileFireParticleSystem );

  // Set it to be able to update every tick
  ProjectileEffects.bUpdateComponentInTick = true;

  // Remove any absolute values for ( Translation, Rotation, Scale )
  ProjectileEffects.SetAbsolute( false, false, false );

  // Attach the particle system to the class so itll move as the
  // class does
  self.AttachComponent( ProjectileEffects );

  // Play the ProjecileFireSound
  self.PlaySound( ProjectileFireSound,,,false );
}
```

This function is private because we don't want any other class to be able to access it as that may result in some functionality that is not desired (such as having TWO Particle Systems spawned for ONE Projectile). We are also using our ProjectileEffects variable here to reference the Particle System being spawned through our WorldInfo.MyEmitterPool class. The SpawnEmitterCustomLifeTime( ) offers us the ability to spawn a Particle System without the worry of where it is spawned. We then make sure that the Particle System does not have a absolute value with SetAbsolute( ) for either translation, rotation, or scale (which will allow the Particle System to move through the world as its absolute location is not locked anywhere) and then we attach the Particle System to the class. The attachment is the important aspect of having a visual Projectile. In order for the Particle System to move along with the class, it must be attached to the Projectile class, which is exactly what the AttachComponent( ) function was designed for; telling the Projectile class to attach the Particle System to the Projectile class.

We used the Init( ) function when we created our Weapon class. Let's write that now:

```
// used to set the rotation, velocity, and acceleration of
// the projectile
```

```
function Init( Vector Direction )
{
    // Set the projectile rotation the same as the rotation used
    // for the direction
    self.SetRotation( rotator( Direction ) );

    // Set the velocity
    self.Velocity = Speed * Direction;

    // Set the acceleration
    self.Acceleration = AccelerationRate * Normal( Velocity );
}
```

We are actually overwriting this function from the native code (though I am not sure that the native code actually does anything, as that is not accessible given the restrictions of UDK. This could just be a declaration of a function on the native side). Since this class is already created when this function is called we are able to use a reference to itself to set the rotation, velocity, and acceleration. We set the rotation with SetRotation( ) to the direction passed into the Init( ) function, from the weapon class; which is the Pawns rotation. Then, we set the velocity to the value of speed (2500) TIMES (*) the value of the direction (Pawns rotation). This tells the projectile to move the way we are aiming, more or less. We then tell the Projectile to accelerate at the speed of the AcclerationRate (3000) TIMES (*) the "normal" value of velocity.

The Normal( ) function is designed to return a UNIT vector with the same orientation as the vector passed into it.

For a visual understanding, this is what Normal( ) does:

Normal Velocity: -0.49,0.87,0.00
Just Velocity: -1466.67,2617.04,0.00

We also need to set the Default Properties to accommodate our class variables and some variables from our parent class, "Projectile". Add the following:

```
DefaultProperties
{
    // Ignore "simple" collision on Static Mesh, react per poly
    bCollideComplex=true

    // If collide actor has non zero extent set to 0, switch to zero
    // extent
    bSwitchToZeroCollision=true

    // Default damage this projectile will do to the enemy
    damageAmount = 10
```

```
    // Will not explode on the actor who owns this projectile
    // ( the weapon )
    bBlockedByInstigator = false

    // Speed of the projectile
    Speed = 3000

    // Absolute max speed of the projectile
    MaxSpeed = 3500

    // How fast this project accelerats
    AccelerationRate = 3000;

    // Particle system for flight
    ProjectileFireParticleSystem =
    ParticleSystem'KismetGame_Assets.Projectile.P_BlasterProjectile_02'

    // Particle system for when the projectile hits something
    ProjectileHitParticleSystem =
        ParticleSystem'KismetGame_Assets.Projectile.P_BlasterHit_01'

    // Sound Cue for fire
    ProjectileFireSound =
        SoundCue'KismetGame_Assets.Sounds.S_Blast_05_Cue'

    // Sound Cue for hit
    ProjectileHitSound =
        SoundCue'KismetGame_Assets.Sounds.S_BulletImpact_01_Cue'
}
```

bCollideComplex gives the ability to ignore the simple brush collision set on Static Mesh Actors and instead, collide per polygon. This gives a more realistic feel to the projectile as it will react to the mesh itself, instead of the collision brush around it. This is especially helpful when some Static Mesh art doesn't have a collision setup for colliding with projectiles.

bSwitchToZeroCollison has to do with the colliding Actors collision settings. It is here to help with the "realism" of the Projectile.

damageAmount is the default amount of damage this projectile will do to the enemy it collides with.

bBlockedByInstigator is designed to tell the class if it should collide with the class who owns it, which would be the weapon. As a precaution, we set this to FALSE, as we don't want the projectile to collide and explode on the weapon.

Speed is just that, the speed at which the Projectile will move.

MaxSpeed is the absolute max speed in which the Projectile class can travel, as sometimes a force may increase the Projectile faster than the original speed in which it is moving. This allows us to keep it from moving too fast.

AccelerationRate is how quickly the projectile will reach it's speed.

Then, we have the TWO Particle Systems that reference the art assets within our game packages.

Our last setup of this class will be for when the projectile touches a Actor and when the Projectile hits a solid "wall". The wall is usually things like BSP and other "solid" collision. When the Projectile "touches" something, it is usually referring to passing into a Trigger Volume or a Collision Cylinder around a Pawn.

To finish, we reference TWO SoundCue files for when the Projectile hits something, as well as when the Projectile is spawned.

To start, let's write the Touch( ) function. Add the following:

```
// When the Projectile touches a non solid collision type
simulated function Touch( Actor Other, PrimitiveComponent OtherComp,
      Vector HitLocation, Vector HitNormal )
{
  // If the Actor the Projectile touches is the EG_AIPawn
  if ( EG_AIPawn ( Other ) != none )
  {
    // Call the AIPawnTakeDamage( ) function, to damage the
    // EG_AIPawn
    EG_AIPawn ( Other ).AIPawnTakeDamage ( damageAmount );

    // Spawn the hit Particle System and destroy the Projectile
    EndOfProjectile ( HitLocation );
  }
}
```

Since our AI enemy Pawns will come from ONE class we are able to check them through the ONE conditional statement. This is done in a way we haven't discussed yet. Since the Actor the Projectile touches is returned through the name "Other", we can use a cast of EG_AIPawn(Other) to see if it is our EG_AIPawn that the Projectile is touching. If it is, then we want to damage that enemy Pawn with a function we haven't written yet: AIPawnTakeDamage( ) which we will get to in the EG_AIPawn chapter. There is also a function call, which has yet to be written, called EndOfProjectile( ). This will be designed to both spawn the ProjectileHitParticleSystem at the location where the Projectile hit and destroy the Projectile, as we don't want it around once it hits something.

Add the HitWall( ) function for when the Projectile hits something solid:

```
// When the Projectile hits a solid object
simulated function HitWall( Vector HitNormal, Actor Wall,
      PrimitiveComponent WallComp )
{
      // Spawn the hit Particle System and destroy the Projectile
      EndOfProjectile( self.Location );
}
```

This is like the Touch( ) function but designed for when the Projectile hits something solid;
things like BSP or "BlockAll" collision. When the Projectile hits one of these call the
EndOfProjectile( ) function to spawn the hit Particle System as well as destroy the
Projectile.

Let's continue by adding the EndOfProjectile( ) function:

```
// Spawns the hit Particle System as well as destroy the Projectile
function EndOfProjectile( Vector hitLoc )
{
      // If the hitLocation passed has a value
      if( hitLoc != Vect( 0,0,0 ) )
      {
            // spawn the Particle System at that location
            WorldInfo.MyEmitterPool.SpawnEmitter
                  ( ProjectileHitParticleSystem, hitLoc );
      }
      else
      {
            // If hitLoc is 0,0,0, spawn the Particle System at the
            // current location of the Projectile
            WorldInfo.MyEmitterPool.SpawnEmitter
                  ( ProjectileHitParticleSystem, self.Location );
      }

      // Play Hit sound
      self.PlaySound( ProjectileHitSound,,,false );

      // Destroy the Projectile
      self.Destroy( );
}
```

This function is passed a Vector location that can be used to spawn the hit Particle System.
If that location is NOT ZERO, ZERO,ZERO (0,0,0), we use PlaySound( ) to play the
ProjectileHitSound and make sure it is NOT destroyed with it's owner. Then, we are going

to use the Destroy( ) function to delete the Projectile class from the World Info. If the variable passed into the function (hitloc) is ZERO, ZERO, ZERO (0,0,0) then spawn the Particle System at the current location of the projectile.

That is the Projectile class. Not quite as challenging as the other classes so far but still a good amount of information to take in.

This is what the entire EG_Projectile class should look like:

```
class EG_Projectile extends UDKProjectile;

// Used for the projectiles acceleration
var float AccelerationRate;

// The visual appearance of the projectile in flight
var ParticleSystem ProjectileFireParticleSystem;

// The visual appearance of the projectile after hitting something
var ParticleSystem ProjectileHitParticleSystem;

// Used to reference the component that is attached to this
// class ( the particle system )
var ParticleSystemComponent ProjectileEffects;

// Used to reference Sound Cues, to play when firing and
// when projectile hits
var SoundCue ProjectileFireSound;
var SoundCue ProjectileHitSound;

// Used to damage enemies
var float damageAmount;

// Called just after this class is created
simulated function PostBeginPlay( )
{
   super.PostBeginPlay( );

   // Spawn the projectile particle system
   SpawnProjectileFireParticleSystem( );
}

// used to set the rotation, velocity, and acceleration of
// the projectile
function Init( Vector Direction )
{
   // Set the projectile rotation the same as the rotation used for the
   // direction
   self.SetRotation( rotator( Direction ) );
```

```
   // Set the velocity
   self.Velocity = Speed * Direction;

   // Set the acceleration
   self.Acceleration = AccelerationRate * Normal( Velocity );
}

// Spawns and attaches the particle system to this class
private function SpawnProjectileFireParticleSystem( )
{
   // Spawn the particle system, using the fire particle system
   ProjectileEffects = WorldInfo.MyEmitterPool.
      SpawnEmitterCustomLifetime( ProjectileFireParticleSystem );

   // Set it to be able to update every tick
   ProjectileEffects.bUpdateComponentInTick = true;

   // Remove any absolute values for ( Translation, Rotation, Scale )
   ProjectileEffects.SetAbsolute( false, false, false );

   // Attach the particle system to the class so itll move as the
   // class does
   self.AttachComponent( ProjectileEffects );

   // Play the ProjecileFireSound
   self.PlaySound( ProjectileFireSound,,,false );

}


// When the Projectile touches a non solid collision type
simulated function Touch( Actor Other, PrimitiveComponent OtherComp,
      Vector HitLocation, Vector HitNormal )
{
   // If the Actor the Projectile touches is the EG_AIPawn
   if ( EG_AIPawn( Other ) != none )
   {
      // Call the AIPawnTakeDamage( ) function, to damage the
      // EG_AIPawn
      EG_AIPawn( Other ).AIPawnTakeDamage( damageAmount );

      // Spawn the hit Particle System and destroy the Projectile
      EndOfProjectile( HitLocation );
   }
}

// When the Projectile hits a solid object
simulated function HitWall( Vector HitNormal, Actor Wall,
      PrimitiveComponent WallComp )
```

```
{
   // Spawn the hit Particle System and destroy the Projectile
   EndOfProjectile( Vect( 0,0,0 ) );
}

// Spawns the hit Particle System as well as destroy the Projectile
function EndOfProjectile( Vector hitLoc )
{
      // If the hitLocation passed has a value
      if( hitLoc != Vect( 0,0,0 ) )
      {
            // spawn the Particle System at that location
            WorldInfo.MyEmitterPool.SpawnEmitter
                  ( ProjectileHitParticleSystem, hitLoc );
      }
      else
      {
            // If hitLoc is 0,0,0, spawn the Particle System at the
            // current location of the Projectile
            WorldInfo.MyEmitterPool.SpawnEmitter
                  ( ProjectileHitParticleSystem, self.Location );
      }

      // Play Hit sound
      self.PlaySound( ProjectileHitSound,,,false );

      // Destroy the Projectile
      self.Destroy( );
}

DefaultProperties
{

   // Ignore "simple" collision on Static Mesh, react per poly
   bCollideComplex=true

   // If collide actor has non zero extent set to 0, switch to zero
   // extent
   bSwitchToZeroCollision=true

   // Default damage this projectile will do to the enemy
   damageAmount = 10

   // Will not explode on the actor who owns this projectile ( the
   // weapon )
   bBlockedByInstigator = false

   // Speed of the projectile
   Speed = 3000
```

```
// Absolute max speed of the projectile
MaxSpeed = 3500

// How fast this project accelerats
AccelerationRate = 3000;

// Particle system for flight
ProjectileFireParticleSystem =
ParticleSystem'KismetGame_Assets.Projectile.P_BlasterProjectile_02'

// Particle system for when the projectile hits something
ProjectileHitParticleSystem =
    ParticleSystem'KismetGame_Assets.Projectile.P_BlasterHit_01'

// Sound Cue for fire
ProjectileFireSound =
    SoundCue'KismetGame_Assets.Sounds.S_Blast_05_Cue'

// Sound Cue for hit
ProjectileHitSound =
    SoundCue'KismetGame_Assets.Sounds.S_BulletImpact_01_Cue'
}
```

Creating An Example Game Player Controller Class

Chapter Ten

The game is setup now to have a visual Pawn, a Weapon, and to shoot a Projectile. The only purpose of the Player Controller is going to setup the input so we are able to fire our Pawns Weapon, which should be relatively quick and easy for you to understand.

Start with adding a PostBeginPlay( ):

```
// Called just after this class is created
simulated function PostBeginPlay( )
{
   super.PostBeginPlay( );

   // Give a reference to this class within the EG_GameInfo
   EG_GameInfo( WorldInfo.Game ).SetPlayerController( self );
}
```

The only thing we are doing here is getting a reference to the EG_GameInfo through the steps talked about in the "classes" chapter. Accessing the SetPlayerController( ) function and then assigning this Player Controller class to that.

As a reminder, we have NOT worked on the Game Info yet. Don't worry if you are getting compiling errors. We will fix them in the Game Info class chapter.

We now want to create a function that we can use in order to communicate with our Weapon class, to tell it when to fire. Add this function:

```
// Used to fire the weapon
private function FireWeapon( bool fire )
{
   // If the bool passed into this function is true
   if ( fire )
   {
      // Turn the bool within the weapon class that fires the
      // weapon, true
      EG_GameInfo( WorldInfo.Game ).GetWeaponClass( )
            .bCanFire = true;
   }
   else
   {
      // If the bool passed is false, turn the bool within the
      // weapon class false
      EG_GameInfo( WorldInfo.Game ).GetWeaponClass( )
            .bCanFire = false;
   }
}
```

This function is designed to take in whatever bool is passed into it and then depending on if it is TRUE or FALSE either turn the bCanFire bool within the Weapon class TRUE or FALSE. If you remember, the bCanFire is checked every frame in the Weapon class so as soon as this changes the next frame will start to fire the weapon, or not, depending on the conditional here.

We want to use the PlayerTick( ) function, which is just like the Tick( ) function but designed for the Player Controller class, to know when the player is inputting a specific key. Add the following:

```
// This is the form of Tick( ) for the player controller,
// called every frame
function PlayerTick( float DeltaTime )
{
   // Keep previous Player Controller PlayerTick( )
   super.PlayerTick( DeltaTime );

   // If the player presses the "LeftMouseButton"
   if ( PlayerInput.PressedKeys.Find( 'LeftMouseButton' ) >= 0 )
   {
      FireWeapon( true );
   }
   // If they are NOT pressing the "LeftMouseButton"
   else
```

```
    {
        FireWeapon( false );
    }
}
```

The most important thing to remember here is the super.PlayerTick( ) call. If you do not have this here, the Pawn class will not respond to any input and will stay still during any game play.

The conditional statement is designed to look into the Player Input (which is a part of the Player Controller) to check the "Pressed Keys" array. It is checking to see f the "LeftMouseButton" is currently being pressed. If it is, then we call the previous FireWeapon( ) function, turning the bool within the Weapon class to TRUE and firing the weapon. If the "LeftMouseButton" is NOT pressed, then the bool within the Weapon class is set to FALSE not firing the weapon.

That is the entire Player Controller class for our example game. The "default" or "base" UDK settings for the Player Controller is set up in a way where the standard input keys are already defined and functional. The only thing we had to do for our game is what is here; allow the player to fire the weapon.

In the next chapter we will look at the Game Info class, so we can create all of our accessors and modifiers, and begin to start playing the game.

The entire class should look like:

```
class EG_PlayerController extends PlayerController;

// Called just after this class is created
simulated function PostBeginPlay( )
{
    super.PostBeginPlay( );

    // Give a reference to this class within the EG_GameInfo
    EG_GameInfo( WorldInfo.Game ).SetPlayerController( self );
}

// Used to fire the weapon
private function FireWeapon( bool fire )
{
    // If the bool passed into this function is true
    if ( fire )
    {
        // Turn the bool within the weapon class that fires the
        // weapon, true
        EG_GameInfo( WorldInfo.Game ).GetWeaponClass( ).bCanFire = true;
```

```
   }
   else
   {
       // If the bool passed is false, turn the bool within the weapon
class false
       EG_GameInfo( WorldInfo.Game ).GetWeaponClass( ).bCanFire =
false;
   }
}

// This is the form of Tick( ) for the player controller,
// called every frame
function PlayerTick( float DeltaTime )
{
   // Keep previous Player Controller PlayerTick( )
   super.PlayerTick( DeltaTime );

   // If the player presses the "LeftMouseButton"
   if ( PlayerInput.PressedKeys.Find( 'LeftMouseButton' ) == 0 )
   {
       FireWeapon( true );
   }
   // If they are NOT pressing the "LeftMouseButton"
   else
   {
       FireWeapon( false );
   }
}
```

Additional Reading:

More in input:
http://udn.epicgames.com/Three/InputOutputHome.html

More on exec functions:
http://udn.epicgames.com/Three/ExecFunctions.html

More on the Player Controller.
http://udn.epicgames.com/Three/CharactersTechnicalGuide.html#Player Controller

Creating An Example Game
Game Info Class

Chapter Eleven

The Game Info class is designed to keep track of everything related to a specific game type. Our game will be quite simple. The player Pawn will be able to run around and shoot at enemy AI. That enemy AI will drop an item for ammo or health to increase the chances of survival for the player.

Given this, the Game Info is also often in charge of keeping tabs on what is going on in the game world it is a part of ; like Pawn(s) and the Player Controller classes. Go ahead and introduce all of those accessors and modifiers we have been using but haven't written.

Start by adding the class variables:

```
// Reference to the EGPawn
var EG_Pawn EGPawn;

// Reference to the EGWeapon
var EG_Weapon EGWeapon;

// Reference to the EGPlayerController
var EG_PlayerController EGPlayerController;
```

These will hold a reference for the EG_Pawn, EG_Weapon, and EG_PlayerController classes.

Add the following functions:

```
// Sets a reference to the EG_PlayerController
function SetPlayerController( EG_PlayerController PC )
{
   // If we do not have a current reference
   if ( EGPlayerController == none )
   {
      EGPlayerController = PC;
   }
   // If we have a current reference, re-assign it with the new one
   else
   {
      EGPlayerController = none;

      EGPlayerController = PC;
   }
}

// Returns the current value of the EGPlayerController variable
function EG_PlayerController GetPlayerController( )
{
   if ( EGPlayerController != none )
   {
      return EGPlayerController;
   }
   else
   {
      `log( "Assign Player Controller before using it" );
   }
}

// Sets a reference to the EG_Weapon class
function SetWeaponClass( EG_Weapon W )
{
   // If we dont have a reference
   if ( EGWeapon == none )
   {
      EGWeapon = W;
   }
   else
   {
      EGWeapon = none;

      EGWeapon = W;
   }
}
// Returns the value of the EGWeapon variable
```

```
function EG_Weapon GetWeaponClass ( )
{
   if ( EGWeapon != none )
   {
       return EGWeapon;
   }
   else
   {
       `log( "Assign Weapon before using it" );
   }
}

// Sets a reference to EG_Pawn
function SetPlayerPawn ( EG_Pawn P )
{
   // If we dont have a current reference
   if ( EGPawn == none )
   {
       EGPawn = P;
   }
   else
   {
       EGPawn = none;

       EGPawn = P;
   }
}

// Returns the value of the EGPawn variable
function EG_Pawn GetPlayerPawn ( )
{
   if ( EGPawn != none )
   {
       return EGPawn;
   }
   else
   {
       `log( "Assign Pawn before using it" );
   }
}
```

There is a lot of repetition here. The idea is that one function (the modifier) will set the value of a class variable. This will hold a reference to it until either the game ends or the function is called again. The reason a modifier function may be called again is let's say our Pawn gets killed. We would have to spawn a new one in order for the player to continue play. We would want to reference the new Pawn when doing that.

The other type of function (the accessor) is designed to return a value of what is being stored. You'll notice that these functions have a type, GetPlayerPawn( ) for instance. This function is designed to return a value of that type. In order for this function to compile you HAVE to have a "return" statement that matches that type. Because we are working with limited classes, we are returning only that type.

The general idea of the accessors is that if the variable doesn't equal none (it is assigned something) return it. For my modifiers, I check if the variable is equal to none first. If it is, I assign what is being passed into the function. If the variable is already assigned, I removed the current assignment and assign the new type being passed into the function. This allows the functions to have a more "secure" process, as without these conditions, it may be easy to get some undesirable bugs.

This is arguable un-needed and is suitable to have the assignment within the functions, without any conditional statements. Such as:

```
EGWeapon = W;
```

Our default properties are the same as before, but here they are again:

```
// Default assignments
DefaultProperties
{
   HUDType = class'USLExampleGame.EG_HUD'
   PlayerControllerClass = class'USLExampleGame.EG_PlayerController'
   DefaultPawnClass = class'USLExampleGame.EG_Pawn'
   bDelayedStart = false
}
```

The HUDType, PlayerControllerClass, and DefaultPawnClass are class paths so the Game Info knows what it should be referencing by default. The bDelatyedStart is a bool value that is used for multi-player games in case you decide to continue on your own with this.

As you can see, the Game Info class for our example game is quite easy. We only really need to keep track of the different class referencesso the other classes have a route to "talk" with each other. Referencing other classes can sometimes be a pain when you're first learning. Luckily the Game Info class offers us the ability to do so without much hassle.

If you debug the game now, you may get an a compiling error from our chapter on the Projectile class, which will call:

```
// Call the AIPawnTakeDamage( ) function, to damage the EG_AIPawn
EG_AIPawn( Other ).AIPawnTakeDamage( damageAmount );
```

If you want to try the game out, comment this line out with two //.

Such as:

```
// Call the AIPawnTakeDamage( ) function, to damage the EG_AIPawn
// EG_AIPawn( Other ).AIPawnTakeDamage( damageAmount );
```

The game should compile with ZERO warnings or errors (as long as AIPawnTakeDamage( ) is commented out). You should be able to move the player character around and shoot the weapon by holding down the LEFT mouse button; the projectiles should stop firing when you let go. When you shoot the Projectiles they should go in a strait line from the tip of the gun to whatever they hit. When they hit any of the art, they should be destroyed and another Particle System should spawn showing a small blue and brown explosion, which resembles the projectile.

Here is the entire EG_GameInfo class:

```
class EG_GameInfo extends GameInfo;

// Reference to the EGPawn
var EG_Pawn EGPawn;

// Reference to the EGWeapon
var EG_Weapon EGWeapon;

// Referfence to the EGPlayerController
var EG_PlayerController EGPlayerController;
```

```
// Sets a reference to the EG_PlayerController
function SetPlayerController( EG_PlayerController PC )
{
   // If we do not have a current reference
   if ( EGPlayerController == none )
   {
      EGPlayerController = PC;
   }
   // If we have a current reference, re-assign it with the new one
   else
   {
      EGPlayerController = none;

      EGPlayerController = PC;
   }
}

// Returns the current value of the EGPlayerController variable
function EG_PlayerController GetPlayerController( )
{
   if ( EGPlayerController != none )
   {
      return EGPlayerController;
   }
   else
   {
      `log( "Assign Player Controller before using it" );
   }
}

// Sets a reference to the EG_Weapon class
function SetWeaponClass( EG_Weapon W )
{
   // If we dont have a reference
   if ( EGWeapon == none )
   {
      EGWeapon = W;
   }
   else
   {
      EGWeapon = none;

      EGWeapon = W;
   }
}

// Returns the value of the EGWeapon variable
function EG_Weapon GetWeaponClass( )
{
```

```
   if ( EGWeapon != none )
   {
       return EGWeapon;
   }
   else
   {
       `log( "Assign Weapon before using it" );
   }
}

// Sets a reference to EG_Pawn
function SetPlayerPawn( EG_Pawn P )
{
   // If we dont have a current reference
   if ( EGPawn == none )
   {
       EGPawn = P;
   }
   else
   {
       EGPawn = none;

       EGPawn = P;
   }
}

// Returns the value of the EGPawn variable
function EG_Pawn GetPlayerPawn( )
{
   if ( EGPawn != none )
   {
       return EGPawn;
   }
   else
   {
       `log( "Assign Pawn before using it" );
   }
}

// Default assignments
DefaultProperties
{
   HUDType = class'USLExampleGame.EG_HUD'
   PlayerControllerClass = class'USLExampleGame.EG_PlayerController'
   DefaultPawnClass = class'USLExampleGame.EG_Pawn'
   bDelayedStart = false
}
```

Next chapter will will work on the HUD class, to show the current ammo count, as well as the Pawns health.

Additional Reading:

http://udn.epicgames.com/Three/UnrealScriptExpressions.html#Ternary%20operators

Creating An Example Game HUD Class

Chapter Twelve

The HUD class is designed to display game relevant information to the player via the game screen. These sorts of things range from health, ammo, pickups, objectives, and so on. There is really no limit to what you're able to display when using UDK, as there are many functions within the HUD class (and sometimes other classes) that allow you to render all sorts of graphical information to the player.

We will be using UDK's internal HUD class and its counterpart (so to say) which is a class called Canvas. Canvas is designed to display all sorts of things in many different ways though it is not as powerful as the other HUD options, such as Scaleform.

Scaleform is a Flash based system that allows a more visually impressive set of HUD data but this is too far outside of the scope of a beginner book. If you feel more comfortable later on read up on Scaleform and its programming language called "Action Script".

Our HUD class is going to be pretty simple. The bottom left side will show a bar that shows the health in red and on the bottom right there will be a bar that shows the ammo in blue. There will also be a number value that updates over the health and ammo bars. At the end, there is a "OUT OF AMMO!" display, when the player reaches ZERO ammo.

Introduce some class variables so we can manage these different aspects. Add this to the USL_HUD.uc class:

```
// Vector2D sizing for health and ammo bars
var Vector2D HealthBar;
var Vector2D AmmoBar;

// When to show bOutOfAmmo text
var bool bOutOfAmmo;

// Used to keep track of game type in seconds
var float fLocalTime;

// Font used to show text
var Font TextFont;
```

And then the **Default Properties** of these **variables**:

```
DefaultProperties
{
    // Default health bar size
    HealthBar = ( X = 256, Y = 64 )

    // Default ammo bar size
    AmmoBar = ( X = 256, Y = 64 )

    // Font
    TextFont = MultiFont'UI_Fonts.MultiFonts.MF_HugeFont'
}
```

The first TWO variables, HealthBar and AmmoBar, are of the type Vector2D. A Vector2D is a struct designed to hold TWO float variables that can be used to represent the X and Y plane of a screen. This is similar to the Vector struct which has THREE floats, for X, Y, and Z. The idea of using the Vector2D struct here is to save in variables used. We could easily use TWO float variables for X and Y and manage them independently, though that will increase the code written and doesn't offer any benefit.

The bOutOfAmmo bool should look familiar from the Weapon class; when we wrote the OutOfAmmo( ) function. This bool is designed to show a "OUT OF AMMO!" text when TRUE.

fLocalTime should also look familiar as we used that during our discussion on variables. This will keep track of game time in seconds so we can display our "OUT OF AMMO!" text for a specific amount of time. That way it's not always in the middle of the screen.

And lastly, the TextFont variable is a type of "Font" which is used to reference a art asset to display text onto the screen. Just like what a text editor would do when you change fonts. Since we only need the ONE font, that is all that we need to define.

The default values for both HealthBar and AmmoBar are set to the same, as the default height and length are going to be the same.

We will now go over the individual functions that will be called, which will render both health and ammo bars, and then the "OUT OF AMMO!" text.

Add:

```
// Render the health of the Pawn onto the screen
private function RenderHealth( )
{
   // Set position of health bar
   Canvas.SetPos( Canvas.ClipX * 0.02, Canvas.ClipY * 0.9 );

   // Set color
   Canvas.SetDrawColor( 255,0,0,255 );

   // If we have full health
   if( EG_GameInfo( WorldInfo.Game ).GetPlayerPawn( ).
      GetPawnHealth( ) >= 100 )
   {
      // healthbar.x is default
      HealthBar.X = default.HealthBar.X;
   }
   else
   {
      // If we dont have full health, get fraction from 100%, times
      // that by default width
      HealthBar.X = ( EG_GameInfo( WorldInfo.Game ).
            GetPlayerPawn( ).GetPawnHealth( ) / 100 ) * 256;
   }

   // Draw the solid color box
   Canvas.DrawRect( HealthBar.X, HealthBar.Y );

   // Black outline
   // Set position of outline
   Canvas.SetPos( Canvas.ClipX * 0.02, Canvas.ClipY * 0.9 );
   // set draw color ( black )
   Canvas.SetDrawColor( 0,0,0,255 );
   // Draw the black outline 2 units bigger and wider than HealthBar
   Canvas.DrawBox( HealthBar.X + 2, HealthBar.Y + 2 );

   // Health text
   // Set position
   Canvas.SetPos( Canvas.ClipX * 0.021, Canvas.ClipY * 0.885 );
   // Set draw color ( white )
   Canvas.SetDrawColor( 255,255,255,255 );
   // Set color
```

186

```
Canvas.Font = TextFont;
// Draw the health value of Pawn
Canvas.DrawText( int( EG_GameInfo(WorldInfo.Game ).
   GetPlayerPawn( ).GetPawnHealth( ) ) );
}
```

There is decent amount of code here but hopefully you do not feel overwhelmed; as there is a lot of repetition. One of the "downsides" of using Canvas is the way it needs to be handled. You'll notice the pattern of "set position, color, drawXX( )". In order for Canvas to know what to you want it to do, you must set each of these each time you want use and update them.

The condition is setting the HealthBar.X (width) value to its default value if the Pawn is at ONE-HUNDRED health. If the Pawns health is less than that, we take the value of the Pawns health, divide it by ONE-HUNDRED (to get a fraction represented as a decimal) and then multiply it by the default length of the health bar (TWO-HUNDRED and FIFTY-SIX), which will result in a bar that is the proper width in relation to the value of health or ammo. ((PawnsHealth / 100) * 256)

The last line calling DrawText( ) is another way of using a cast to display something more desirable for the player, as displaying something like "92.0000" might be distracting, which is what would display if we did not use the cast. If you remember, the difference between a "float" and "int" variable type is the concept of "floating point numbers". Because "int" variables do not have these, if we cast a "float" into an "int", the "int" will drop the decimal numbers and instead display the TWO whole values. This way, we will see something like "92", instead of "92.00000", when the player loses health or ammo.

You may also be wondering why I did not set up any arguments like I did during the "functions" chapter. It is a judgment call and since I feel that passing positions, colors, or fonts as arguments is an extra step (since it is all contained in the class anyway), I just do everything within the block of the function itself.

The RenderAmmo( ) function should look very close to the RenderHealth( ):

```
// Used to render the ammo amount onto the HUD
private function RenderAmmo( )
{
   // Set position to show the color box
   Canvas.SetPos( Canvas.ClipX * 0.8, Canvas.ClipY * 0.9 );
   // set color ( blue )
   Canvas.SetDrawColor( 0,0,255,255 );

   // If we have full ammo
   if ( EG_GameInfo( WorldInfo.Game ).GetWeaponClass( ).
      GetAmmoCount( ) >= 100 )
```

```
    {
        // AmmoBar.X is default
        AmmoBar.X = default.AmmoBar.X;
    }
    else
    {
        // If we dont have full ammo, render what % is left of
        // the default 256 length
        AmmoBar.X = ( EG_GameInfo( WorldInfo.Game ).
            GetWeaponClass( ).GetAmmoCount( ) / 100 ) * 256;
    }

    // Render colored box
    Canvas.DrawRect( AmmoBar.X, AmmoBar.Y );

    // Black outline
    // Set position of outline
    Canvas.SetPos( Canvas.ClipX * 0.8, Canvas.ClipY * 0.9 );
    // Set color ( black )
    Canvas.SetDrawColor( 0,0,0,255 );
    // Render out the box
    Canvas.DrawBox( AmmoBar.X + 2, AmmoBar.Y + 2 );

    // Ammo Text
    // Set position of text
    Canvas.SetPos( Canvas.ClipX * 0.801, Canvas.ClipY * 0.885 );
    // Set draw color ( white )
    Canvas.SetDrawColor( 255,255,255,255 );
    // Set font
    Canvas.Font = TextFont;
    // Render ammo count to screen
    Canvas.DrawText( int( EG_GameInfo( WorldInfo.Game ).
        GetWeaponClass( ).GetAmmoCount( ) ) );
}
```

This function is doing the exact same thing as RenderHealth( ), it is just pointing to the iAmmoCount within the Weapon class.

The next function is to display our "OUT OF AMMO!" warning. Add the following:

```
// Render out text "OUT OF AMMO" with a black background
private function RenderOutOfAmmo( )
{
  // Black
  // Set Position for text
  Canvas.SetPos( Canvas.ClipX * 0.4485, Canvas.ClipY * 0.4985 );
  // Set the color
  Canvas.SetDrawColor( 0,0,0,255 );
```

```
   // Set the font
   Canvas.Font = TextFont;
   // Display the text with 0.5x, 0.5y in sizing
   Canvas.DrawText( "OUT OF AMMO!",, 0.5, 0.5 );

   // Red
   // Set position for text
   Canvas.SetPos( Canvas.ClipX * 0.45, Canvas.ClipY * 0.5 );
   // Set the color
   Canvas.SetDrawColor( 255,0,0,255 );
   // Set the font
   Canvas.Font = TextFont;
   // Display the text with 0.5x, 0.5y in sizing
   Canvas.DrawText( "OUT OF AMMO!",, 0.5, 0.5 );
}
```

This should look close to the previous functions, aside from the repetition of what looks like the same thing. The reason for the repetition is something purely esthetic; to have a black "shadow" to the text, so it doesn't sit on the screen with only a bright red.

The last thing we need to do is tell the HUD class to render all of these things when they need to be rendered. If you remember, the "main" draw loop (meaning it gets called every frame) is a function called DrawHUD( ). The DrawHUD( ) function is designed to be called every frame, and then render out what should be rendered depending on the conditions in that frame.

Add the following:

```
// Called per frame : used to render onto screen
function DrawHUD( )
{
   // If our pawn exists, render health and ammo
   if( EG_GameInfo( WorldInfo.Game ).GetPlayerPawn( ) != none )
   {
      RenderHealth( );
      RenderAmmo( );
   }

   // If bOutOfAmmo is true
   if( bOutOfAmmo )
   {
      // Keep track of game time, in seconds
      fLocalTime += RenderDelta;

      // Render "OUT OF AMMO!"
      RenderOutOfAmmo( );
```

```
        // When the fLocalTime is more than 3 ( seconds )
        if ( fLocalTime > 3 || EG_GameInfo( WorldInfo.Game ).
            GetWeaponClass( ).GetAmmoCount( ) > 0 )
        {
                // Turn off bOutofAmmo ( hide text )
                bOutOfAmmo = false;

                // Reset fLocalTime back to ZERO
                fLocalTime = 0;
        }
    }
}
```

The first condition is there to check that the EG_Pawn class exists. If it does, we call the RenderHealth( ) and RenderAmmo( ) functions. This is saying if the Pawn exists, show the bars.

We then check to see if bOutOfAmmo is TRUE. As you remember, this is changed in the Weapon class when the Weapon is out of ammo. Instead of always showing the "OUT OF AMMO!" text, there is another condition that will either be TRUE if "fLocalTime" is more than THREE (seconds) or the player has picked up more ammo (the ammo count is now more than ZERO). We then reset the bOutOfAmmo bool and the fLocalTime value.

If you debug the game, the blue ammo bar (one on the right) should decrease when you shoot. Remember that if you do NOT have the "AIPawnTakeDamage( )" function inside of the Projectile class commented out, you will get a compiling error. If you want to debug the game, comment out the line in EG_Projectile:

```
//EG_AIPawn( Other ).AIPawnTakeDamage( damageAmount );
```

This is what the HUD should look like in game:

Nothing in this HUD class should be overly complicated. The practice of creating functions should be starting to click and the idea of using some of the programming including with

UDK should also be starting to make more sense. Don't worry too much if you are still a bit confused on some aspects, that is perfectly normal! You can bet that nobody instantly understands every aspect of this stuff.

If you happen to be looking at different ways to use the HUD class, check out the additional reading below.

The entire EG_HUD class should be:

```
class EG_HUD extends HUD;

// Vector2D sizing for health and ammo bars
var Vector2D HealthBar;
var Vector2D AmmoBar;

// When to show bOutOfAmmo text
var bool bOutOfAmmo;

// Used to keep track of game type in seconds
var float fLocalTime;

// Font used to show text
var Font TextFont;

// Called per frame : used to render onto screen
function DrawHUD( )
{
   // If our pawn exists, render health and ammo
   if( EG_GameInfo( WorldInfo.Game ).GetPlayerPawn( ) != none )
   {
      RenderHealth( );
      RenderAmmo( );
   }

   // If bOutOfAmmo is true
   if( bOutOfAmmo )
   {
      // Keep track of game time, in seconds
      fLocalTime += RenderDelta;

      // Render "OUT OF AMMO!"
      RenderOutOfAmmo( );

      // When the fLocalTime is more than 3 ( seconds )
      if ( fLocalTime > 3 || EG_GameInfo
            ( WorldInfo.Game ).GetWeaponClass( ).GetAmmoCount( ) > 0 )
      {
            // Turn off bOutofAmmo ( hide text )
```

```
            bOutOfAmmo = false;

            // Reset fLocalTime back to ZERO
            fLocalTime = 0;
        }
    }
}

// Render the health of the Pawn onto the screen
private function RenderHealth( )
{
    // Set position of health bar
    Canvas.SetPos( Canvas.ClipX * 0.02, Canvas.ClipY * 0.9 );
    // Set color
    Canvas.SetDrawColor( 255,0,0,255 );

    // If we have full health
    if( EG_GameInfo( WorldInfo.Game ).GetPlayerPawn( ).
        GetPawnHealth( ) >= 100 )
    {
        // healthbar.x is default
        HealthBar.X = default.HealthBar.X;
    }
    else
    {
        // If we dont have full health, get fraction from 100%, times
        // that by default width
        HealthBar.X = ( EG_GameInfo( WorldInfo.Game ).
            GetPlayerPawn( ).GetPawnHealth( ) / 100 ) * 256;
    }

    // Draw the solid color box
    Canvas.DrawRect( HealthBar.X, HealthBar.Y );

    // Black outline
    // Set position of outline
    Canvas.SetPos( Canvas.ClipX * 0.02, Canvas.ClipY * 0.9 );
    // set draw color ( black )
    Canvas.SetDrawColor( 0,0,0,255 );
    // Draw the black outline 2 units bigger and wider than HealthBar
    Canvas.DrawBox( HealthBar.X + 2, HealthBar.Y + 2 );

    // Health text
    // Set position
    Canvas.SetPos( Canvas.ClipX * 0.021, Canvas.ClipY * 0.885 );
    // Set draw color ( white )
    Canvas.SetDrawColor( 255,255,255,255 );
    // Set color
    Canvas.Font = TextFont;
```

```
   // Draw the health value of Pawn
   Canvas.DrawText( int( EG_GameInfo
      ( WorldInfo.Game ).GetPlayerPawn( ).GetPawnHealth( ) ) );
}

// Used to render the ammo amount onto the HUD
private function RenderAmmo( )
{
   // Set position to show the color box
   Canvas.SetPos( Canvas.ClipX * 0.8, Canvas.ClipY * 0.9 );
   // set color ( blue )
   Canvas.SetDrawColor( 0,0,255,255 );

   // If we have full ammo
   if ( EG_GameInfo( WorldInfo.Game ).GetWeaponClass( ).
      GetAmmoCount( ) >= 100 )
   {
      // AmmoBar.X is default
      AmmoBar.X = default.AmmoBar.X;
   }
   else
   {
      // If we dont have full ammo, render what % is left of the
      //default 256 length
      AmmoBar.X = ( EG_GameInfo( WorldInfo.Game ).
            GetWeaponClass( ).GetAmmoCount( ) / 100 ) * 256;
   }

   // Render colored box
   Canvas.DrawRect( AmmoBar.X, AmmoBar.Y );

   // Black outline
   // Set position of outline
   Canvas.SetPos( Canvas.ClipX * 0.8, Canvas.ClipY * 0.9 );
   // Set color ( black )
   Canvas.SetDrawColor( 0,0,0,255 );
   // Render out the box
   Canvas.DrawBox( AmmoBar.X + 2, AmmoBar.Y + 2 );

   // Ammo Text
   // Set position of text
   Canvas.SetPos( Canvas.ClipX * 0.801, Canvas.ClipY * 0.885 );
   // Set draw color ( white )
   Canvas.SetDrawColor( 255,255,255,255 );
   // Set font
   Canvas.Font = TextFont;
   // Render ammo count to screen
   Canvas.DrawText( int( EG_GameInfo( WorldInfo.Game ).
      GetWeaponClass( ).GetAmmoCount( ) ) );
```

```
}

// Render out text "OUT OF AMMO" with a black background
private function RenderOutOfAmmo( )
{
  // Black
  // Set Position for text
  Canvas.SetPos( Canvas.ClipX * 0.4485, Canvas.ClipY * 0.4985 );
  // Set the color
  Canvas.SetDrawColor( 0,0,0,255 );
  // Set the font
  Canvas.Font = TextFont;
  // Display the text with 0.5x, 0.5y in sizing
  Canvas.DrawText( "OUT OF AMMO!",, 0.5, 0.5 );

  // Red
  // Set position for text
  Canvas.SetPos( Canvas.ClipX * 0.45, Canvas.ClipY * 0.5 );
  // Set the color
  Canvas.SetDrawColor( 255,0,0,255 );
  // Set the font
  Canvas.Font = TextFont;
  // Display the text with 0.5x, 0.5y in sizing
  Canvas.DrawText( "OUT OF AMMO!",, 0.5, 0.5 );
}

DefaultProperties
{
  // Default health bar size
  HealthBar = ( X = 256, Y = 64 )
  // Default ammo bar size
  AmmoBar = ( X = 256, Y = 64 )

  // Font
  TextFont = MultiFont'UI_Fonts.MultiFonts.MF_HugeFont'
}
```

Additional Reading:

More on Canvas:
http://udn.epicgames.com/Three/CanvasTechnicalGuide.html

More on Scaleform:
http://udn.epicgames.com/Three/ScaleformTechnicalGuide.html

More on Action Script:
http://udn.epicgames.com/Three/ScaleformTechnicalGuide.html#UnrealScript%20and%20_ActionScript

Creating An Example Game Drop Actor Class

Chapter Thirteen

Sometimes it is handy to have a single Actor responsible for a couple tasks, as long as they are relatively alike. In this instance, since the enemy AI will drop a ammo and a health pickup,we can use one type of Actor and decide what type it'll be right after it spawns. This way we can keep the logic for both within the same class, then spawn them with a chance to pick between the two player perks.

We have used the Spawn( ) function before but have yet to go over some of how it works.

The Spawn( ) function is designed to create a Actor class instance. Generally, Actors have a physical representation of something; a Static Mesh, a Skeletal Mesh, or a Particle System. Later down the road if you are in need of spawning a class instance but do not want a physical appearance of it, the class should probably be extending Object, as the the Object class doesn't refer to a Static Mesh, Skeletal Mesh, or Particle System. The catch is, you cannot spawn a class extending Object with Spawn( ), you must use "new". Such as:

```
myObjectClassReference = new class'MyObjectClass';
```

If we wanted to spawn an class that extends Actor, it would be as we have been doing previously, with Spawn( ):

```
myActorClassReference = Spawn( class'MyActorClass', WhoOwnsThisSpawn,
```

```
SpawnTag, SpawnLocation, SpawnRotation, ActorTemplate,
SpawnInCollisionBool );
```

You can see that the two vary quite a bit. Also, if you remember, you can access specific classes through a "static" function, so sometimes direct reference isn't needed, if you plan ahead and use "static" functions, instead of relying on Spawn( ) and "new".

Our item Drop Actor is going to have TWO types, one for ammo and one for health. The type will be chosen by an UDK function called RandRange( ). RandRange( ) is designed to pick a random number by the TWO float values past into it. Depending on the result of RandRange( ), the Drop Actor will be assigned a Static Mesh and a name. From there, if the player Pawn class gets close enough to it, the Drop Actor will move towards the player Pawn and when the Drop Actor touches the Pawn the Pawn will receive a random range of either health or ammo; depending on the name of the Drop Actor.

To start, add the following class variables:

```
// Used to determine what time of visual for item
var StaticMesh Pickup[2];

// Used to reference the mesh of the item
var StaticMeshComponent PickupComponent;

// The name of the item ( Health - Ammo )
var name LootType;
```

And then, the Default Properties:

```
DefaultProperties
{
    // Art asset paths for pickup art
    Pickup[0] =
        StaticMesh'Pickups.Health_Large.Mesh.S_Pickups_Health_Large_Keg'
    Pickup[1] =
        StaticMesh'Pickups.Berserk.Mesh.S_Pickups_Berserk'

    // Light environment so the Actor is lit
    begin object class=DynamicLightEnvironmentComponent name=LightEnv
        bEnabled = true
    end object
    Components.Add( LightEnv )

    // Static mesh component so we can assign the Actor an appearance
    begin object class=StaticMeshComponent name=LootItem
        LightEnvironment = LightEnv
    end object
    Components.Add( LootItem )
```

```
    // Used to assign and reference the Static Mesh
    PickupComponent = LootItem

    // Used to know what is colliding with the Actor
    Begin Object Class=CylinderComponent NAME=CollisionCylinder
        CollideActors=true
        CollisionRadius=+0020.000000
        CollisionHeight=+0035.000000
        bAlwaysRenderIfSelected=true
    End Object
    CollisionComponent=CollisionCylinder
    Components.Add(CollisionCylinder)

    bHidden=false
    bCollideActors=true
    bCollideWorld=true
    bBlockActors=true
}
```

The first variable type is used to reference a Static Mesh art asset. Since the Jazz Jackrabbit art assets do not include Static Mesh art for either health or ammo we are using some Unreal Tournament assets.

The next variable is so we can both assign and reference one of these Static Mesh art assets during the process in which this Actor is assigned a art asset.

Part of keeping track of what type of perk this Drop Actor will give is knowing what it is. The LootType variable will allow us to assign the proper name and then compare these names so we know what to do with them.

The beginning of the Default Properties reflects the variables. The Actor Component list is nothing you have not seen yet. We have a DynamicLightEnvironmentComponent, a StaticMeshComponent, and a CylinderComponent so properly light, show, and interact with the Drop Actor.

This class also starts with a PostBeginPlay( ) function so properly assign both the Static Mesh and name of the Drop Actor. It will also call a yet unwritten function to "toss" the item upwards after it spawns, simulating an effect like it is "exploding" out of the enemy AI Pawn.

Add the following:

```
// Called just after this class is created
simulated function PostBeginPlay( )
{
    // Make sure we include the parent class code for PostBeginPlay( )
```

```
    super.PostBeginPlay( );

    // If the random range is greater than 50 and pawn health is
    // less than 100
    if ( RandRange( 1, 100 ) > 50 && EG_GameInfo( WorldInfo.Game ).
            GetPlayerPawn( ).GetPawnHealth( ) < 100 )
    {
        // Display health Static Mesh
        PickupComponent.SetStaticMesh( Pickup[ 0 ] );

        // Name the item by type
        SetLootType( 'Health' );
    }
    else
    {
        // Display ammo Static Mesh
        PickupComponent.SetStaticMesh( Pickup[ 1 ] );

        // Name the item type
        SetLootType( 'Ammo' );
    }

    // Toss the item a bit up in the air, to simulate it coming out of
    // the AI Pawn
    TossLootItem( );
}
```

After calling the "super" to make sure we are including the parent class code for PostBeginPlay( ) we have a conditional. This conditional is using a UDK function RandRange( ) which will accept TWO float values and then create a "random" number between them. We use this in conjunction with the conditional that the Pawns health is LESS than ONE-HUNDRED. This way we will only spawn the health pickup when the Player needs it.

In order to assign the proper Static Mesh, we are again referencing our StaticMeshComponent through a class variable, and then using a UDK function called SetStaticMesh( ) to assign one of the Pickup array Static Mesh art assets to the Drop Actor. If the RandRange( ) is more than FIFTY, set the Drop Actor to the "health" Static Mesh and name the LootType variable "Health". If it less than FIFTY, assign the "ammo" Static Mesh and name the LootType variable "Ammo".

Create the TossLootItem( ) function. Add the following:

```
// Used to toss the item up in the air a little bit
function TossLootItem( )
{
    // Change physics to falling so it moves in the air
```

```
   // By default, physics are changed back when item hits the ground
   self.SetPhysics( PHYS_Falling );

   // Velocity is set upwards of 256 from spawn point
   self.Velocity.Z += 256;
}
```

When this TossLootItem( ) function is called we use a UDK function to set the physics of the class to "PHYS_Falling" which allows the class to simulate gravity by falling down the world Z axis (if it is not touching anything). Then, we assign the Velocity.Z of the class to itself plus TWO-HUNDRED and FIFTY SIX. This simulates the Drop Actor "popping" up into the air and then falling back down the ground. One cool thing about using the PHYS_Falling physics type is that when the Actor hits anything solid, the physics will automatically change so it doesn't fall through the world.

We now want to setup the accessor and modifier for the LootType variable. This will allow us to both assign a value to LootType and get the value of LootType. Add the following functions:

```
// Names the item
function SetLootType( name type )
{
   // Only assign if the item is not named
   if ( LootType == 'None' )
   {
      LootType = type;
   }
}

// Returns the type of item assigned
function name GetLootType( )
{
   return LootType;
}
```

These should both look familiar to you, as we have used many of them in the Game Info chapter. The idea is that when the SetLootType( ) function is called it accepts ONE argument for the variable type of "name". Name is a type that is used to hold characters like what you see here, limited to SIXTY-FOUR characters. When the SetLootType( ) function is called, it checks the variable for if it is named "None" (if it has not been assigned yet). If this is TRUE, it assigned the name variable type passed into the function.

The GetLootType( ) returns the current value of the LootType variable.

Since we need to know when the player Pawn has touched the Drop Actor, we will use the Touch( ) function to know when that happens.

Add the following:

```
// When the class touches a non solid Actor in the world
simulated function Touch( Actor Other, PrimitiveComponent
      OtherComp, Vector HitLocation, Vector HitNormal )
{
   // If what it touched is our player Pawn
   if( EG_Pawn( Other ) != none )
   {
      // If the item type is of 'Health'
      if( GetLootType( ) == 'Health' )
      {
         // Give the player a random range of health: 0 - 25
         EG_Pawn( Other ).SetPawnHealth( RandRange( 0, 25 ) );
      }
      // If the item type is not 'Health' - by process of
      // elimination it's 'Ammo'
      else
      {
         // Give the player a random range of ammo: 0 - 50
         EG_GameInfo( WorldInfo.Game ).GetWeaponClass( ).
               SetAmmoCount( RandRange( 0, 50) );
      }

      // Destroy this class
      self.Destroy( );
   }
}
```

The Touch( ) function is designed to be called whenever the Actor associated with it "touches" an Actor or Primitive Component within the world. When this happens the type of Actor or Primitive Component is passed in as an argument that we can use to compare, to know if that type or class of that Actor or Primitive Component is what we are looking for.

Our if statement is checking to see if the class (which extends Actor) is our EG_Pawn class. If that is TRUE (or, as it's written, if the Actor that touched the Drop Actor doesn't equal none) then we run the next block of code. The if statement within the if that checks for EG_Pawn checks the name of the Drop Actor variable LootType of either "Health" and then uses the modifier functions written within either the Weapon or Pawn class to change either health or uses else to assign to ammo. Again, we use the RandRange( ) function to pick an amount of ZERO to TWENTY-FIVE for health or ZERO to FIFTY for ammo.

The last function this class needs is the Tick( ) function so we know if the player Pawn is close enough to the Drop Actor for the Drop Actor to move towards the player Pawn.

Add the following:

```
// Called per frame, as long as this class exists
function Tick( float DeltaTime )
{
  // If the distance between the item and the player is less than 512
  if ( VSize( self.Location - EG_GameInfo
     ( WorldInfo.Game ).GetPlayerPawn( ).Location ) < 512 )
  {
    // Set physics to falling
    self.SetPhysics( PHYS_Falling );
    // Move the item closer to the Pawn at the rate of distance
    // between item and Pawn * speed of  2500
    self.Velocity = Normal( ( EG_GameInfo( WorldInfo.Game ).
        GetPlayerPawn( ).Location ) - self.Location ) * 2500;
  }
}
```

Again, remember that the Tick( ) function is called every frame.

Inside of the Tick( ) function we have a if statement that uses the Vsize( ) function to get a float value that represents the distance between the location of the Drop Actor and the location of the player Pawn. If the distance between the two is less than FIVE-HUNDRED and TWELVE set the physics of the Drop Actor to PHYS_FALLLING and change the velocity of the Drop Actor to the direction between the Drop Actor and the player Pawn multiplied by the speed of TWO-THOUSAND and FIVE-HUNDRED. The speed value is completely arbitrary here. The higher the value the faster it will move towards the Pawn. The lower the number the slower it will move.

The Normal( ) function is designed to return the unit vector with the same orientation as the vector passed into it. In this case, it returns a vector that points from the player Pawn to the Drop Actor. We use that direction to set the velocity of the Drop Actor to that direction TIMES the "speed" or value of TWO-THOUSAND and FIVE-HUNDRED. This will make the Drop Actor "shoot" at the player Pawn quickly when the player Pawn gets within FIVE-HUNDRED and TWELVE units of it.

Nothing in this class should look scary or overwhelming to you. One thing that we have not worked with is what is going on in the Tick( ) function, where we check the distance between the Drop Actor and the player Pawn and then move the Drop Actor to the player Pawn. This is a simple way to manage how the player picks up the Drop Actor. Outside of that, we are still working with variable types and conditionals, and "talking" with other classes to manage what sort "loot" this Drop Actor represents.

In the next chapter we will begin to work on the enemy AI by creating the EG_AIPawn class.

This is what the entire class should look like:

```
class EG_DropActor extends Actor;

// Used to determin what time of visual for item
var StaticMesh Pickup[2];
// Used to reference the mesh of the item
var StaticMeshComponent PickupComponent;
// The name of the item ( Health - Ammo )
var name LootType;

// Called just after this class is created
simulated function PostBeginPlay( )
{
    // Make sure we include the parent class code for PostBeginPlay
    super.PostBeginPlay( );

    // If the random range is greater than 50 and pawn health is
    // less than 100
    if ( RandRange( 1, 100 ) > 50 && EG_GameInfo( WorldInfo.Game ).
        GetPlayerPawn( ).GetPawnHealth( ) < 100 )
    {
        // Display health Static Mesh
        PickupComponent.SetStaticMesh( Pickup[ 0 ] );
        // Name the item by type
        SetLootType( 'Health' );
    }
    else
    {
        // Display ammo Static Mesh
        PickupComponent.SetStaticMesh( Pickup[ 1 ] );
        // Name the item type
        SetLootType( 'Ammo' );
    }

    // Toss the item a bit up in the air, to simulate it coming out
    // of the AI Pawn
    TossLootItem( );
}

// Used to toss the item up in the air a little bit
function TossLootItem( )
{
    // Change physics to falling so it moves in the air
    // By default, physics are changed back when item hits
    // the ground
    self.SetPhysics( PHYS_Falling );
```

```
        // Velocity is set upwards of 256 from spawn point
        self.Velocity.Z += 256;
}


// Names the item
function SetLootType( name type )
{
        // If the item is not named
        if ( LootType == 'None' )
        {
                LootType = type;
        }
        // If the item happens to be named ( un likely but still here to
        // check )
        else
        {
                LootType = 'None';

                LootType = type;
        }
}


// Returns the type of item assigned
function name GetLootType( )
{
        return LootType;
}


// When the class touches a non solid Actor in the world
simulated function Touch( Actor Other, PrimitiveComponent OtherComp,
Vector HitLocation, Vector HitNormal )
{
        // If what it touched is our player Pawn
        if( EG_Pawn( Other ) != none )
        {
                // If the item type is of 'Health'
                if( GetLootType( ) == 'Health' )
                {
                        // Give the player a random range of health
                        EG_Pawn( Other ).SetPawnHealth( RandRange( 0, 25 ) );
                }
                // If the item type is not 'Health' - by process of
                // elimination it's 'Ammo'
                else
                {
                        // Give the player a random range of ammo
                        EG_GameInfo( WorldInfo.Game ).GetWeaponClass( ).
                                SetAmmoCount( RandRange( 0, 50 ) );
                }
```

```
                // Destroy this class
                self.Destroy( );
        }
}


// Called per frame, as long as this class exists
function Tick( float DeltaTime )
{
        // If the distance between the item and the player is less
        // than 512
        if ( VSize( self.Location - EG_GameInfo
                ( WorldInfo.Game ).GetPlayerPawn( ).Location ) < 512 )
        {
                // Set physics to falling
                self.SetPhysics( PHYS_Falling );
                // Move the item closer to the Pawn at the rate of
                // distance between item and Pawn * speed of 2500
                self.Velocity = Normal( ( EG_GameInfo( WorldInfo.Game ).
                        GetPlayerPawn( ).Location ) - self.Location ) * 2500;
        }
}


DefaultProperties
{
        // Art asset paths for pickup art
        Pickup[0] =
        StaticMesh'Pickups.Health_Large.Mesh.S_Pickups_Health_Large_Keg'

        Pickup[1] = StaticMesh'Pickups.Berserk.Mesh.S_Pickups_Berserk'

        // Light environment so the Actor is lit
        begin object class=DynamicLightEnvironmentComponent name=LightEnv
                bEnabled = true
        end object
        Components.Add( LightEnv )

        // Static mesh component so we can assign the Actor
        // an appearance
        begin object class=StaticMeshComponent name=LootItem
                LightEnvironment = LightEnv
        end object
        Components.Add( LootItem )
        // Used to assign and reference the Static Mesh
        PickupComponent = LootItem

        // Used to know what is colliding with the Actor
        Begin Object Class=CylinderComponent NAME=CollisionCylinder
                CollideActors=true
```

```
        CollisionRadius=+0020.000000
        CollisionHeight=+0035.000000
        bAlwaysRenderIfSelected=true
    End Object
    CollisionComponent=CollisionCylinder
    Components.Add(CollisionCylinder)

    bHidden=false
    bCollideActors=true
    bCollideWorld=true
    bBlockActors=true
    bProjTarget=true
    bAlwaysRelevant = true
}
```

Creating An Example Game
AI Pawn Class
Chapter Fourteen

As mentioned before, the Pawn class is designed to display a physical representation in the world of a character, monster, NPC, and so on; which is why this game requires TWO. In order for our player to have enemies to fight against, we need to setup the AI Pawn class to be something different than the Pawn itself. In this case, we will be using the TWO turtle models that come along with Jazz Jackrabbit.

Before we begin any code, there has to be some alterations to the AnimTree(s) for both of these types, as we need to reference animations for their attacks and deaths.

Start by opening the editor, using the short-cut you made and saved to wherever you found convenient. If you don't remember, refer back to chapter ONE.

Once the editor is open, open the Content Browser (if it isn't already) and go to the following folder within the Packages drop-downs:

UDKGame – Content – Mobile – Misc – KismetGame_Assets – Anims.

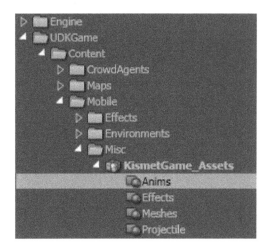

Scroll down within the Content Window to the "Turtle_AnimTree".

DOUBLE-CLICK it to open it, which will open the AnimTree Editor. You should see something like this:

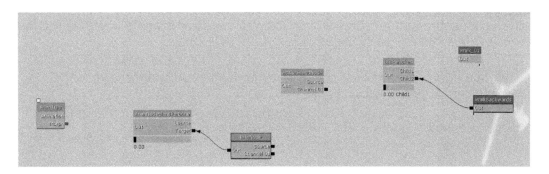

RIGHT-CLICK on the "Source" output block on the "AnimNodeBlendPerBone" box and select "Break Link"

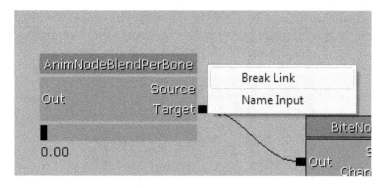

From there, RIGHT-CLICK anywhere next to this box, on the gray background and select "NewAnimationNode" and then "AnimNodePlayCustomAnim"

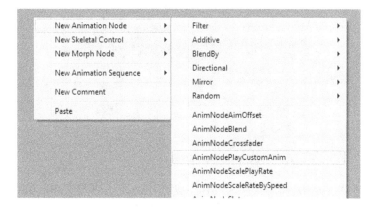

Select the "ActionBlendNode", "bIsPaniced", "Walk_01", and "WalkBackwards" by holding down CONTROL and using LEFT-CLICK; once all of them are selected continue to hold down CONTROL and use LEFT-CLICK and HOLD to move the boxes to the right.

Select the "CustomAnim" and move it closer to the "ActionBlendNode" box, which should be connected to the "AnimNodeBlendPerBone" box; as seen below. Then LEFT-CLICK the "Out" on the "CustomAnim" box and drag the line to the "Source" box on the "ActionBlendNode" box.

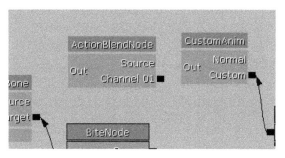

Then select the small node named "Walk_01" with LEFT-CLICK, press CONTROL + C, then CONTROL + V. This will create a copy of this box. Select the copy of the "Walk_01" box and move it over to the "Custom" output box on the "CustomAnim" box, then connect the "Out" of the "Walk_01" to the "Custom" of the "CustomAnim" box.

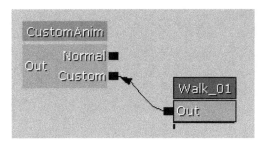

Select the new "Walk_01" and in the "Properties" bar on the bottom of the screen, change the "Anim Seq Name" to: "Bite_01". Keep "Playing" checked but UNCHECK "Looping".

▼ Anim Node Sequence	
Anim Seq Name	Bite_01
Rate	1.000000
Playing	✔
Looping	☐
Cause Actor Anim End	☐

After that select both the new "CustomAnim" and "Bite_01" boxes and again, CONTROL + C and then CONTROL + V. Then move the two pasted boxes to the right of the original and connect the "Out" of the newest "CustomAnim" to the "Normal" of the previous "CustomAnim". Then, select the second "Bite_01" and rename it to: Die_01

You can keep the rest of the settings the same as the "Bite_01" box.

Once that is done, take the "Out" from the "ActionBlendNode" and connect it to the "Normal" of the "CustomAnim" box that holds "Die_01".

After everything is connected, make sure the "CustomAnim" box is selected for "Playing" but NOT "Looping".

The whole tree should now look like:

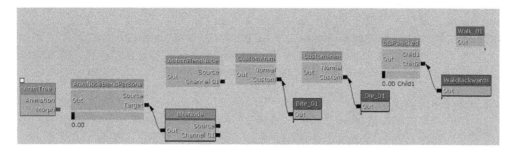

You can now close the AnimTree editor but DON'T close out of the editor. Instead, RIGHT-CLICK the Turtle_AnimTree box within the Content Window and select "Save".

Open up the AnimTree labled: TurtleBomb_AnimTree. As before, RIGHT-CLICK the "Source" output in "AnimNodeBlendPerBone" and then "Break Link".

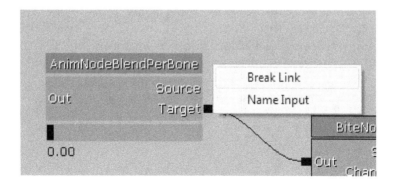

Again, select the FOUR boxes that have been broken off the link and move them out of the way. Then, RIGHT-CLICK - "New Animation Node" → "AnimNodeCustomNodeAnim". Select the "Walk_01" box, CONTROL + C and then CONTROL + V. Connect that new "Walk_01" to the recently created "CustomAnim" box, through the "Custom" output box. Select the

211

"Walk_01", if not already selected and rename it to: Die_01

Break off the "ActionBlendNode" from the "bIsPaniced" and then connect the "Out" of the "ActionBlendNode" to the "Source" of the "AnimNodeBlendPerBone" box. After that, connect the "Out" of the "CustomAnim" to the "Source" of the "ActionBlendNode".

The whole tree should look like:

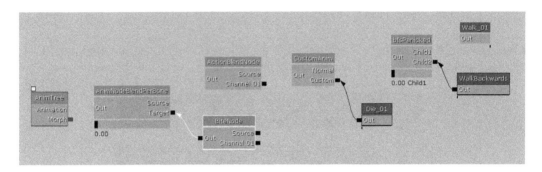

Make sure the "CustomAnim" box is selected for "Playing" but NOT "Looping".

Save this one as well by RIGHT-CLICK on the "TurtleBomb_AnimTree" AnimTree, within the Content Window, then SAVE.

Once this AnimTree is saved, you can close the editor.

The reason we needed to setup the CustomAnim nodes is so we can reference them through the ActionBlendNode within the code. This will allow use to call the animations, "Die_01" and "Bite_01" when we want them. There are more dynamic ways of handling things like this but they involve setting up these AnimTrees in a much more complicated way. If you want a good reference to a more elaborate AnimTree, look inside of the UT3 – Characters folder, for the "AT_CH_Human" AnimTree.

To start on our code, we are going to be using a enum list as well as a couple structs. Open up Visual Studio and then the EG_AIPawn.uc class, then start by adding the following:

```
// Type of AI
enum AIType
{
   EG_MELEE,
   EG_EXPLOSION,
};

// Classes and variable that makes up the Pawn
```

```
struct PawnComponents
{
   var SkeletalMesh MeshList[AIType];
   var AnimTree AnimTreeList[AIType];
   var AnimSet AnimSetList[AIType];
   var float fHealth;
   var name PawnType;
   var bool bIsDead;
};

// Different animations based on AI type
struct PawnAnimations
{
   var name Death;
   var name Attack;
   var name Explode;
   var name ToCompare;
   var AnimNodeSlot ActionBlendNodeReference;
};
```

If you remember from the "Classes, Structs, and Enums" chapter, an enum list is a way to keep a name in relation to a number, in a list. In this instance, the "EG_MELEE" name is actually just a ZERO within the code, but is accessible through the term "EG_MELEE". This allows us to use it as the value of ZERO without the hassle of trying to understand what ZERO means, because it is named.

The first struct, "PawnComponents" is used to store a SkeletalMesh, AnimTree, AnimSet, a float value that will represent the AI Pawns health, a name to keep track of what type of AI it will be, and a bool value to know if the Pawn is "dead". Because this class is going to hold multiple types of SkeletalMesh, AnimTree, and AnimSet(one for the "melee" turtle, one for the "explosion" turtle) having a struct will allow us to easily assign and understand what each art asset we will be referencing.

The second struct is just as useful as the first but is used to keep track of the animations the Pawn(s) will be using. The purpose is the same as the first struct, to keep track of what each animation the AI type will be referencing. There is also a name variable "ToCompare" used to compare the name of the last animation played, for conditionals on what should happen.

Let us create a reference for each struct as well as a couple more variables, one to reference the bool value to know when animations are playing, an "explosion" Particle System, and the other to reference the SkeletalMeshComponent. Add the following class variables:

```
// Used to keep track of when a custom animation is playing
var bool bAnimPlaying;

// Reference to the mesh
```

```
var SkeletalMeshComponent MeshReference;

// Used when the AI Pawn dies
var ParticleSystem BarrelExplosion;

// Variable to reference PawnComponents struct
var PawnComponents AIPawn;

// Variable to reference PawnAnimations struct
var PawnAnimations PawnAnims;
```

bAnimPlaying is to keep track when we are playing the "custom" animations we setup within the AnimTree.

The MeshReference variable is there so we can access the SkeletalMeshComponent that will be assigned within the DefaultProperties. With this reference, we can access things like Socket locations.

The BarrelExplosion is used to reference a Particle System within the art files of the editor. It will be used when the AI Pawn is destroyed.

The next TWO variables, AIPawn and PawnAnims are both so we can use the structs, which will be in charge of getting references to Skeletal Mesh, AnimTrees, AnimSets, and then assignment for animation names.

Setup the DefaultProperties for these class variables. Within the DefaultProperties, add this:

```
DefaultProperties
{
   // Default references for art assets
   AIPawn={(MeshList[EG_MELEE]=
       SkeletalMesh'KismetGame_Assets.Anims.SK_Turtle',
   MeshList[EG_EXPLOSION]=
       SkeletalMesh'KismetGame_Assets.Anims.SK_TurtleBomb_01',
   AnimTreeList[EG_MELEE]=
       AnimTree'KismetGame_Assets.Anims.Turtle_AnimTree',
   AnimTreeList[EG_EXPLOSION]=
       AnimTree'KismetGame_Assets.Anims.TurtleBomb_AnimTree',
   AnimSetList[EG_MELEE]=
       AnimSet'KismetGame_Assets.Anims.SK_Turtle_Anims',
   AnimSetList[EG_EXPLOSION]=
       AnimSet'KismetGame_Assets.Anims.SK_TurtleBomb_01_Anims',
   fHealth=100.0f , PawnType=' ' )}

   // Default names for animtions used by both melee and explosion
   // types
   PawnAnims={( Attack="Bite_01", Death="Die_01", Explode="Die_01" )}
```

```
   // Reference to Particle System for when the pawn dies
   BarrelExplosion = ParticleSystem'WP_RocketLauncher.Effects.
      P_WP_RocketLauncher_RocketExplosion'

   // Default movement speeds
   GroundSpeed = 120
   AirSpeed = 120
}
```

The AIPawn default values may look a bit complicated, mainly because it is quite a bit more than anything we have done before. Just remember that all the reference assignments are just like any other, just within the variable "AIPawn" which is referencing the struct. If you remember, the struct is made up of THREE arrays for SkeletalMesh, AnimTree, and AnimSet types. The amount of elements in each array is set to the amount of the enum list (which we know is TWO). Because the enum list gives us a name for each number value, we can use the naming EG_MELEE and EG_EXPLOSION to reference ZERO and ONE in the array elements. With each of these, there are art reference for the SkeletalMesh, AnimTree, and AnimSet.

Another thing you make notice is the brackets ({}) around the AIPawn and PawnAnims assignments. These are here to break up the assignment references into multiple lines. Without this, you will get a compiling error that says something like: "Missing key name in: (struct assignment)".

The PawnAnims assignments are all default names so we can use easier to read naming, for the animation names. Though the animation names are quite simple as is, this can be a handy practice when dealing with a vast library of animation names. In our case, I do believe that referring to "Bite_01" as "Attack" and "Die_01" as "Death" (for melee) and "Explode" (for explosion) types, will make understanding what is going on a little be easier, when calling animations.

The final assignments here is for the BarrelExplosion, which is a art asset path for a Particle System that is usually used for the Rocket Launcher, as it explodes. This will be used to "hide" the AI Pawn when it disappears, after we use the Destroy() function. We also set the default values for the Pawns movement speeds. This will keep the animations in line with how fast it is moving.

The rest of the DefaultProperties are very similar to the EG_Pawn class. Add the following UNDER the BarrelExplosion assignments:

```
begin object class=DynamicLightEnvironmentComponent
name=LightEnvironment
      // Whether a SH light should be used to synthesize all
      // light not accounted for by the synthesized directional light.
```

```
        bSynthesizeSHLight=TRUE
        // Whether this light environment is being applied to a
        // character
        bIsCharacterLightEnvironment=TRUE
        // Whether to use cheap on/off shadowing from the environment
        // or allow a dynamic preshadow.
        bUseBooleanEnvironmentShadowing=FALSE
        // Whether the light environment is used or treated
        // the same as a LightEnvironment=NULL reference.
        bEnabled = TRUE
    end object
    Components.Add( LightEnvironment )

    begin object class=SkeletalMeshComponent name=AIMeshComponent
        // How far off the "ground" this mesh will be
        Translation=( Z=-67 )
        // Size of skeletal mesh based on its original size
        Scale=1.00

        // Whether to cast any shadows or not
        CastShadow=TRUE
        // Should this block rigid body phyics
        BlockRigidBody=TRUE
        // If true, update skeleton/attachments even when our Owner
        // has not been rendered recently
        bUpdateSkelWhenNotRendered=FALSE
        // If true, do not apply any SkelControls when owner
        // has not been rendered recently.
        bIgnoreControllersWhenNotRendered=TRUE
        // If we are running physics, should we update bFixed bones
        // based on the animation bone positions.
        bUpdateKinematicBonesFromAnimation=TRUE
        // Controls whether the primitive should cast shadows
        // in the case of non precomputed shadowing
        bCastDynamicShadow=TRUE
        // Enum indicating what type of object this should
        // be considered for rigid body collision.
        RBChannel=RBCC_Untitled3
        // Types of objects that this physics objects will collide with.
        RBCollideWithChannels=( Untitled3=true )
        // The lighting environment to take the primitive's
        // lighting from.
        LightEnvironment=LightEnvironment
        // if set, components that are attached to us have their
        // bOwnerNoSee and bOnlyOwnerSee properties overridden by ours
        bOverrideAttachmentOwnerVisibility=true
        // If TRUE, this primitive accepts dynamic decals
        bAcceptsDynamicDecals=FALSE
        // Indicates whether this SkeletalMeshComponent should have a
```

```
        // physics engine representation of its state.
        bHasPhysicsAssetInstance=true
        // The ticking group this component belongs to
        TickGroup=TG_PreAsyncWork
        // If non-zero, skeletal mesh component will not update
        // kinematic bones and bone springs when distance factor
        // is greater than this (or has not been rendered for a while).
        // This also turns off BlockRigidBody, so you do
        // not get collisions with 'left behind' ragdoll setups.
        MinDistFactorForKinematicUpdate=0.2
        //If true, DistanceFactor for this SkeletalMeshComponent will
        // be added to global chart.
        bChartDistanceFactor=true
        // Used for creating one-way physics interactions (via
        // constraints or contacts) Groups with lower RBDominanceGroup
        // push around higher values in a 'one way' fashion. Must be
        // less than 32.
        RBDominanceGroup=20
        // If TRUE, dynamically lit translucency on this primitive will
        // render in one pass,
        bUseOnePassLightingOnTranslucency=TRUE
        // If true, use per-bone motion blur on this skeletal mesh.
        bPerBoneMotionBlur=true
    end object
    Components.Add( AIMeshComponent )
    MeshReference = AIMeshComponent

    Begin Object Name=CollisionCylinder
        // How round the collision cylinder is
        CollisionRadius=+0021.000000
        // How tall the collision cylinder is
        CollisionHeight=+0044.000000
    End Object
    CylinderComponent=CollisionCylinder
```

Just like the EG_Pawn class, we have a DynamicLightEnvironmentComponent, a SkeletalMeshComponent, and a CollisionCylinder extension. The DynamicLightEnvironmentComponent will give the AI Pawn real-time or, dynamic lighting. The SkeletalMeshComponent will give it a Skeletal Mesh to appear as, and the CollisionCylinder will allow us to know when the Pawn is touching or colliding with another Actor in the world.

The first function to add to the class is the PostBeginPlay( ) function. Add the following:

```
// Called just after this class is created
simulated function PostBeginPlay( )
{
```

```
   // Keep parent code for this PostBeginPlay( )
   super.PostBeginPlay( );

   // Set physics for this Pawn to walking
   self.SetPhysics( PHYS_Walking );
}
```

The purpose of this is to set the classes physics to PHYS_Walking. If this is not set, the Pawn won't be able to move and maybe cause some headaches when trying to move the Pawn within the Controller.

We now need to initiate the reference to the AnimTree, so we are able to access the proper AnimNode. That way we can call the proper animations. Add the following:

```
// Initiate AnimTree for AI Type
simulated function PostInitAnimTree( SkeletalMeshComponent SkelComp )
{
   // If SkelComp matches our MeshReference
   if ( SkelComp == MeshReference )
   {
      // Assign our AnimNodeSlot variable to 'FullBodySlot', so we can
      // reference animations
      PawnAnims.ActionBlendNodeReference = AnimNodeSlot
            ( MeshReference.FindAnimNode( 'ActionBlendNode' ) );
   }
}
```

This will be called for us, as that is what it setup to do within a parent class. The idea is that if the SkelComp argument is equal to the MeshReference variable within our class, then assign the ActionBlendNodeReference within our PawnAnims struct varibale, to the "ActionBlendNode" within the AnimTree (the ones we setup during the first part of this chapter).

We want to create FOUR accessor functions to get the type of SkeletalMesh, AnimTree, AnimSet, and to name the class to what type we want to use, depending on the type of AI we want this class to be; melee or explosion. Add the following functions:

```
// Returns a SkeletalMesh, depending on bool value passed in
function SkeletalMesh GetMesh( bool melee )
{
   // If passed bool is true
   if ( melee )
   {
      // Return "melee" mesh
      return AIPawn.MeshList[EG_MELEE];
   }
```

```
   else
   {
      // If false, return the "explosion" mesh
      return AIPawn.MeshList[EG_EXPLOSION];
   }
}

// Returns a AnimSet, depending on bool passed in
function AnimSet GetAnimSet( bool melee )
{
   // If passed bool is true
   if ( melee )
   {
      // Return "melee" AnimSet
      return AIPawn.AnimSetList[EG_MELEE];
   }
   else
   {
      // If false, return "explosion" AnimSet
      return AIPawn.AnimSetList[EG_EXPLOSION];
   }
}

// Returns a AnimTree, depending on bool passed in
function AnimTree GetAnimTree( bool melee )
{
   // If passed bool is true
   if ( melee )
   {
      // Return "melee" AnimTree
      return AIPawn.AnimTreeList[EG_MELEE];
   }
   else
   {
      // If false, return "explosion" AnimTree
      return AIPawn.AnimTreeList[EG_EXPLOSION];
   }
}

// Returns the name of the Pawn type.
function name GetPawnNameType( bool melee )
{
   // Assigns a name to know what type this AI Pawn is
   if ( melee )
   {
      return 'Melee';
   }
   else
   {
```

```
            return 'Explosion';
    }
}
```

Each of these are design to return their specific type, depending on the bool value that is passed into each. An important thing to keep in mind is that all of the values passed into each of these should match, or you'll get a cross between what reference is returned.

The simple process is, if the argument "melee" is TRUE, return the proper reference to the EG_MELEE array element within each type, held in our AIPawn variable, which comes from the PawnComponents struct. If "melee" is FALSE, return the explosion reference.

We need to create a function that will be used to initiate the values for this class, depending on the type of turtle we want to use. Add the following:

```
// Used to assign what type of AI this Pawn will be, at spawn
function InitAIPawn ( bool melee )
{
    // Assign what mesh, depending on what bool value is passed in
    MeshReference.SetSkeletalMesh ( GetMesh ( melee ) );

    // Assign what AnimTree, depending on what bool value is passed in
    MeshReference.SetAnimTreeTemplate ( GetAnimTree ( melee ) );

    // Assign what AnimSet is set, depending on what bool value is
    // passed in
    MeshReference.AnimSets [0] = GetAnimSet ( melee );

    // Assigns a name to know what type this AI Pawn is
    AIPawn.PawnType = GetPawnNameType ( melee );
}
```

As you can see, this takes advantage of all of the accessor functions we created to properly assign some of the class references by using SetSkeletalMesh( ), SetAnimTreeTemplate( ), and then to directly assign a reference to the first element within the AnimSets[ ] array. This works by using the return type of the function to act as the type that is being assigned through the TWO modifier functions (SetSkeletalMesh( ) and SetAnimTreeTemplate( )) as well as a direct reference to the AnimSets[ ] array.

All of these assignments are dependent on the function argument "melee", which will be passed just after we spawn this class via a Actor within the world, which will be programmed later on.

It is the time to write that function that's been holding up our debugging, which is being used inside of the Projectile class: AIPawnTakeDamage( ). Add the following:

```
// Sets the value of fHealth for the Pawn unless fHealth is
// lower than ZERO
function AIPawnTakeDamage( float damage )
{
   // If Pawn health is more than zero
   if ( AIPawn.fHealth > 0 )
   {
      // Subtract health
      AIPawn.fHealth -= damage;
   }
   // Also need to check if the health is not below ZERO
   else if ( AIPawn.fHealth <= 0 )
   {
      if ( AIPawn.PawnType == 'Melee' )
      {
            PlayAIPawnAnimation( PawnAnims.Death );
      }
      else
      {
            PlayAIPawnAnimation( PawnAnims.Explode );
      }
   }
}
```

The float value passed into this function, through the argument "damage" will be SUBTRACTED from the value of fHealth if it a positive value. If the value passed in happens to be a negative, the value will be ADDED to the fHealth value. This works a lot like our SetPawnHealth( ) function inside of EG_Pawn.

In order for this function to work "properly" we should have a check after we assign the new fHealth value, to make sure that damage didn't "kill" the AI Pawn. So after checking that the fHealth value is MORE than ZERO, we also check to make sure that the new fHealth value didn't fall BELOW or EQUAL to ZERO. If it happened to, we then we want to check what type of AI this is set to, either "Melee" or "Explosion", depending on what type this AI is. We then call a function not yet written, called: PlayAIPawnAnimation( ) which will play an animation and set our bAnimPlaying bool to TRUE.

We will now write the PlayAIPawnAnimation( ) function. Add the following:

```
// Used to play specific animations, passed by name
function PlayAIPawnAnimation( name AnimName )
{
   if ( AnimName == PawnAnims.Death || AnimName == PawnAnims.Explode )
   {
      // Plays the custom animation depending on the AnimName passed
      // into this function
      PawnAnims.ActionBlendNodeReference.PlayCustomAnim
```

```
        ( AnimName, 1.0, 0.25 );

    bAnimPlaying = true;
  }

  if ( AnimName == PawnAnims.Attack && PawnAnims.
     ActionBlendNodeReference.GetPlayedAnimation( ) !=
     PawnAnims.Attack )
  {
     // Plays the custom animation depending on the AnimName passed
     // into this function
     PawnAnims.ActionBlendNodeReference.PlayCustomAnim
          ( AnimName, 1.0, 0.25 );

     bAnimPlaying = true;
  }
}
```

This is another fairly strait forward function. It takes in a name variable, called "AnimName". If "AnimName" matches any of our PawnAnim variable assignments, then use the PlayCustomAnim( ), which comes from the AnimNode reference, "ActionBlendNodeReference" which is held in our PawnAnims struct variable. Within the PlayCustomAnim( ), we play the animation by reference of AnimName, at the rate of ONE (normal speed), and blend the animation over ZERO point TWO-FIVE (0.25) seconds. The, we set our bAnimPlaying to TRUE if we are call either of the "death" animations, so the next function we write: Tick( ) will know what to do when bAnimPlaying is TRUE.

If we just want to use the "attack" animation, we can call it, if it's not already being played. This will prevent us from calling the same animation over and over, causing issues with how the Skeletal Mesh may look when attacking.

Add the following:

```
// Used to check animations to call AIDeath( ) they finish
function Tick( float DeltaTime )
{
  // If bAnimPlaying is true
  if ( bAnimPlaying )
  {
     // If there is a custom animation player - comes from
  // AnimNodeSlot
  if ( PawnAnims.ActionBlendNodeReference.bIsPlayingCustomAnim )
  {
     // If the current animation play is "death", "explode", or
     // "attack"
     if( PawnAnims.ActionBlendNodeReference.GetPlayedAnimation( ) ==
          PawnAnims.Death || PawnAnims.ActionBlendNodeReference.
```

```
            GetPlayedAnimation( ) == PawnAnims.Explode ||
            PawnAnims.ActionBlendNodeReference.GetPlayedAnimation( )
            == PawnAnims.Attack )
    {

            // Reference that animation name through "ToCompare"
            PawnAnims.ToCompare = PawnAnims.
                ActionBlendNodeReference.GetPlayedAnimation( );

            // Set the ground speed, air speed, and velocity of
            // this Pawn to ZERO
            self.GroundSpeed = 0;
            self.AirSpeed = 0;
            self.Velocity = Vect( 0,0,0 );

            // Break out of this code block
            return;
    }

}
else // If NOT playing a custom Animation
{
    // Is "ToCompare" equal to "Attack"
    if ( PawnAnims.ToCompare == PawnAnims.Attack )
    {
            // Do TEN damage to the Player Pawn
            EG_GameInfo( WorldInfo.Game ).GetPlayerPawn( )
                .SetPawnHealth( -10 );
    }

    // Is "ToCompare" equal to "Death" or "Explode"
    if ( PawnAnims.ToCompare == PawnAnims.Death || P
            PawnAnims.ToCompare ==  PawnAnims.Explode )
    {
            // Call AIDeath( ) function
            AIDeath( );
    }

    // Turn bAnimPlaying false
    bAnimPlaying = false;
    // Set ToCompare to " "
    PawnAnims.ToCompare = ' ';
  }
 }
}
```

As you remember, the Tick( ) function is called every frame. So, we are checking to see if "bAnimPlaying" is TRUE. If so, we then check to make sure that "bIsPlayingCustomAnim" from our ActionBlendNodeReference, which is referencing our AnimNodeSlot, is also TRUE.

In order for us to compare each of these animations and then make sure we are doing the right thing with it, we have to keep both of these seemingly redundant if statements because if we didn't, it would make comparing the animation last played difficult.

We want to make sure that the animation that is currently playing is one of our "Death", "Attack", or "Explode" animations. If so, we assign a reference to the name of the animation that is playing to our "ToCompare" name variable from the PawnAnimations struct.

Since we now know that a animation is playing, we want to stop the AI Pawn from moving. This is because if the Pawn is moving around while animating, it is going to look as if it is sliding around. Then, we do something we haven't done yet, and use the return statement to "leave" the block of code. You have been used to seeing "return" used to return a type. In this case, we can use return to stop the code there.

The reason we are using the return here, is that there is no longer a reason to check anything else, as we have accomplished our goal for when the bIsPlayingCustomAnim is TRUE.

When bIsPlayingCustomAnim is FALSE, it will skip the reference to the last animation name played and instead use that ToCompare reference to tell the program what to do with it. If it is the same as "Attack" we do TEN damage to the player. If it is the same as "Death" OR "Explode" we call the AIDeath( ) function.

We then turn the bAnimPlaying to FALSE and "reset" the ToCompare name variable to ' ' (which is just a space).

Write the AIDeath( ) function. Add the following:

```
// Set to private to prevent other classes from calling this
private function AIDeath( )
{
   // Set the Pawn to "Dead"
      AIPawn.bIsDead = true;

   // Spawn explosion
   WorldInfo.MyEmitterPool.SpawnEmitter( BarrelExplosion,
      self.Location );

   // Spawn DropActor ( Random type by code within EG_DropActor )
   Spawn( class'EG_DropActor',,,self.Location, self.Rotation );

   // Destroy this class
   self.Destroy( );
}
```

Because this function could result in some strange bugs, if called by accident (such as continually spawning a Drop Actor), we set it to private. Also, if you look at the last AIPawnTakeDamage( ) function, the only time this function gets called is when the fHealth value is LESS than or EQUAL to ZERO, limiting the amount of times it's possible to actually call this function.

We start by first declaring the Pawn as "Dead", so our Controller will know what to do in case of that. Then, in order to "hide" the Pawns death, we use the SpawnEmitter( ) function to call an explosion as the Pawn is destroyed, with the Destroy( ) function.

Between the Particle System being spawned with the SpawnEmitter( ) function, we also create a EG_DropActor at the location and rotation of the Pawn. In this case, we do NOT need a reference to the Drop Actor, so we use Spawn( ) to create one.

That is our EG_AIPawn class. Here is what it should look like:

```unrealscript
class EG_AIPawn extends Pawn;

// Type of AI
enum AIType
{
   EG_MELEE,
   EG_EXPLOSION,
};

// Classes and variable that makes up the Pawn
struct PawnComponents
{
   var SkeletalMesh MeshList[AIType];
   var AnimTree AnimTreeList[AIType];
   var AnimSet AnimSetList[AIType];
   var float fHealth;
   var name PawnType;
   var bool bIsDead;
};

// Different animations based on AI type
struct PawnAnimations
{
   var name Death;
   var name Attack;
   var name Explode;
   var name ToCompare;
   var AnimNodeSlot ActionBlendNodeReference;
};

// Used to keep track of when a custom animation is playing
```

```
        var bool bAnimPlaying;

        // Reference to the mesh
        var SkeletalMeshComponent MeshReference;

        // Used when the AI Pawn dies
        var ParticleSystem BarrelExplosion;

        // Variable to reference PawnComponents struct
        var PawnComponents AIPawn;

        // Variable to reference PawnAnimations struct
        var PawnAnimations PawnAnims;

        // Called just after this class is created
        simulated function PostBeginPlay( )
        {
              // Keep parent code for this PostBeginPlay( )
              super.PostBeginPlay( );

              // Set physics for this Pawn to walking
              self.SetPhysics( PHYS_Walking );
        }

        // Initiate AnimTree for AI Type
        simulated function PostInitAnimTree( SkeletalMeshComponent SkelComp )
        {
              // If SkelComp matches our MeshReference
              if ( SkelComp == MeshReference )
              {
                    // Assign our AnimNodeSlot variable to 'FullBodySlot',
                    // so we can reference animations
                    PawnAnims.ActionBlendNodeReference = AnimNodeSlot
                          ( MeshReference.FindAnimNode( 'ActionBlendNode' ) );
              }
        }

        // Returns a SkeletalMesh, depending on bool value passed in
        function SkeletalMesh GetMesh( bool melee )
        {
              // If passed bool is true
              if ( melee )
              {
                    // Return "melee" mesh
                    return AIPawn.MeshList[EG_MELEE];
              }
              else
              {
                    // If false, return the "explosion" mesh
```

```
                return AIPawn.MeshList[EG_EXPLOSION];
        }
}


// Returns a AnimSet, depending on bool passed in
function AnimSet GetAnimSet( bool melee )
{
        // If passed bool is true
        if ( melee )
        {
                // Return "melee" AnimSet
                return AIPawn.AnimSetList[EG_MELEE];
        }
        else
        {
                // If false, return "explosion" AnimSet
                return AIPawn.AnimSetList[EG_EXPLOSION];
        }
}


// Returns a AnimTree, depending on bool passed in
function AnimTree GetAnimTree( bool melee )
{
        // If passed bool is true
        if ( melee )
        {
                // Return "melee" AnimTree
                return AIPawn.AnimTreeList[EG_MELEE];
        }
        else
        {
                // If false, return "explosion" AnimTree
                return AIPawn.AnimTreeList[EG_EXPLOSION];
        }
}


// Returns the name of the Pawn type.
function name GetPawnNameType( bool melee )
{
        // Assigns a name to know what type this AI Pawn is
        if ( melee )
        {
                return 'Melee';
        }
        else
        {
                return 'Explosion';
        }
}
```

```
// Used to assign what type of AI this Pawn will be, at spawn
function InitAIPawn( bool melee )
{
      // Assign what mesh, depending on what bool value is passed in
      MeshReference.SetSkeletalMesh( GetMesh( melee ) );

      // Assign what AnimTree, depending on what bool value is
      // passed in
      MeshReference.SetAnimTreeTemplate( GetAnimTree( melee ) );

      // Assign what AnimSet is set, depending on what bool value
      // is passed in
      MeshReference.AnimSets[0] = GetAnimSet( melee );

      // Assigns a name to know what type this AI Pawn is
      AIPawn.PawnType = GetPawnNameType( melee );
}

// Sets the value of fHealth for the Pawn unless fHealth is
// lower than ZERO
function AIPawnTakeDamage( float damage )
{

      // If Pawn health is more than zero
      if ( AIPawn.fHealth > 0 )
      {
            // Subtract health
            AIPawn.fHealth -= damage;
      }
      // Also need to check if the health is not below ZERO
      else if ( AIPawn.fHealth <= 0 )
      {
            // Set the Pawn to "Dead"
            AIPawn.bIsDead = true;

            // If this AI Pawn is 'Melee'
            if ( AIPawn.PawnType == 'Melee' )
            {
                  PlayAIPawnAnimation( PawnAnims.Death );
            }
            else
            {
                  // If not melee, do the explosion animation instead
                  PlayAIPawnAnimation( PawnAnims.Explode );
            }
      }
}
```

```
// Used to play specific animations, passed by name
function PlayAIPawnAnimation( name AnimName )
{
      if ( AnimName == PawnAnims.Death ||
          AnimName == PawnAnims.Explode )
      {
            // Plays the custom animation depending on the
            // AnimName passed into this function
            PawnAnims.ActionBlendNodeReference.PlayCustomAnim
                  ( AnimName, 1.0, 0.25 );

            bAnimPlaying = true;
      }

      if ( AnimName == PawnAnims.Attack &&PawnAnims.
          ActionBlendNodeReference.GetPlayedAnimation( ) !=
                PawnAnims.Attack )
      {
            // Plays the custom animation depending on the
            // Anim Name passed into this function
            PawnAnims.ActionBlendNodeReference.PlayCustomAnim
                  ( AnimName, 1.0, 0.25 );

            bAnimPlaying = true;
      }
}

// Set to private to prevent other classes from calling this
private function AIDeath( )
{
      // Spawn explosion
      WorldInfo.MyEmitterPool.SpawnEmitter
            ( BarrelExplosion, self.Location );

      // Spawn DropActor ( Random type by code within EG_DropActor )
      Spawn( class'EG_DropActor',,,self.Location, self.Rotation );

      // Destroy this class
      self.Destroy( );
}

// Used to check animations to call AIDeath( ) they finish
function Tick( float DeltaTime )
{
      // If bAnimPlaying is true
      if ( bAnimPlaying )
      {
            // If there is a custom animation player -
            // comes from AnimNodeSlot
```

```
if ( PawnAnims.ActionBlendNodeReference.
     bIsPlayingCustomAnim )
{
     // If the current animation play is "death",
     // "explode", or "attack"
     if ( PawnAnims.ActionBlendNodeReference.
     GetPlayedAnimation( ) == PawnAnims.Death ||
     PawnAnims.ActionBlendNodeReference.
     GetPlayedAnimation( ) == PawnAnims.Explode ||
     PawnAnims.ActionBlendNodeReference.
     GetPlayedAnimation( ) == PawnAnims.Attack )
     {
          // Reference that animation name through
          // "ToCompare"
          PawnAnims.ToCompare = PawnAnims.
          ActionBlendNodeReference.GetPlayedAnimation( );

          // Set the ground speed, air speed, and
          // velocity of this Pawn to ZERO
          self.GroundSpeed = 0;
          self.AirSpeed = 0;
          self.Velocity = Vect( 0,0,0 );

          // Break out of this code block
          return;
     }

}
else // If NOT playing a custom Animation
{
     // Is "ToCompare" equal to "Attack"
     if ( PawnAnims.ToCompare == PawnAnims.Attack )
     {
          // Do TEN damage to the Player Pawn
          EG_GameInfo( WorldInfo.Game ).
               GetPlayerPawn( ).SetPawnHealth( -10 );

     }

     // Is "ToCompare" equal to "Death" or "Explode"
     if ( PawnAnims.ToCompare == PawnAnims.Death
          || PawnAnims.ToCompare == PawnAnims.Explode )
     {
          // Call AIDeath( ) function
          AIDeath( );
     }

     // Turn bAnimPlaying false
     bAnimPlaying = false;
```

```
                // Set ToCompare to " "
                PawnAnims.ToCompare = ' ';
            }
        }
    }


DefaultProperties
{
    // Default references for art assets
    AIPawn={(MeshList[EG_MELEE]=
        SkeletalMesh'KismetGame_Assets.Anims.SK_Turtle',
    MeshList[EG_EXPLOSION]=
        SkeletalMesh'KismetGame_Assets.Anims.SK_TurtleBomb_01',
    AnimTreeList[EG_MELEE]=
        AnimTree'KismetGame_Assets.Anims.Turtle_AnimTree',
    AnimTreeList[EG_EXPLOSION]=
        AnimTree'KismetGame_Assets.Anims.TurtleBomb_AnimTree',
        AnimSetList[EG_MELEE]=
        AnimSet'KismetGame_Assets.Anims.SK_Turtle_Anims',
    AnimSetList[EG_EXPLOSION]=
        AnimSet'KismetGame_Assets.Anims.SK_TurtleBomb_01_Anims',
    fHealth=100.0f, PawnType=' ' )}

    // Default names for animtions used by both melee and
    // explosion types
    PawnAnims={( Attack="Bite_01", Death="Die_01", Explode="Die_01" )}

    // Reference to Particle System for when the pawn dies
    BarrelExplosion=
ParticleSystem'WP_RocketLauncher.Effects.P_WP_RocketLauncher_RocketExplosion'

    // Default movement speeds
    GroundSpeed = 120
    AirSpeed = 120

    begin object class=DynamicLightEnvironmentComponent
        name=LightEnvironment
        // Whether a SH light should be used to synthesize all light not
        // accounted for by the synthesized directional light.
        bSynthesizeSHLight=TRUE
        // Whether this light environment is being applied to a
        // character
        bIsCharacterLightEnvironment=TRUE
        // Whether to use cheap on/off shadowing from the environment or
        // allow a dynamic preshadow.
        bUseBooleanEnvironmentShadowing=FALSE
        // Whether the light environment is used or treated the same as
        // a LightEnvironment=NULL              // reference.
        bEnabled = TRUE
```

```
end object
Components.Add( LightEnvironment )

begin object class=SkeletalMeshComponent name=AIMeshComponent
    // How far off the "ground" this mesh will be
    Translation=( Z=-67 )
    // Size of skeletal mesh based on its original size
    Scale=1.00

    // Whether to cast any shadows or not
    CastShadow=TRUE
    // Should this block rigid body phyics
    BlockRigidBody=TRUE
    // If true, update skeleton/attachments even when our Owner has
    // not been rendered recently
    bUpdateSkelWhenNotRendered=FALSE
    // If true, do not apply any SkelControls when owner has not
    // been rendered recently.
    bIgnoreControllersWhenNotRendered=TRUE
    // If we are running physics, should we update bFixed bones
    // based on the animation bone positions.
    bUpdateKinematicBonesFromAnimation=TRUE
    // Controls whether the primitive should cast shadows in the
    // case of non precomputed shadowing
    bCastDynamicShadow=TRUE
    // Enum indicating what type of object this should be considered
    // for rigid body collision.
    RBChannel=RBCC_Untitled3
    // Types of objects that this physics objects will collide with.
    RBCollideWithChannels=( Untitled3=true )
    // The lighting environment to take the primitive's lighting
    // from.
    LightEnvironment=LightEnvironment
    // if set, components that are attached to us have their
    // bOwnerNoSee and bOnlyOwnerSee properties overridden by ours
    bOverrideAttachmentOwnerVisibility=true
    // If TRUE, this primitive accepts dynamic decals spawned during
    // gameplay.
    bAcceptsDynamicDecals=FALSE
    // Indicates whether this SkeletalMeshComponent should have a
    // physics engine representation of its state.
    bHasPhysicsAssetInstance=true
    // The ticking group this component belongs to
    TickGroup=TG_PreAsyncWork
    // If non-zero, skeletal mesh component will not update
    // kinematic bones and bone springs when distance factor
    // is greater than this (or has not been rendered for a while).
    // This also turns off BlockRigidBody, so you do
    // not get collisions with 'left behind' ragdoll setups.
```

```
        MinDistFactorForKinematicUpdate=0.2
        //If true, DistanceFactor for this SkeletalMeshComponent will be
        // added to global chart.
        bChartDistanceFactor=true
        // Used for creating one-way physics interactions (via
        // constraints or contacts) Groups with lower RBDominanceGroup
        // push around higher values in a 'one way' fashion. Must be
        // less than 32.
        RBDominanceGroup=20
        // If TRUE, dynamically lit translucency on this primitive will
        // render in one pass,
        bUseOnePassLightingOnTranslucency=TRUE
        // If true, use per-bone motion blur on this skeletal mesh.
        bPerBoneMotionBlur=true
    end object
    Components.Add( AIMeshComponent )
    MeshReference = AIMeshComponent

    Begin Object Name=CollisionCylinder
        // How round the collision cylinder is
        CollisionRadius=+0021.000000
        // How tall the collision cylinder is
        CollisionHeight=+0044.000000
    End Object
    CylinderComponent=CollisionCylinder
}
```

This class is probably the most complicated so far. We are using a variety of custom and UDK included functions, as well as some higher level logic (in comparison to what we have been doing prior to this) to deal with some of the issues of using TWO "types" of Pawns within one class. If you are having some issues with this go back to the EG_Pawn class to become acquainted again with a less complicated class.

We will now create the Controller for this class, so it knows how and when to attack the player Pawn.

Additional Reading:

More on the AnimTree Editor:
http://udn.epicgames.com/Three/AnimTreeEditorUserGuide.html

More on the AnimSet Editor:
http://udn.epicgames.com/Three/AnimSetEditorUserGuide.html

Creating An Example Game AI Controller Class

Chapter Fifteen

The Controller is designed to keep tabs on a Pawn character. You know our Player Controller class is responsible for taking input from the Player itself. It turns out that when creating a Controller for a AI Pawn, it can get quite tedious, as you have to govern all of its movement and "abilities" within the one class. Luckily, UDK comes with a declaration called a "state". A state is a bit like a class within a class. For each state you are able to call things as the Controller "enters" a state, as well has keep functions within each state. It is a way to separate actions from each other, while keeping the class as a whole.

To further explain the purpose of our AI Controller class:

The premise of our AI is quite simple. We have a "Melee" type and a "Explosion" type. Each will have ONE attack ability that is called when the AI Pawn is within a specific range. A part of this attack is an animation, which will display as a "bite" if the AI Pawn is melee, or it will explode if it is an explosion type.

The movement of the AI Pawn is done through some UDK functions to set a location and then a bool value that will move to that location, once it is set as a "focal point". When the AI Pawn is in its "idle" state, it will "find" a random location to walk to. If it makes it to that spot or gets stuck on something, it will "find" a new one. Only when the Player Pawn is close enough will the AI Pawn "attack".

Lets get started by adding some class variables in our EG_AIController class:

```
// Used to reference "enemy" Player Pawn
var Pawn EGPlayerPawn;

// Used to reference what Pawn this is controlling
var EG_AIPawn EGAIPawn;

// Used to dynamically reference all Path Nodes in the level
var array<PathNode> PN;

// Used to move the AI Pawn if it doesn't "see" the enemy Pawn
var Vector NextLocation;
```

Both the EGPlayerPawn and the EGAIPawn variables are so we can reference their like classes: Pawn and EG_AIPawn. We are using the general class "Pawn" here because there is no need to directly access EG_Pawn, as we are using it to check distances.

The array<PathNode> is a Dynamic Array, which allows us to add thing to an array without knowing the exact number of elements will be included into it. This is great for storing many of any ONE type of Object, to use for referencing later. In this case, we will store all of the PathNodes within the level and then use that array to find the "nearest" ones to the AI Pawn, so it has a location to move to.

NextLocation is so we can know how far the AI Pawn is from its destination. This is helpful for when the AI Pawn needs to find a new location to move to; if it is less than an amount from the NextLocation, find a new one.

Add the PostBeginPlay( ) function:

```
// Called just after this class is created
simulated function PostBeginPlay( )
{
  // Local reference to assign to dynamic array: PN
  local PathNode LPN;

  // Keep parent code of same function included
  super.PostBeginPlay( );

  // Assign reference to the "enemy" Player pawn
  EGPlayerPawn = EG_GameInfo( WorldInfo.Game ).GetPlayerPawn( );

  // Assign a refernce to each Path Node in the world, using the PN
  // dynamic array
  foreach WorldInfo.AllActors( class'PathNode', LPN )
  {
```

```
    // Adds each of the Path Nodes to the dynamic array: PN
    PN.AddItem( LPN );
  }
}
```

We have to have a local reference to a PathNode here as well because we need to know what to add to our PathNode Dynamic array.

We then assign the EGPlayerPawn reference to the return value of GetPlayerPawn( ), which is within our EG_Pawn class; which we access through our EG_GameInfo class.

At the end, we run a foreach iterator to add each of the Path Nodes in the game world to our Path Node Dynamic Array. This is done because the foreach will run for each Path Node, and then, for each one it finds, it adds it to the array: PN

To continue, we start with our states. Again, remember that these are a bit like having a class within a class. They will include unique functions that may be confusing, as they can repeat; which CAN'T be done within the class scope.

To start, let's add the "auto state", which is designed to automatically be the state the Controller will start in.

```
// Automatically enter this state, "look" for enemy Pawn
auto state SearchForPawn
{
  // called per frame
  function Tick( float DeltaTime )
  {
    // If the enemy Player Pawn is closer than 1024 units
    if ( VSize( EGAIPawn.Location - EGPlayerPawn.Location ) < 1024 )
    {
        GotoState( 'SeeEnemyPlayer' );
    }

    // If the location of the AI is within 100 units of the
    // NextLocation or the NextLocation is 0,0,0
    // Of if the AI Pawns velocity drops below 40 ( it's stuck )
    else if ( VSize( EGAIPawn.Location - NextLocation ) < 100 ||
        NextLocation == Vect( 0,0,0 ) || VSize( EGAIPawn.Velocity )
        < 40 && !EGAIPawn.AIPawn.bIsDead )
    {
        // Turn off bool that controls movement
        bPreciseDestination = false;

        // Move to the next location using "random" PathNode
        // location
```

```
            MoveToNextLocation( GetSearchPathLocation( ) );
        }
    }

begin:
    // Set AI Pawn ground speed to default
    EGAIPawn.GroundSpeed = EGAIPawn.default.GroundSpeed;
}
```

You'll notice a few things here that might be confusing. First, the creation of the state visually doesn't look quite like creating a function, as the state name is in that light blue color. Second, you will see the Tick( ) function within the state. This is where it may get even more confusing: each state can have its own functions as well as access any other functions within the class but, each state CAN'T communicate with each other. This means that if you create a function within one state, it can only be used in that state. If you create a function within the class, then ALL states can use it. And lastly, after the Tick( ) function, there is the "begin:". Consider this a PostBeginPlay( ) for states but called immediately after the Controller enters it. This is just as useful as what PostBeginPlay( ) does and is used for similar reasons.

As for what this state does. Since this is the state the Controller will enter first, we first want to make sure that the ground speed for the AI Pawn is set to its default speed (as this state will be called from other states later, which will change the ground speed to be more fitting for them). We then run an if statement that checks the distance between the AI Pawn and the Player Pawn. If the distance is less than ONE-THOUSAND and TWENTY-FOUR, the Controller is instructed to go to the "SeeEnemyPlayer" state. We then run an else if, because if the first if is TRUE, there is no reason to run the second if, we check to see if the AI Pawn is within ONE-HUNDRED units of its pathing target location OR if the NextLocation has not been assigned yet, OR if the Velocity is less than FORTY and the AI Pawn is NOT dead.

If these conditions are met, we stop the AI Pawns movement with bPreciseDestination to FALSE and then we MoveToNextLocation( ) by getting a "random" location from GetSearchPathLocation( ).

A lot of this code isn't written yet, but take the names of the functions for what they appear to be, as that will be their end goal; moving to a new location and getting a new location.

The next state is going to be for when the AI Pawn "sees" the Player Pawn; when it gets within a specific range of the Player Pawn. Add the following:

```
// When the AI "sees" the enemy Pawn
state SeeEnemyPlayer
{
    function Tick( float DeltaTime )
```

```
    {
        // If distence between Player and AI is less than 100
        if( VSize( EGPlayerPawn.Location - EGAIPawn.Location ) < 100 )
        {
            GotoState( 'AttackEnemyPlayer' );
        }
        else
        {
            GotoState( 'SearchForPawn' );
        }
    }

begin:
    // Set AI speed to 400 ( fast )
    EGAIPawn.GroundSpeed = 400;

    // Move the AI to the location of the Player Pawn
    MoveToNextLocation( EGPlayerPawn.Location );
}
```

When the Controller enters this state, the first thing that happens is the AI Pawns ground speed is set to FOUR-HUNDRED and it is instructed to move to the location of the Player Pawn.

Within the Tick( ) function of this state we check the distance of the AI Pawn and the Player Pawn. If that location is LESS than ONE-HUNDRED units, the Controller goes to the "AttackEnemyPlayer" state. If that is not TRUE, the Controller goes back to the "SearchForPawn" state.

This is another example of why working with states can be a bit tedious. Since the MoveToNextLocation( ) is called only when the Controller enters this state and it isn't practical to have it in the Tick( ) function, we use the conditions of the SearchForPlayer state to "jump" back and forth between itself and this SeeEnemyPlayer state, so the AI Pawn will continually update its location to the Player Pawn, as long as the Player Pawn is within ONE-THOUSAND and TWENTY-FOUR units of the AI Pawn.

The next state is to "attack" the Player Pawn. Add the following:

```
// When the AI can attacks the player
state AttackEnemyPlayer
{
    function Tick( float DeltaTime )
    {
        // Goes back to the 'SearchForPawn' state when anim is done
        // playing
        if( !EGAIPawn.bAnimPlaying )
```

```
        {
            GotoState( 'SearchForPawn' );
        }
    }

begin:

    // If the Pawn type is 'Melee' and is NOT dead
    if ( EGAIPawn.AIPawn.PawnType == 'Melee' && !
        EGAIPawn.AIPawn.bIsDead )
    {
        // Play attack animation
        EGAIPawn.PlayAIPawnAnimation( EGAIPawn.PawnAnims.Attack );
    }

    // Instead of attacking the enemy Pawn with a bite, explode and do
    // damage if the enemy Pawn is close enough
    if ( EGAIPawn.AIPawn.PawnType == 'Explosion' &&
         !EGAIPawn.AIPawn.bIsDead )
    {

        // Spawn barrel explosion to simulate explosion
        EGAIPawn.WorldInfo.MyEmitterPool.SpawnEmitter
                ( EGAIPawn.BarrelExplosion, EGAIPawn.Location );

        // If the AI Pawn is within 256 units of the player Pawn
        if ( VSize( EGAIPawn.Location - EGPlayerPawn.Location ) < 256  )
        {
            // Do 25 damage to the player Pawn
            EG_GameInfo( WorldInfo.Game ).
                GetPlayerPawn( ).SetPawnHealth( -25 );
        }

        // Spawn a pickup
        Spawn( class'EG_DropActor',,, EGAIPawn.Location );

        // Destroy the AI Pawn
        EGAIPawn.Destroy( );

        // Go to "dead" state
        GotoState( 'AIIsDead' );
    }
}
```

Because this state is meant to be very quick, the "begin:" is quite thorough. We start by checking if the AI Pawn is a "melee" type and is NOT dead. If that is TRUE, we use the PlayAIPawnAnimation( ) function that we wrote in the AI Pawn class to play the "Attack" animation.

If that is FALSE, we then check the AI Pawn type for "explosion" and if it is NOT dead. If this is TRUE (which is likely based on the process of elimination), we spawn the BarrelExplosion Particle System at the location of the AI Pawn. We then check the distance of the AI Pawn to the Player Pawn and if that is under TWO-HUNDRED and FIFTY-SIX units, we do TWENTY-FIVE damage to the Player Pawn.

We then spawn a Drop Actor at the location of the AI Pawn and Destroy( ) the AI Pawn. Then, finally, we move the Controller to the "AIIsDead" state.

Within this states Tick( ) function, we make sure that bAnimPlaying is FALSE before moving the Controller back to SearchForPawn state. This is in case the AI Pawn is the melee type and we don't want the "Attack" animation to continually repeat itself, so we check to make sure it is finished playing before moving states.

The final Controller state is the AIIsDead state. Add the following:

```
// When the Pawn is "Dead"
state AIIsDead
{
begin:
  // Stop AI Pawn from moving
  bPreciseDestination = false;

  // Destroy the controller
  self.Destroy( );
}
```

As you can see, this is a very simple state. It is designed to "end" the Controller class. It stops the AI Pawn from moving and it destroys the Controller itself.

The states are not overly complicated themselves, in principal. It is when you have many of them doing many sorts of things in relation to each other that it because difficult to keep track of what is going on and where the Controller is within the states. One practice I've picked up is using a function to print text to the screen in key locations (such as when the Controller enters a state) so you can get an idea of what is going on, when.

We have used this function before, in the beginning chapters, so using it now should be familiar. It is called:

```
DebugMessagePlayer( "Debug Text Here" );
```

Let's start with the function that sets a reference to the currently controlled AI Pawn.

Add the following:

```
// Assigns reference to what Pawn this controller is controlling
function SetControlledPawn( EG_AIPawn P )
{
   // If not already assigned a reference
   if ( EGAIPawn == none )
   {
      EGAIPawn = P;
   }
   // If already assigned
   else
   {
      // Remove current assignment
      EGAIPawn = none;

      // Assign new one
      EGAIPawn = P;
   }
}
```

Because we need to directly access the EG_AIPawn to get reference to some of its variables and functions, we have to assign a reference directly to it. Also, this looks a lot like most of the modifier functions we have been writing. If the EGAIPawn reference doesn't have a value, assign it the passed value. If it is assigned a reference, remove that reference and assign the one passed into the function.

Let's add the function that will return a vector value for the "random" Path Node location.

Add the following:

```
// Returns a "random" vector value from the Path Node locations
// within 1536 units of the AI
private function vector GetSearchPathLocation( )
{
   // Stores nearby PathNode locations for AI movement
   local array<Vector> NearbyPathNodeLocation;
   // Used for for loop and local RandRange( )
   local int i;

   // For loop to cycle through Path Nodes in class variable PN
   for( i = 0; i < PN.Length; i++ )
   {
      // If the distance between the AI Pawn and the pathnode is under
      // 1536 add its location to the NearbyPathNodeLocation array
      if ( VSize( EGAIPawn.Location - PN[ i ].Location ) < 1536 )
      {
            NearbyPathNodeLocation.AddItem( PN[ i ].Location );
      }
```

```
    }

    // reuse "i" to hold random range between 0 and how many elements
    // are in  NearbyPathNodeLocation
    i = RandRange( 0, NearbyPathNodeLocation.Length );

    // Return the "random" element within the array, as a vector
    return NearbyPathNodeLocation[ i ];
}
```

Because there is no need for any other class to use this function, it is set to private. The return type is a Vector, which will represent a location for the AI Pawn to move to.

The first of the TWO local variables is NearbyPathNodeLocation, which is a Dynamic Array. The second local variable is a int, named "i", which is used in the for loop as well as to keep a random value, depending on how many Path Nodes are within a specific distance of the AI Pawn.

Because the code is compiled one line at a time, we are able to re-use the "i" variable because once the for loop finishes, there is no need for us to keep any assignment as the "i" variable is to reference the element that is being added to the NearbyPathNodeLocation array.

The for loop will continue as long as it is LESS than the length of the class Dynamic Array "PN" (which holds all the worlds Path Node Actors). If the distance between the AI Pawn and any Path Node in the PN element list is LESS than FIFTEEN-HUNDRED and THIRTY-SIX, the vector location of where they are within the world are added to the NearyPathNodeLocation Array.

We then assign "i" a random number between ZERO and the length of the local vector array NearybyPathNodeLocation. Then, we return that random number element within the NearbyPathNodeLocation array.

The next function is to move the AI Pawn to a location.

Add the following:

```
// Used to move the player to the next location
private function MoveToNextLocation( Vector Loc )
{
    // If the AI Pawn isnt dead
    if ( !EGAIPawn.AIPawn.bIsDead )
    {
        // Assign class variable to passed variable
        NextLocation = Loc;
```

```
        // SetDestinationPosition to the NextLocation
        SetDestinationPosition( NextLocation );
        // Set the "absolute" location to the same
        SetFocalPoint( NextLocation );
        // Turn bPreciseDestination to TRUE - moves the player
        bPreciseDestination = true;
    }
    else
    {
        // If AI Pawn is dead
        bPreciseDestination = false;
    }
}
```

Again, since there is no reason for any other class to access this function, it is set to private. This function isn't designed to return any type but does take in ONE vector argument, which will be used to move the AI Pawn to.

We first check that the AI Pawn is NOT dead. If that is TRUE. We assign are class vector variable NextLocation to the value of the argument passed into the function. Then, we use some Controller based functions to first set the destination the AI Pawn will move to with SetDestinationPostion( ). Then, we set the absolute focal point, which is usually design so that the controlled Pawn will be moving to maybe an offset location. In our case, it is the same location as the SetDestinationPosition( ). This is done with the SetFocalPoint( ) function. Then, we use the bPreciseDestination to TRUE, and that's it. The Pawn will continue to move until bPreciseDestination is set to FALSE.

There is another method within states to move the AI Pawn called MoveTo( ) and MoveTowards( ) but I have found this method easier to control and often more reliable.

If the AI Pawn is dead, we turn bPrecieDestination to FALSE, stopping it's movement. This is more of a safety check, as this function shouldn't be called anyways, if the AI Pawn is dead.

The last function is the one being called within the Tick( ) functions, inside the states.

That is the AI Controller class. Hopefully not too much of this was overly complicated, as this is a basic AI Controller. Also, there is not a whole lot going on in here that is outside of the relative difficulty of the past chapters.

The entire class should look like:

```
class EG_AIController extends Controller;

// Used to reference "enemy" player Pawn
var Pawn EGPlayerPawn;
```

```
// Used to reference what Pawn this is controlling
var EG_AIPawn EGAIPawn;

// Used to dynamically reference all Path Nodes in the level
var array<PathNode> PN;

// Used to move the AI Pawn if it doesn't "see" the enemy Pawn
var Vector NextLocation;

// Called just after this class is created
simulated function PostBeginPlay( )
{
   // Local reference to assign to dynamic array: PN
   local PathNode LPN;

   // Keep parent code of same function included
   super.PostBeginPlay( );

   // Assign reference to the "enemy" player pawn
   EGPlayerPawn = EG_GameInfo( WorldInfo.Game ).GetPlayerPawn( );

   // Assign a refernce to each Path Node in the world, using the PN
   // dynamic array
   foreach WorldInfo.AllActors( class'PathNode', LPN )
   {
      // Adds each of the Path Nodes to the dynamic array: PN
      PN.AddItem( LPN );
   }
}

// Automatically enter this state, "look" for enemy Pawn
auto state SearchForPawn
{
   // called per frame
   function Tick( float DeltaTime )
   {
      // If the enemy player Pawn is closer than 1024 units
      if ( VSize( EGAIPawn.Location - EGPlayerPawn.Location ) < 1024 )
      {
          GotoState( 'SeeEnemyPlayer' );
      }

      // If the location of the AI is within 100 units of the
      // NextLocation or the NextLocation is 0,0,0
      // Of if the AI Pawns velocity drops below 40 ( it's stuck )
      else if ( VSize( EGAIPawn.Location - NextLocation ) < 100 ||
              NextLocation == Vect( 0,0,0 )|| VSize( EGAIPawn.Velocity )
              < 40 && !EGAIPawn.AIPawn.bIsDead )
```

```
            {
                // Turn off bool that controls movement
                bPreciseDestination = false;
                // Move to the next location using "random" PathNode
                // location
                MoveToNextLocation( GetSearchPathLocation( ) );
            }
    }

begin:
    // Set AI Pawn ground speed to default
    EGAIPawn.GroundSpeed = EGAIPawn.default.GroundSpeed;
}

// When the AI "sees" the enemy Pawn
state SeeEnemyPlayer
{
    function Tick( float DeltaTime )
    {
        // If distance between Player and AI is less than 100
        if( VSize( EGPlayerPawn.Location - EGAIPawn.Location ) < 100 )
        {
            GotoState( 'AttackEnemyPlayer' );
        }
        else
        {
            GotoState( 'SearchForPawn' );
        }
    }

begin:

    // Set AI speed to 400 ( fast )
    EGAIPawn.GroundSpeed = 400;

    // Move the AI to the location of the Player Pawn
    MoveToNextLocation( EGPlayerPawn.Location );
}

// When the AI can attacks the player
state AttackEnemyPlayer
{
    function Tick( float DeltaTime )
    {

        // Goes back to the 'SearchForPawn' state when anim is done
        // playing
        if( !EGAIPawn.bAnimPlaying )
        {
```

246

```
            GotoState( 'SearchForPawn' );
        }
    }

begin:

    // If the Pawn type is 'Melee' and is NOT dead
    if ( EGAIPawn.AIPawn.PawnType == 'Melee' &&
         !EGAIPawn.AIPawn.bIsDead )
    {
        // Play attack animation
        EGAIPawn.PlayAIPawnAnimation( EGAIPawn.PawnAnims.Attack );
    }

    // Instead of attacking the enemy Pawn with a bite, explode and do
    // damage if the enemy Pawn is close enough
    if ( EGAIPawn.AIPawn.PawnType == 'Explosion'
         && !EGAIPawn.AIPawn.bIsDead )
    {

        // Spawn barrel explosion to simulate explosion
        EGAIPawn.WorldInfo.MyEmitterPool.SpawnEmitter
                ( EGAIPawn.BarrelExplosion, EGAIPawn.Location );

        // If the AI Pawn is within 256 units of the player Pawn
        if ( VSize( EGAIPawn.Location - EGPlayerPawn.Location ) < 256  )
        {
            // Do 25 damage to the player Pawn
            EG_GameInfo( WorldInfo.Game ).
                GetPlayerPawn( ).SetPawnHealth( -25 );
        }

        // Spawn a pickup
        Spawn( class'EG_DropActor',,, EGAIPawn.Location );

        // Destroy the AI Pawn
        EGAIPawn.Destroy( );

        // Go to "dead" state
        GotoState( 'AIIsDead' );
    }
}

// When the Pawn is "Dead"
state AIIsDead
{
begin:
    // Stop AI Pawn from moving
    bPreciseDestination = false;
```

```
   // Destroy the controller
   self.Destroy( );
}


// Assigns reference to what Pawn this controller is controlling
function SetControlledPawn( EG_AIPawn P )
{
   // If not already assigned a reference
   if ( EGAIPawn == none )
   {
      EGAIPawn = P;
   }
   // If already assigned
   else
   {
      // Remove current assignment
      EGAIPawn = none;

      // Assign new one
      EGAIPawn = P;
   }
}


// Returns a "random" vector value from the Path Node locations within
// 1536 units of the AI
private function vector GetSearchPathLocation( )
{
   // Stores nearby PathNode locations for AI movement
   local array<Vector> NearbyPathNodeLocation;
   // Used for for loop and local RandRange( )
   local int i;

   // For loop to cycle through Path Nodes in class variable PN
   for( i = 0; i < PN.Length; i++ )
   {
      // If the distance between the AI Pawn and the pathnode
      // is under 1536
      // Add its location to the NearbyPathNodeLocation array
      if ( VSize( EGAIPawn.Location - PN[ i ].Location ) < 1536 )
      {
            NearbyPathNodeLocation.AddItem( PN[ i ].Location );
      }
   }

   // reuse "i" to hold random range between 0 and how many
   // elements are in NearbyPathNodeLocation
   i = RandRange( 0, NearbyPathNodeLocation.Length );

   // Return the "random" element within the array, as a vector
```

```
       return NearbyPathNodeLocation[ i ];
}

// Used to move the player to the next location
private function MoveToNextLocation( Vector Loc )
{
    // If the AI Pawn isnt dead
    if ( !EGAIPawn.AIPawn.bIsDead )
    {
        // Assign class variable to passed variable
        NextLocation = Loc;
        // SetDestinationPosition to the NextLocation
        SetDestinationPosition( NextLocation );
        // Set the "absolute" location to the same
        SetFocalPoint( NextLocation );
        // Turn bPreciseDestination to TRUE - moves the player
        bPreciseDestination = true;
    }
    else
    {
        // If AI Pawn is dead
        bPreciseDestination = false;
    }
}
```

In the next chapter we will create the Kismet Sequence Actor that will actually spawn the AI Pawns and assign them this Controller class, so they know what to do.

Additional Reading:

More on AI & Navigation with UDK:
http://udn.epicgames.com/Three/AIAndNavigationHome.html

More on the AI system:
http://udn.epicgames.com/Three/AIOverview.html

More on UnrealScript States:
http://udn.epicgames.com/Three/UnrealScriptStates.html

Creating An Example Game Sequence Action Class

Chapter Sixteen

Kismet is a designer tool that is aimed to help designers in performing game functions without extensive programming knowledge. But, with every designer tool aimed to ease the complication of traditional game programming, there is traditional game programming. UDK has made the experience of programming Kismet actions fairly easy. Let's get started in make a Kismet node to spawn our AI Pawn.

Add the following to SeqAct_EGAISpawner file:

```
// Refernces to class types
var( ) class<EG_AIPawn> EGAIPawn;
var( ) class<EG_AIController> EGAIController;
```

These TWO variables have a couple new aspects to how they are declared. The first is the opening and closing parentheses. This declaration means that the variable is able to be edited by the designer, within the editor. Later on, if you become more advanced and, this sort of practice will become quite normal, as things such as Archetypes and world Actors are very common.

The next function is the "main" Kismet function. This function will be the same for all Sequence Actions you may write. Add the following:

```
// When this Kismet node is activated
function Activated( )
{
   // Local refernces to the Linked Actor
   local Actor LocationActorReference;

   // Local reference to the Linked Actor location
   local Vector Loc;

   // If there is a connected Actor
   if ( VariableLinks[0].LinkedVariables.length > 0 )
   {
      // Cast and set reference to connected Actor
      LocationActorReference = Actor( SeqVar_Object( VariableLinks[0].
         LinkedVariables[0] ).GetObjectValue( ) );

      // Set reference to location of Actor
      Loc = LocationActorReference.Location;

      // If the first "melee" input is connected
      if ( InputLinks[0].bHasImpulse )
      {
         SpawnAITypes( 'Melee', Loc, EGAIPawn, EGAIController );
      }

      // If the second "explosion" input is connected
      if ( InputLinks[1].bHasImpulse )
      {
         SpawnAITypes( 'Explosion', Loc, EGAIPawn,
            EGAIController );
      }

      // If the third "random" input is connected
      if ( InputLinks[2].bHasImpulse )
      {
         SpawnAITypes( 'Random', Loc, EGAIPawn, EGAIController );
      }


   }
   // If there is no Object connected to Linked Variables
   else
   {
      ScriptLog( "No Actor connnected to Kismet node." );
   }
}
```

Kismet works by connected different Kismet "nodes" to each other with a line system. Each node has a input and an output. Every time a Kismet action is called through the input, this function Activated( ) is called. After the Activation is called, the output for the node is called, continuing onto the next Kismet node, if there is one.

We need TWO local variables, one to reference the Object that is attached to the Kismet node and the other to reference the Vector location of that Object.

Then, we use an if statement to make sure that there is an Object connected to the Kismet node because if there isn't, there isn't much point in trying to use it. This is done with accessing the LinkedVariable array, with is apart of the VariableLinks array, and make sure that it is above ZERO.

We then assign our Actor reference by doing a "double" cast. Because Kismet variables are based off SeqVar_Object, we can cast the value of the connected Object by getting the Objects value, with GetObjectValue( ). Once we have that value, we can cast it as a SeqVar_Object, and then we can cast that as an Actor. So, it is the Object value, cast into the SeqVar_Object, which is cast as an Actor.

After that, we use the recently referenced Object connected to the Kismet node and set a Vector to the location of that Object.

The next few conditional statements check to see what input links are being fired. InputLink[0] is for the melee, InputLink[1] is for explosion, and InputLink[2] is for a "random" choice between the two. Each of these will call the same SpawnAIType( ) function, but with a different argument, to call the proper AI Type.

The end of the Activated( ) code block is an else statement that will be called if there is NO Object connected to the Variable Links of the Kismet node.

The next function governs what type of AI to spawn. Add the following:

```
// Spawns Pawn and Controller, assigns references
function SpawnAITypes( name Type, Vector Loc, class<EG_AIPawn> P,
    class<EG_AIController>  C )
{
    // Local.A.I.Pawn reference
    local EG_AIPawn LAIP;
    // Local.A.I.Controller reference
    local EG_AIController LAIC;

    // Spawn and reference Controller
    LAIC = GetWorldInfo( ).Spawn( C,,, Loc );

    // Spawn and reference Pawn
    LAIP = GetWorldInfo( ).Spawn( P,,, Loc );
```

```
// Possess Pawn with Controller
LAIC.Possess( LAIP, false );

// Set reference to Pawn within Controller
LAIC.SetControlledPawn( LAIP );

// If a melee type
if ( Type == 'Melee' )
{
    // Assign AI Pawn as melee type
    LAIP.InitAIPawn( true );
}

// If NOT a melee and NOT a random
if ( Type == 'Explosion' )
{
    // Assign AI Pawn as explosion type
    LAIP.InitAIPawn( false );
}

// If random, choose type based on condition and
// RandRange( ) function
if ( Type == 'Random' )
{
    if ( RandRange( 0, 100 ) < 50 )
    {
        // Melee
        LAIP.InitAIPawn( true );
    }
    else
    {
        // Explosion
        LAIP.InitAIPawn( false );
    }
}
}
```

This function will take in FOUR arguments. A name to know what type to spawn, a Vector to know where to spawn it, and TWO class references to know what to spawn. These classes are the EG_AIPawn and the EG_AIController, which are being passed in from the designer assignments of the class references, from within the editor.

In order to reference what classes are being spawned, we need to have the TWO local variables for both EG_AIPawn and EG_AIController. We then access the world info with GetWorldInfo( ) and then with that, we can use the Spawn( ) function, as directly using the Spawn( ) function within the Sequence Action class is not possible; which is one of the reasons GetWorldInfo( ) exists.

We spawn both the Pawn and the Controller at the location of the connected Object. We then Possess( ) the AIPawn, assign a reference to it within the Controller class and then run the conditionals to assign the proper AI Type within the EG_AIPawn class, by using the InitAIPawn( ) function.

Each conditional is strait forward. If the name being passed in is "Melee", it uses TRUE within the InitAIPawn( ) function, assigning the "melee" SkeletalMesh, AnimTree, and AnimSet. If the name is "Explosion", spawn the associated content for that, and if it is "Random" use a RandRange( ) function to get a "random" spawn of either "Melee" or "Explosion".

The last bit of this class is the DefaulProperties. Add the following:

```
DefaultProperties
{
    // Name of Kismet Node
    ObjName="Spawn EG AI"

    // Where this is located within Actions
    ObjCategory="Example Game: USL Book"

    // Remove default Input Links
    InputLinks.empty

    // Add three for Melee, Explosion, Random
    InputLinks( 0 ) = ( LinkDesc="Melee" )
    InputLinks( 1 ) = ( LinkDesc="Explosion" )
    InputLinks( 2 ) = ( LinkDesc="Random" )

    // Remove default Variable Links
    VariableLinks.Empty

    // Add one named "Location" that looks for an Object
    VariableLinks( 0 ) = ( ExpectedType=class'SeqVar_Object',
        LinkDesc="Location", PropertyName=ObjectType, MaxVars=1 )
}
```

This doesn't look like any other DefaultProperties we have written. The ObjName assigns the name of the Kismet node itself. Then, depending on what type of Kismet node it is, the ObjCategory is where it will be in the drop-down of that Kismet node type. In our case, it will be in "Actions" as this class is a SequenceAction.

InputLinks.empty removes any of the default InputLinks. Then, we create THREE more for "Melee", "Explosion", and "Random". These will serve as the InputLinks that are called to spawn specific types, which is delegated within the Activated( ) function if statements.

Just like the InputLinks, we empty out any default VariableLinks with VariableLinks.Empty. Then, we create ONE for our Object Actor to connect to. The expected type is so the Kismet node knows what type should be connected. The LinkDesc is the name of the VariableLink and is displayed on the Kismet node itself. We then name the PropertyName to ObjectType, and then set the maximum number of VariableLinks to connect to ONE.

That is our SequenceAction designed to spawn our EG_AIPawn and EG_AIController.

K. If you compile the code and open the editor, then click on the Kismet button, located on the top tool-bar. You will get a window with a empty gray background. RIGHT-CLICK on this and mouse over "New Action", then "Example Game: USL Book", then select our "Spawn EG AI" Kismet action.

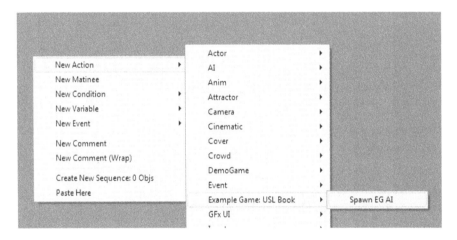

You will then get a Kismet node that will be used to spawn the type of AI you want, at the location of the Actor or Object you decide.

This is the makings of our Kismet node, as we know them in code:

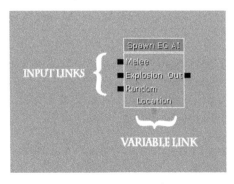

Using the Kismet node(s) are not very complicated. The idea of Kismet is to create a "line" of connected nodes that will perform an action. Because I could probably write another book about how to use Kismet, instead, download the following map file:

http://tinyurl.com/JazzExampleGameMap

You should see this in the Kismet window, as well as many Path Nodes in the level:

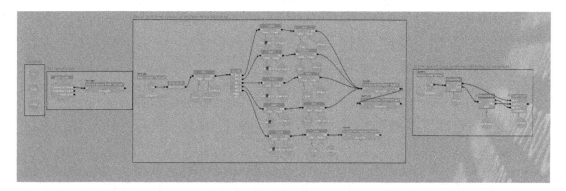

To give a warning: If you plan on using our Kismet node in different ways. You MUST set the class references in it's properties. In order to do this, select our Kismet node in the Kismet window, then look at the "Properties" window at the bottom. Change the selections for EGAIPawn and EGAIController, under the "Seq Act EGAISpawner" drop-down, to their proper assignments.

Such as:

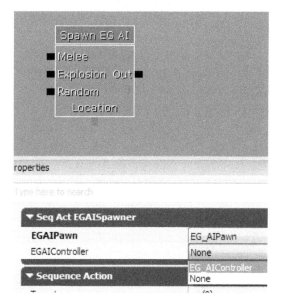

As you can see, Kismet can become a mess quick. For as complicated as it may appear at a distance, it is actually quite simple.

Starting on the far left, we have a list of "Variables". These are used by reference with a Kismet tool called a "Named Variable". Consider the "Variables" on the left our class variables and any of the Named Variables a reference to those.

The process that is going on there, is on Level Load, we call the Remote Event "SetType". This is set have a ZERO point TWO-FIVE (0.25) second delay, then to reset both of the bool values, and final enter a switch statement.

The switch statement works a bit like what we went over in our Switch statement chapter. The difference for Kismet is that for every time this node is called, the output of the switch statement will increment by ONE. So the first time it is called, it uses the top output. The second time, it uses the second output, and so on.

What is going on for each output for the switch statement is to set the location of the "Location" Object, set what type of AI we want to spawn with the bMelee or bRandom. Then for the first FOUR switch statement outputs, we call another Remote Event "Spawn". The reason the last switch statement doesn't use "SetType" like the rest, is that we don't want the switch statement to loop again.

Inside of the Spawn Remote Event is TWO comparisons. If bMelee is TRUE, we spawn the melee AI with our Kismet node. If it is FALSE, we check bRandom. If bRandom is TRUE, we spawn the random AI Type, if bRandom is FALSE, we spawn the Explosion type.

That is our Example Game! You should be able to play in the editor or with the debugger in Visual Studio. When you spawn you should have FIVE AI running around that will attack you (if you don't kill them first).

Don't let this be the end of this project. You may have noticed that subtle things have yet to be completed within this game type; such as a death for the player Pawn. Continue the practices you have been learning and explore further.

Additional Reading:

More on programming for Kismet:
http://udn.epicgames.com/Three/MasteringUnrealScriptDelegates.html#TUTORIAL%2012.16%20-%20DELEGATES%20%20KISMET,%20PART%20I:%20INTRODUCTION%20%20INITIAL%20CLASS%20SETUP

More on using Kismet:
http://udn.epicgames.com/Three/KismetHome.html

Wrap Up

Chapter Seventeen

At this point you should have an understanding of how to pass data around through functions and classes. You should understand the difference between the data types associated with UDK as well as how these data types represent the information being stored in them. You should understand the way a class hierarchy works, as a "super" class will pass non-private information to its inherited classes. In regards to UDK, you should understand the following terms: Object, Actor, Pawn, HUD, Weapon, Projectile, as well as how all of these classes are related. The idea of referencing different variables and classes should also be something that you can do with accessors and modifiers. On top of all of that, you should have a basic understanding of some of the problems associated with making games, as well as how to tackle them; including things like for loops, conditional statements, and arrays.

You may now be wondering, what now? If you want to continue forward with learning Unreal Script, there is one Epic supported site that holds the complete resource. It is as follows:

http://udn.epicgames.com/Three/UnrealScriptHome.html

If you want to learn more about programming in general there is not only a huge amount of information available online but also a vast amount of literature associated with the practice of programming. Depending on what language you would like to learn, I can personally recommend the following books:

- *C++ Primer Plus (6th version +)* – Stephen Prata
- *Principles and Practice Using C++ - Bjarne Stroustrup*
- *Effective C++ 3rd edition* – Scott Meyers
- *More Effective C++* – Scott Meyers
- *Accelerated C++* – Andrew Koenig and Barbara E. Moo
- *Beginning C++ Game Programming* – Michael Dawson
- *OGRE 3D 1.7 Beginners Guide* – Felix Kerger
- *Game Programming All In One 3rd Edition* – Jonathan S. Harbour
- *Game Programming Gems* - http://www.gameprogramminggems.com/
- *Artificial Intelligence for Games, 2nd Edition* – Ian Millington and John Funge
- *Programming Game AI by Example* – Mat Buckland
- *Modern C++ Design: Generic Programming and Design Patterns Applied* – Andrei Alexandrescu

If you want to find people to work with or ask questions, check out the following communities:

> http://forums.epicgames.com/forums/366-UDK
> http://www.reddit.com/r/udk/
> http://www.reddit.com/r/unrealengine/
> http://www.3dbuzz.com/forum/forums/277-Unreal-Technology

If you have questions or insight about this book, including but not limited to grammatical errors, code compiling issues, confusion, or a question, you can email me at:

> Kyle@EmotionalRobots.com